PROFESSIONAL EDUCATION
FOR LIBRARIANSHIP
International Perspectives

PROFESSIONAL EDUCATION FOR LIBRARIANSHIP
International Perspectives

Olu Olat Lawal

B.A. Hons. *Birmingham* M.A. Ph.D
Loughborough, FCLIP *Lond.* Cert. in Lib. *Ibadan.*
University Librarian
University of Calabar Library, Calabar,
Cross River State, Nigeria

Spectrum Books Limited
Ibadan
Abuja •Benin City •Lagos •Owerri

Spectrum titles can be purchased on line at
www.spectrumbooksonline.com

Published by
Spectrum Books Limited
Spectrum House
Ring Road
PMB 5612
Ibadan, Nigeria
*e-mail: admin*1@*spectrumbooksonline.com*

in association with
Safari Books (Export) Limited
1st Floor
17 Bond Street
St Helier
Jersey JE2 3NP
Channel Islands
United Kingdom

Europe and USA Distributor
African Books Collective Ltd
The Jam Factory
27 Park End Street
Oxford OX1, 1HU, UK

© O.O. Lawal

First published, 2003

ISBN: 978-029-415-5

Printed by Printmarks Ventures, Ososami, Ibadan

Dedication

This book is dedicated to my wife Jumoke (a.k.a. 'the official') and our children Segun, Folake, Bolaji and Bunmi, and to the fond memory of late Professor Peter Havard-Williams of Loughborough and Botswana Universities.

Contents

Contents

Preface

One of the essential criteria on professionalism is the knowledge-base theory, which in practical terms forms the core for assessing whether or not an occupation fulfils the requirements necessary for a calling. Knowledge is self-generating and it generally functions and expands on the basis of existing occupational techniques. In view of its self-generating process, knowledge becomes naturally continuous and normally should be kept under review by the occupation's practitioners. Such knowledge is usually supplemented by the skill factor. A professional librarian who arguably is at the vortex of community service, both social and academic, should be aware of the information needs of his clients and how best such needs can be met.

Education and training of the professional therefore forms the focus of this book in terms of the genesis of professional education in librarianship through the decades to the threshold of a new millennium. There is no gainsaying that the 21st century portends new changes in the application of technology and how this affects services and career opportunities. However, one must know his roots before embarking on a destination so as not to be consumed by it. The undergraduate students of librarianship and other categories of students in Education or Communication Technology, in interdisciplinary terms, would find this work useful. In addition, the fresh first degree professional embarking on a masters degree in librarianship will find this work very informative and useful in preparing for the world of work in which the librarian and information professionals find themselves in this rapidly changing world of information. This book is recommended as a text for library educators, degree and postgraduate students and library/information practitioners keenly interested in professional education.

Olu Lawal
Calabar, June 2000

Acknowledgements

The author wishes to acknowledge the works of several colleagues cited in this study regardless of the often lively debates we have engaged in at various national and international fora. I also wish to acknowledge the serious level of encouragement received from Late Professor Peter Havard-Williams, my former Head of Department and Director of Research of my Doctoral programme 1980 – 83; also Professor John Dean of Queens University, Belfast, my external examiner and mentor on professional education; my degree, especially postgraduate. students who beneficially challenged me to document my expositions on professional education for posterity.

Finally, I wish to thank my very dear wife Jumoke for her endurance and assistance in training three graduate children and preparing another one for future academic achievement. Grateful thanks to Mrs. Pat Ekanem, my Chief Confidential Secretary for typing a large portion of the manuscript.

Introduction

In comparison with older established library schools and institutions in countries such as Britain, Canada, Germany, India, the U.S.A. and Russia, the professionalisation of education for librarianship in Nigeria is a recent phenomenon. This study examines in detail the important factors which, in the process of professionalisation, have either aided or impeded the development of the library and information profession in Nigeria.

The general aim of this study is to attempt to delineate those factors which have contributed to this process by surveying aspects of library education provision from an international perspective.

Special emphasis will be placed on the post-independence period, 1960-1980, since it was during that period that visible expansion in library and information services occurred, and library schools emerged, offering courses at graduate and non-graduate levels in universities, comparable to provisions made by other schools educating workers for other professions.

Different writers have in the past made significant contributions to the study of library education in Nigeria. The works of Dean[1], Harris[2], Akinyotu[3], Obi[4] and Ogunsheye[5] have *inter alia* focused on events leading up to, and immediately following, the establishment of formal library education in Nigeria. While they have been concerned with historical developments in library education provision, very little attempt has been made at a thorough evaluation of the content and objectives of courses in order to show their relative importance to professional objectives.

Library education must concern itself profoundly with changes in the character of the library profession and in so doing, it is important to recognise and formulate objectives which are not only likely to reflect present library problems but also relate to future professional needs. This study examines the objectives of this academic preparation of the libraries as well as the vocational contents needed for learning skills. Thus, one of the features of concern in this study is the educational setting in which the aspirant professional prepares for formal involvement in the library and information work force.

It is quite fundamental to probe the theoretical basis of curriculum development, and how this is reflected in librarianship's definition and practice of the concept in providing the kind of education that will equip its practitioners to perform their various assignments. It is also essential to consider the curriculum development concept if only as a prognostic for determining the educational development which will emerge in response to local needs in Nigerian librarianship.

Two trends of thought seem to have characterised the development of library education in Nigeria since 1960: (i) *The desire and search for a theoretically-based education* which would provide the initiate with the principles and philosophy of the profession and leave the technical aspects of training to his employer, i.e graduate education to provide 'leaders' for the profession ; (ii) *The insistence on providing vocational type training* – which is rich in technical skills and would provide the profession with the urgently required level of staffing needs in librarians, i.e., non-graduate education to provide paraprofessionals.

The various factors influencing the development of education for librarianship in respect of the above two schools of thought will be examined to enhance better understanding in the evaluation of library schools' programmes.

According to one of the sociological criteria on professionalism, a profession is based on a substantial body of knowledge which can be transmitted to students. It follows that attention needs to be paid to the divergent definitions of what that knowledge should consist of. In particular, it will be illuminating to consider how these divergent definitions either inhibit or promote the development of an educational system which could be termed *professional*. We would be examining this in the ensuing chapters.

References

1. Dean, J., 'Training and Management for Library Personnel: Professional Education in Nigeria', *Nigerian Libraries* 2(2), 1966: 68-70.

2. Harris, J., 'Libraries and Librarianship in Nigeria of Mid-century,' *Nigerian Libraries* 6 (1 & 2), 1970: 26-40.

3. Akinyotu, A., 'Training and Education of Library Personnel in Nigeria – Comments and Proposals on its Objectives and Content,' *Nigerian Libraries* 8(2), 1972: 103-166.

4. Obi, D. S., 'Education for Librarianship in Nigeria,' *Nigerian Libraries* 11(3), 1975: 221-251.

5. Ogunsheye, F. A., 'Formal Programme Development in Library Education in Nigeria,' *Journal of Education for Librarianship* 19(2), (Fall) 1978: 140-150.

Note: Recent theses and academic dissertations on Nigerian library education

6. Ajia, S. A., 'Library Education in Nigeria,' (M.A. Dissertation), Loughborough, L. U. T. 1977.

7. Lawal, O. O., 'Elements of Degree Courses in Librarianship and Information Science' (M.A. Thesis), Loughborough. L.U.T. 1979.

8. Olden, E. A., 'The Development of the Department of Library Science Ahmadu Bello University', (M.L.S. Thesis) Zaria, Nigeria: Ahmadu Bello University, 1980.

References

1.

2.

3.

4.

5.

6.

7.

8.

1

Conceptual Framework for Curriculum Development

In the field of education, an analysis of curriculum development seems to yield categories and relationships which can be arranged and studied in a 'conceptual framework'. This has been considered as a prerequisite for any theoretically sound curriculum work as stressed in the studies of contemporary curriculum scholars like: Hoyle, Hooper, Banks, Musgrave, Lawton and others (United Kingdom); Vergil Harrick, Ralph Tyler, Hilda Taba and others (America). The general task of a systematic approach to curriculum development seems to be based on the formation of hypotheses on three classes of curriculum variables, and on the relationship between them:

(a) That the purpose of education is to enable the individual to deal with various *situations* in life;
(b) That the individual gains this ability through acquiring certain *qualifications* and dispositions; and,
(c) That since it is through the various *elements* of the *curriculum* that such qualifications are to be generated, a rationally planned curriculum should be developed on the basis of an identification of these situations, qualifications, and curriculum elements to an optimal degree of correctness and objective.[1]

Given the above hypotheses, one could identify 'situations' by deducing and applying criteria for such identifications, for example, through combining reasoned value statements, analytic appraisals of objective (present and future) needs, evidence on the effects of learning and instruction, elements of cultural tradition and other variables. 'Situations' in this context, may be defined as consisting of personal, social, political and vocational life of the individual, and needed 'qualifications' may be defined through an analysis of these situations, thereby enabling a distinction to be made between cognitive and affective structures required to develop the structures of the disciplines. The scheme as outlined above, will enhance differentiation of the levels of curriculum development too often confused in practice, namely: the identification of aims; the definition of specific objectives into which aims must be translated; the selection of content; and, organisation of teaching methodology. These points may seem obvious enough but it must be stressed that it is important to develop a logic within which curriculum development in the librarianship discipline can be objectively considered.

Furthermore, it seems logical to assume that any hypothesis on the effect of the content of the curriculum (consisting of all the elements) in generating behaviour has to be explicitly stated and, in principle, verified. Nor can there be generalisations on the value of disciplines in building a universe of 'meaning' for the learner. Such 'philosophic realism' as Phenix[2] calls it, needs to be checked in detail. Robinson[3] considers that it is largely through the established system of arts and sciences, through their substance, principles and methods that curriculum developers undertake to observe, appreciate and interpret reality and are thus enabled to deal with it.

The potent motives for curriculum change are shared by all countries;

(a) the 'explosion of knowledge', so called especially in English speaking countries, termed the 'progress of sciences' in Eastern Europe, has evolved as a motive concept which may be defined as a vastly extended body of information and rapidly changing concepts and methods, all of which require new programmes and rationalised ways of planning curricula and teaching methodology;

(b) the extension of the scope and instruments of the sciences, natural and social, has challenged the curriculum in a more profound manner;

(c) changes in the structure of society, in the share of its members in economic and political responsibilities and in individual aspirations have brought about considerable quantitative and qualitative expansion of the school population.

One may submit that since curriculum development therefore is in the form of a continuum, it is the task of those responsible for changes to articulate value systems and have rational insight into social and individual needs prevailing in a society, to translate the value systems and insight into detailed educational objectives, and to integrate with them reflected practical experience and empirical evidence on the effect of learning and teaching, and thereby attempt to draw forth a consensus on the curriculum. In practical terms, however, the attainment of a consensus on the curriculum seems to be an utopian ideal as evidenced in the literature of education.

Within the conceptual framework of the curriculum it is possible to review theory with current practice in the field especially as it relates to library and information studies.

Defining the Curriculum

In all human societies, children are initiated into particular modes of making sense of their experience and the world about them. This socialisation process continues into adulthood in which experience is transformed into a set of norms, knowledge and skills which the society requires for its continuance. In most societies most of the time, this 'curriculum' of initiation is not questioned; frequently it is enshrined in myths, rituals and immemorial practices, which have absolute authority. In the sociology of education, one condition of pluralism is the conflict and argument about what this curriculum of initiation should contain. This argument is, however, not the feature of concern here, but the emphasis must be that today, such conflicts and arguments are even more profound and tend to undermine rational discussion of what the curriculum should contain in the educational context.

Some clarity is needed over what is generally understood by the term 'curriculum'. A survey of the literature suggests several meanings being attached to the use of the term. In the meantime it may be helpful to distinguish the use of the word to denote the content of a particular subject or area of study from the use of it to refer to the total programme of an educational institution. Often, conflicts do arise as attempts are made to reconcile the competing demands of these two aspects of curriculum planning. Inadequacies of previous attempts at curriculum planning can be attributed to the fact that they have tended to proceed in a rather piecemeal fashion within subjects rather than according to some overall rationale, so that the curriculum is seen as 'the amorphous product of generations of tinkering'.[4]

Kelly considers that the term curriculum concerns 'the overall rationale for the educational programme of the institution'.[5] This definition may be acceptable in the context of planning but surely it is lacking in meaning for considering problems relevant to individual subject content. There are four basic elements of the curriculum: objectives, content, methods and evaluation – these do not constitute neat, absolute categories but at least they help to streamline the search for a definition. They are closely interrelated and each element is influenced by, and influences, the others. The curriculum therefore constitutes a 'system' and curriculum development (or 'change' as some writers prefer to call it) is in one sense a form of 'systems analysis'. This view is consistent with system theories proposed by Kerr[6], Taba[7], Taylor[8], Mervitt[9], and Hirst.[10]

A curriculum may be externally or internally justified based on assumptions regarding the nature of the environment, student and institutional needs. The curriculum is the nerve centre for relating the various facets of change in the environment. It incorporates an understanding of:

(i)   the nature of the student: meaning of his life, his self-perception, his needs as a person and as a librarian, how he learns, and his previous learnings;

(ii)   the nature of librarianship; the objectives, the tasks, the certification system, and expert opinion on problems;

(iii)   the state of education: the teaching profession, the educational institution, organisation of education in national, state and other parastatal institutions; and

(iv)   the political, social and economic climate.

In addition to defining the curriculum its educational role could be put into greater perspective through an understanding of the evolution of the concept. Historically, 'curriculum' is a Latin word carried directly over into English. Its first Latin meaning was 'a running', 'a race', 'a course', 'a career'. By picking out just two of Cicero's uses of the word it is possible to trace the direction in which the term has developed. Defending Rabivius, Cicero stated: *'Exiguum nobis vitae curriculum natura circumscripsit, immensum gloriae'* (Nature has confined our lives within a short space, but that for our glory is infinite).[11] 'Curriculum' is used here to refer to the temporal space in which we live, to the confines within which things may happen, to the container as opposed to the contents.

Conversely, while writing the scripts for the seventh volume of *Antiquities*, Cicero described the work – involving the study of law and Greek literature – as *'Hae sunt exercitationers ingenii, haec curricula mentis'* (These are the spurs of my intellect, the course of my mind runs on).[12] 'Curriculum' here refers to the things he is studying — the content. This metaphorical extension, firstly from the race-course and running to intellectual pursuits, and then from the reference to the things that happen within the constraints; prefigures the general movement of the term through the ancient and modern world. One may wish to enquire about the length and obstacles of a race-course. In particular, one may wish to relate this kind of enquiry to the intellectual curriculum. These considerations remained the important curriculum questions throughout the medieval world.

The term curriculum apparently did not find its way into the vernacular in England until the nineteenth century. In 1643, the Munimenta of Glasgow University referred to the *'curriculum quinquae annorum'* (curriculum of five years), maintaining the ancient Latin ambiguity of the container and the contained: that is, reference is made to the content of the curriculum while design changed little during this period, though the common seventeenth century opinion assumed that all the faculties of the mind, both active and passive are 'mightily heightened and improved by exercise'. In this respect, Rymer argues that there were profound disagreements about **what** content should be used to exercise the mind.[13]

The use of the term curriculum in England, following the German lead, still had some way to go along the metaphorical extension from indicating the container – period of study – to indicating the contained – course content. For example, item 39 of Glasgow University's calendar for 1829 states: 'The curriculum of students who mean to take a degree in surgery (is) to be three years'. However, by the end of the nineteenth century, the term had changed very rapidly, and typical uses seem to have lost any lingering sense of the contained or temporal constraints, and mean simply the content. One aspect of development in curriculum studies during this century is the emphasis placed upon the question of **how**, as distinct from **what** should constitute the curriculum. This has led to focusing on the individual learner as an important variable.

Thus, in recent years the meaning of curriculum has widened to include detailed plans of student activities, a variety of study materials, suggestions for learning strategies, and arrangements for putting the programme into use.[14] Decisions about the content of the curriculum are now being based on an analysis of the nature of society. A survey of the literature suggests differing views as to what is to be taught in schools and whether this should be decided by reference to the culture of the society the schools have been created to serve. A leaning towards this interpretation of the curriculum even when the problems of definition are recognised, is likely to lead to a view of two or more cultures. This is not necessarily disadvantageous to educational practice as some writers seem to indicate. For example, Eliot[15] and Bantock[16,17] have argued that having a view of two or more cultures could have serious implications for curriculum planning and educational practice in general. However, it seems impossible to isolate wholly the ideal elements in culture without incurring grave falsifications. According to Benge[18], those who try to understand imaginative literature or art without reference to its social context are guilty of 'intellectual triviality'. The important point is to enable connections to be made among the elements of culture and it does not seem that the problem is what the connections are but how they should be established especially in the planning of curricula.

The curriculum may therefore be viewed as comprising several interrelated components: precise statement of objectives for each area of study, the knowledge and learning experiences most likely to **achieve** the stated objectives, and the means of deciding the degree to which the objectives are being achieved (evaluation).

The Core: Purpose and Function

A characteristic example of controversy generated in the literature of curriculum studies is the purpose and function of the common core concept. The controversy in this area centres on whether or not there is in fact a core of knowledge central to the study of all disciplines. Librarians with keen interest in professional education, as well as professional library educators seem to have joined in the questioning of the importance and significance of the core concept as it applies to library education practice.

A basic assumption that underlies any core programme, for example in library and information studies, should be: is there a body of knowledge that is central to librarianship, sufficiently central that all prospective librarians should be required to master it, no matter what their library types or specialisation may be? Any answer may not be perfect since the knowledge considered to be 'sufficiently central' cannot be precisely defined. On this basis, the assumption itself may not be universally acceptable since librarians and educators have differing views with regards to the fundamental reasoning of a body of knowledge considered central to librarianship.

Brief History of the Common Core in British Librarianship

The question of a common core in British library and information studies dates back to the 1882 Library Association Syllabus and 1906 six sectional certificates which in addition to English and European literature had 'the principles of classification, the elements of bibliography and cataloguing, library administration, and a cataloguing knowledge of at least two languages besides English'[19]. The Library Association's Annual Report for 1929-30 reported a drastic restructuring of the entire syllabus. The six sectional certificates were discontinued and replaced by a three-tier examination structure: elementary, intermediate and final.

According to Bramley:

> ... the new syllabus represented a bold attempt to emulate the work of other professional bodies and make the examinations of the LA a true test of competence to practise as a librarian.[20]

A case in point of the core elements was the inclusion in the final examination of compulsory papers such as General Bibliography and Book Selection, with a somewhat unusual choice in the further papers between Historical Bibliography, Paleography, and Archives, or Indexing and Abstracting. The compulsory paper had five main areas: The Essentials of Good Book Production; The Collation and Description of Books; The Materials of Bibliographic Compilation of Bibliographies; and Book Selection. The advanced library administration consisted of two compulsory papers: part (a) Fundamental and General, covering all types of library; and part (b) Giving a specialised alternative – either (i) public, or (ii) university and special libraries.[21] Thus, professional librarians were required to have a grasp of the basic techniques of classification and cataloguing and a knowledge of other subjects in the elementary examination.

With regards to the final examination, Bramley argues that the objectives of testing and revealing the candidates' advanced knowledge of library practice could not have been realised because the core was rigid in the Library Association's new syllabus and did not reflect advances in library practice.[22]

Between 1930 and 1970, the core was persistently the focus of argument in the library profession with questions raised as to its inflexibility. In the late seventies, a curriculum workshop considered demands for increased specialisation in the profession.[23] Similarly in 1980 a curriculum development project[24] seminar critically examined the common core concept, with most participants acknowledging existing changes in library schools curricula most of which are unrecorded outside the official documents of the schools.[25] The old troika inherited from the Library Association syllabuses: cataloguing and classification, management and bibliographical organisation, were still seen substantively in many teaching syllabuses. But were now overlaid with many new elements and not simply the teaching of library operations.

Following the British Library report on computer teaching in schools of librarianship and information science (1979)[26], one could understand why the seminar concerned itself on the role of the computer in library and information work and how this affects courses. The Library Association's Working Party on the new technologies currently stresses the need for post-qualification re-training in this field but educators found that the Working Party discussions had little regard to the impact of technology on library school courses other than the request that the courses should cover the effective management of the new technologies, while in terms of methodology the bulk was shifted to the library schools to respond in some way with regard to the curricula.[27] The findings of the seminar can be summarised as follows:

> ...management courses still exhibit a wide variety of approaches and levels. Librarians, not unexpectedly, lay great stress on skills in so-called 'inter-personal relations' and the need for 'self-management'. Cataloguing skills seem to have acquired a new lustre in schools, with some reflected light from AACR2 and the burgeoning databases. The links with bibliographical skills are in some schools being more clearly established.[28]

It can be observed that the core in the United Kingdom has so far displayed a remarkable resilience in the process of curriculum reform. For example, an element of a common core which for long was submerged beneath the traditional three elements was the use of books and information, and the needs and problems of the user. This central professional concern is now so evident in practice and teaching that participants at the seminar felt it has become part of a common core. In the past two decades, 1980-2000, Information Communications Technology (ICT) has in the foresight of the seminar, formed the central focus of library school curricula.

In the view of Edward Dudley, the structure of a common core which stipulate the extent and level of treatment of commonly identified subjects can no longer be spelt out in British teaching syllabuses. A quantitative approach along the three traditional lines, which was attempted in the sixties by the Library Association when it was asked to approve the rapidly growing number of internally organised and examined courses, was considered by the seminar as no longer valid.[29]

Furthermore, emphasis is now being placed upon 'a more effective assessment' of the relevance of the core to professional practice of the future. Such assessment, it was argued, could be achieved through examining the objectives of courses and teaching syllabuses and the relationship between them. The new function of the core, as may seem likely, would require to make an impact on practice but as one library school head remarked, "the common core may be a valuable unifying myth, but it will be difficult to find that much common ground between the core teaching of all courses in all seventeen schools."[30]

American Library Schools and the Common Core

A survey of professional literature reveals that even among those who support the idea of a core, library educators in the United States seem to be moving decidedly in the direction of reducing as much as possible the amount of compulsory elements in the content of library schools' curricula, thereby increasing the number of different optional courses from which the student may freely choose. Asheim states that in almost all cases where syllabuses have been examined there is some kind of requirement or compulsory course elements, i.e., if not a single requirement for all students, then separate requirements for all students in each specialty: 'a bunch of little cores.'[31] The author suggests that the common core which is presented in separate forms usually consists of two or three courses that turn up in every core, thus incorporating the general core concept *sub rosa.*[32]

British writers on library education have sometimes implied developments in the field as being predetermined by events in the American library education scene. For example Bramley, an accomplished library education historian, while commenting on the LA's three-tier examination syllabus, wrote thus:

> ...the optional papers which had been introduced at the final level were but pale copies of the elective subjects which were being offered by the schools of librarianship in the U.S.[33]

The literature of library education is replete with traces of developments in the field in both countries. However, the approach to the core concept in American library schools is slightly different from that of British schools as shall be explained in detail later.

The core concept in American education for librarianship can be traced to the beginning of formal library training in the U.S.A. Melvil Dewey's school, starting as a required programme of a few months' duration, was essentially all core – based on a kind of task analysis of what desk workers do in libraries. As schools began to expand, the basic general information began to be supplemented by elective courses as well, and by the time of the 1923 Williamson Report, the programme was about one-half required courses (which may be one way of defining the core), and one-half electives. The required courses continued to consist essentially of the content of Dewey's early programme: cataloguing and classification, reference and bibliography, book selection, and administration of libraries. The emphasis was highly practical even though the one concession to a more humanistic and less obviously-practical content was the history of books and libraries.

In 1923, Williamson surveyed library schools' programmes and suggested that book selection, reference work, and classification were the 'heart of the curriculum.'[34]

The term 'core' gradually came into use when in 1936 Reece in his book, *The Curriculum in Library Schools,* refers to 'a common core', but as a descriptor not a generic name.[35] In the post-war period of the 1940s when a shortage of trained personnel began to focus attention on the need to train a large number of persons in the basic skills, a more formal identification of basic content began to take shape, and the term 'core' began to be used for a specific component of the curriculum. In the same period, despite the influence of Williamson's call for a more professionally-oriented education rather than just technical training, there was a reversion toward the Dewey-programme in American library education. The basic skills were to a great extent taught at the undergraduate level, and consisted of the kind of training which now typifies the present Library Technical Assistants' curricula.

Increasingly,. such 'core' content was seen as a prerequisite for the professional education that led to the fifth-year degree with the continuing pressure from the profession to condense such core content to as short a period as possible. Many librarians and library educators in the U.S. were concerned that the introduction of core content into the college curriculum would dilute the librarian's background of general education, and the consensus began to be in favour of placement of both core and elective courses at the post-bachelor level as part of the master degree programme. By the time of the 1951 revision of the Standards for Accreditation, the master's degree had become the official level of the first professional degree, despite the large number of undergraduate programmes that were producing candidates for library positions which carried professional status. And in both the undergraduate and the fifth-year programmes, the core idea persisted.

Several important educational conferences were held in the 1940s and in the period immediately after, but perhaps the most memorable in the early 1950s was the University of Chicago Workshop on 'The core of education for librarianship', which in 1953 reaffirmed the core idea but did suggest that some of the library content could be taught at the undergraduate level concurrently with the general courses without reducing the amount of general education in the total programme.[36] Elsewhere in the literature, Asheim reports that this recommendation did not find wide acceptance in practice, but that the idea of the core continued to characterise library education even though in its application there does not seem to be necessarily an agreement on its content or structure. This suggests the elusive nature of the core curriculum.

The core has since then been variously modified as shown on the programmes of American library schools, to the old Dewey basics, certain new areas of attention were added: 'The Library in Society', for example, and in the Chicago Workshop – 'Research'. In the intervening years after 'Materials Selection' has replaced 'Book Selection'; 'Documentation' showed up for a while then changed its title, thus: 'School Libraries' became 'Media Centres', 'Information Science', 'Library Automation' and 'Multi-media' approaches became almost unanimously part of the required content. Attention has been focused on the effects on the curriculum in regards of change of titles. Marco for example observes that:

> A serious level-error in library training is found in the United States, in the approach to preparation of librarians for elementary schools. (These librarians are now more often referred to as media specialists, and their libraries are known as media centres). While librarians in public and university librarians are expected to have master's degrees, bachelors specialists are normally employed with only bachelors degrees. It seems that the function of the media specialist has not been correctly assessed; such a person does in fact require a knowledge base of great complexity, and an educational experience no less complete than that of colleagues in other types of libraries.[37]

This idea of changing titles can distort the function of the core especially in a changing profession such as librarianship even though it is recognised that the required content of course is perhaps defined by area of need in library practices.

Horrocks [38] in examining the concept of the core, suggests that the idea in modified form, dates back to the initiative at the University of Pittsburgh in 1964 when the university introduced a new orientation course taken by all students in their first month of study. Students were introduced to the literature of librarianship, library history and the current professional situation, to the teaching methodology, i.e., within and outside the faculty. Team-teaching is the significant element in this new approach by Pittsburgh.

Reed [39] in 1971 published a report of a survey of American library schools in the context of the core. Nine out of the fifty library schools surveyed still required Library History course (one of the core components); thirty-two schools demanded a course in Book Selection; forty-two required Cataloguing; forty-two required Reference. But the fundamental Library in Society course showed that twenty-six schools required it. Reed also discovered that the information science course offered by most schools earlier, had by 1970 dwindled to just eight schools. The implication of Reed's findings is that the core idea was falling out of favour with many schools in key areas of study.

The Association's (A.L.A.) Standards for Accreditation expressed continued support for the belief that library education should include 'the study of principles and procedures common to all types of librarians and library services.[40] But the Standards did not specify these principles and procedures, leaving it to each school to identify and justify its own set of basic essentials. Because of this general reluctance to be specific, there are those who hold the belief that librarians and library educators really do not have any idea what the essentials of librarianship are. If there is no common agreement on what the core should be, then it follows that there is no such thing as the core, they submit.

Rees,[41] for example, argues that a library school that has a core programme is dedicated to turning out generalists and is therefore indifferent to the needs of specialists. Asheim expands on this argument by stating that the schools with a core programme are dedicated to turning out both generalists and specialists and also desire their specialists to have a thorough grounding in general principles.[42] Each library school has its own set of required content and each one, when it comes up with its (presumably unique) definition of the common core turns out to be where everyone else is; advocating the premise that anyone holding a degree from the particular school should know something about materials that carry information, the needs and interests of the users of those materials, and the means, devices, processes, and mechanisms that will bring the user and information together. Usually, the disagreement about details of courses and the comparative amount of attention given to the different areas of study is seldom **about** the study areas themselves.

Marco[43] conducted a survey of library schools showing recent trends in respect of the core curriculum in graduate education. The study was limited to courses offered at the master's degree level which have been accredited by the A.L.A. The findings of the survey suggest that there is a 'threat' to the core, although, what constitutes this threat remained undefined. Marco's findings exposed an emerging attitude which he proposed in four new axioms:

(a) While basic principles and professional concerns are central to the programme, they do not necessarily remain constant. Changes of emphasis are to be expected.

(b) Basic principles and professional concerns do not have to be shaped into particular courses such as those which have been found in the traditional core curriculum.

(c) A convenient approach to the teaching of basic principles and basic professional concerns is through the device of a single 'integrated' course.

(d) Curricula structure is employed, the educational objectives must be clear and specific, and the measurement of success – for the curriculum and for the student – is the extent to which educational objectives are attained.

These educational objectives are based upon the tasks which librarians will be expected to perform.[44]

Of the four axioms outlined, axiom three (c) seems to present a new approach to the core — an integrated approach to the organisation of contents especially in the core areas. The theme of an integrated approach to the core was carried further in the workshop titled 'Integrated Core Curriculum: Alternative Approaches,'[45] held in March 6-8, 1977, at the University of North Carolina, Chapel Hill. The workshop was organised by the library schools of the University of South Carolina, Drexel University and the University of North Carolina at Chapel Hill. Seventy-one library educators from forty schools were in attendance. The findings of the workshop indicate that the integrated core curriculum concept did not receive universal enthusiasm.[46] For example, when asked in a survey if an integrated core curriculum might be considered for their school, 32% of the participants said 'yes': 16% said 'may be', and 45% 'no'. When asked why not: tradition, faculty resistance, financial considerations and the presence of part-time students in the programme were some of the reasons given. Thus, the results of the survey show that some library educators were dissatisfied with their programmes as they now exist, but such educators remain unconvinced that an integrated core curriculum is the solution.[47]

This attitude, as exemplified in the above results, does not detract from the major arguments in favour of providing a core programme: i.e., it is wasteful to duplicate the teaching of basics in multiple contexts; that librarianship loses its integrity and identity as a result of a fragmentation of the profession which impedes the ability of librarians to communicate with one another,[48] and that the existence of a core strengthens the specialist courses which follow, by sparing them the necessity of repeating over and over again the core content at the expense of the more intensive specialist study which can be built upon the assurance that all students in the class have already been exposed to the principles on which the specialist operations rest or from which they depart for specialist reasons.[49] This seems to be the present situation of the American core curriculum.

Implications of the Common Core for Developing Countries

The 'curriculum' as a whole is the instrument by which the objectives of a programme (or body of programmes) are translated through a series of lectures, seminars and tutorials, into knowledge (i.e. learning) skills that are required to cause affective and behavioural changes in those recruited into the profession. Within this broad definition of the curriculum, one may argue that a core programme is *sine qua non* in the planning of basic professional courses in the library school. The function of the core could be defined as, 'that part of the total curriculum which requires to be learned, no matter what specialisation the student aims for, or at what level the student is taught.[50] Whatever modifications there are to the core concept, the function remains the same. The purpose of the core is to contain 'those features of the educational programme which have common application to all librarians whether they work in a small public library or large university library, a high school or college library, or a special library in a technical organisation. The link between the 'purpose' and 'function' of the core is the educational preparation of both the generalist and specialist in all spheres of library and information work.

There are implications, in the adoption of the core concept, for curriculum planning in the developing countries. According to Dean:

> For various reasons the idea of a core curriculum is favoured in the developing countries, since the demand for flexibility and mobility requires every librarian to have an overall mastery of the essential elements of librarianship as they apply in any library situation. Where professionals are often few and far between the necessity of producing people who, for example are adaptable enough to move from a special library to a public library or from a cataloguing department to a reference department is paramount. The argument in favour of the acceptance of a core idea is really an argument for the production of the generalist or *Johannes fac totum* at the basic professional level and for training in depth in specialist fields at the post-professional level.[51]

It is clear that the author considered the core concept *in situ* by revealing the relative importance of the concept to the developing countries based on the urgent needs of libraries and library schools in those countries. The situation is often more confused especially when with economic boom as experienced by Nigeria in the seventies, sudden expansion in library services occur with the attendant urgent staffing needs to meet the demands of a rapidly changing society. The argument put forward by Dean in the above quotation is very pertinent today as when it was made in the early seventies. Provision for the educational preparation of librarians in Africa is still inadequate, bearing in mind that in the U.K. alone there were seventeen library schools which is equivalent to the whole of library schools in Africa. The responsibility lies with curriculum planners in the profession to ensure that the common core concept is used to good effect in preparing professionals for work in the expanding library and information services.

It is recognised that the emphasis on each constituent subject varies according to local needs of the country in which the library schools are situated, and this is likely to affect the functioning of the core. The effects of modifications to the core are considered in detail later with reference to Nigerian library schools.

Thus, in the case of developing countries, Dean states that the professional course is normally structured to cover core subjects and ancillary electives, the latter giving students an opportunity of pursuing individual interests without detracting from the general appreciation and comprehension of the essential aspects of librarianship.[52] Elsewhere in the literature, Professor Peter Havard-Williams refers to the importance of the core concept for the developing countries, stating that the idea of a core programme is a useful one if only to set educators thinking of the possibility of using resources economically, and more importantly to initiate, where this is necessary, a more unified approach to the education and training of library, information and archive staff.[53] The extent to which this objective has been achieved in the planning of library education programmes in Nigeria can be evaluated. However, the objective of a unified approach to the core seems to have taken off quite well in Nigerian educational programmes, and this study presents an opportunity for reviewing and reporting progress that has been made. Emphasis in the objectives of library and information studies programmes now seem to have moved from training for narrow special areas to training of library and information personnel for information studies based on a harmonised structure of the common core curriculum. For example, Professor Ogunsheye[54] of the Ibadan Library School has demonstrated the application of the harmonised core in the curricula of two library schools in Nigeria, based on the seminal work of Havard-Williams and Franz, 'Planning Information Manpower' (Conference Document Com 74/NATIS/REF 5).

In the past decade, various contributory factors have emerged to stimulate curriculum reform in library and information studies. One could consider the development of information systems and resource sharing, information network systems, planning of national information agencies, and international efforts directed at planning information manpower through seeking standardisation in educational practice in librarianship for developed and developing countries alike. In particular, one could consider the role of NATIS concerning its discernible efforts in the provision of qualified manpower for information services, bearing in mind universal technological innovations and the impact on libraries and library education – the Inter-Governmental Conference of UNESCO in September 1974 is an example of such efforts; to ensure a minimum supply of suitably qualified manpower. For NATIS, attention was paid to the programme for professional education and training of information personnel in its Objective 13. Objective 13 states *inter alia* that, '…basic elements of this programme are: (i) the harmonisation of curricula for documentalists, librarians and archivists.…'[55] The common core concept has incurred added significance and importance through this unified approach to the curriculum.

The varied patterns of educational systems in different countries, it is recognised, often incur varied structures which tend to relate to the relevant needs of the local community.

The common core programme as proposed in the NATIS document has a broad framework from which it would be possible for individual countries to interpret its adoption according to needs; the needs of students, staff and institution. According to the Objective 8 of NATIS, UNESCO states its course of action as follows:

> A core subject area, in harmony with equivalent programmes and objectives at national, regional and international levels, should be adopted as a guide for preparing basic professional curricula for information specialists, librarians and archivists at a level consistent with that of other university programmes of graduate standing.[56]

It is not always possible to follow up an objective which is as international in character as in the above quotation. It is therefore to the credit of UNESCO that recent developments indicate a continuity of action as envisaged in the framework of NATIS and UNISIST programmes. For example, second Inter-Governmental Conference on Scientific and Technological Information for Development (UNISIST 11) was held in Paris 28 May – 1 June 1979, where support was reaffirmed for the harmonisation and co-ordination of programme in the education and training of information personnel. UNESCO also convened a meeting at its headquarters in Paris from 26 to 30 November 1979, with the aim:

> ...to examine the possible measures to be taken for the harmonization of archival training programmes and the co-ordination of these programmes with those designed for the training of librarians and information specialists.[57]

This follow-up conference is a positive sign of progress being made in the attempt to harmonise the structure of the common core programme. Examples of individual library school's implementation stages are few in published form, although, Beraquet in a recent study provides a survey of schools offering combined training programmes for information studies:

> At the 'Ecole des Charters', Paris, archivists and librarians are trained together since its foundation in 1821; documentalists are added to these two (groups) in the U.K. at the School of Archive, Library and Information Studies at University College, London, and at the Department of Library and Information Studies at Loughborough University of Technology; in Africa at the well-known school at Accra and in Senegal at the School of Librarians, Archivists and Documentalists at the University of Dakar; and in Spain, at the 'Escuela de Documentalistas, Archiverosy Bibliotecarios' in Madrid where they have a post-university programme for archivists and librarians, and a common programme on the sub-professional level for assistant archivists, documentalists and librarians.[58]

A significant omission is a mention of other efforts at a combined training, as currently being done at the Ibadan Library School, even though evidence has been made available in this respect in professional literature, since 1977.[59]

In general, the post-World War II decades have brought into being new social, economic, political, scientific and technological changes which have re-shaped the traditional elements of library provision and practice and have therefore left their mark on the content of library and information studies.

The growth of literature and world literacy have complemented educational expansion. This has led to increased specialisation and the emergence of new subject-matter, especially, in the sciences and technology; introduced new materials and equipment; and also brought about the increasingly large and literate user population in libraries. These new elements call for complex skills and a specialised knowledge that could be most systematically conveyed in library schools.

With library and information studies still faced with the challenge of providing principles and guidelines for these new library situations, the notion of a core programme is invaluable in curriculum planning. One cannot propose that the mastering of detailed knowledge and skills in certain areas of library work, once essential and highly valued, is any longer a substantial part of library education. The important aspect of education for librarianship in terms of organising the curricula of library schools is to recognise the new function of the common core element in order to achieve the desired result of producing a **professional** capable of handling situations in library and information work.

References

1. Robinson, S. B., 'A Conceptual Structure of Curriculum Development', *Comparative Education*, 5(3), 1969: 223.

2. Phenix, P. N., *Realms of Meaning*, New York: McGraw-Hill, 1964.

3. Robinson, S. B. *op. cit*, : 224

4. Taba, H., *Curriculum Development Theory and Practice*, New York: Harcourt, Brace and World, 1962:8.

5. Kelly, A. Y., *The Curriculum: Theory and Practice*, London: Harper and Row, 1977: 3.

6. Kerr, J. F., *Changing the Curriculum*. London: University of London Press, 1968, (The problem of curriculum reform: 13-38)

7. Taba, H., *op. cit*.

8. Taylor, P. , 'Purpose and Structure in the Curriculum' *Educational Review*, (University of Birmingham), 19(3) & 20(1), 1967: 159-172: 19-29.

9. Merritt, J., *Reading and the Curriculum*, London: Ward Lock Educational, 1971.

10. Hirst, P. H., 'The Logic of the Curriculum', *Journal of Curriculum Studies*, 1(2), 1969: 142-158.

11. Cicero., *Cratio pro Rabirio Perduellonis Reo:* 10:30 Quoted in: Egan, K. 'What is Curriculum?' *Curriculum Inquiry*, 8, Spring 1978, 66.

12. Cicero., *De Senectute*, 11.38. Quoted in: Egan ... 'What is curriculum,' *Ibid*.

13. Rymer, T., *An Essay Concerning Critical and Curious Learning*, Reprinted. Los Angeles: University of California, Augustan Reprint Society, publication number 113, 1965 (1998).

14. Lewy, A., *Planning the School Curriculum*, Paris, UNESCO International Institute for Educational Planning, 1977: 11.

15 Eliot, T. S., *Notes Towards a Definition of Culture*, London: Routledge and Kegan Paul, 1968.

16. Towards a theory of popular education, In: Hooper, R. ed. *The Curriculum: Context, Design and Development*, Edinburgh: 1971: 251-264

17. Benge, R. C., *Cultural Crisis and Libraries in the Third World*, London: Clive Bingley, 1979:121.

18. Bramle, G., *A History of Library Education*, London: Clive Bingley, 1969:11.

19. Bramley, G., *Apprentice to Graduate: A History of Library Education in the U.K,* London: Clive Bingley, 1981: 88.

20. *Ibid:* 91

21. *Ibid:* 91

22. The papers referred to here are discussed in detail in the appropriate section of this work in the review of literature on curriculum development in librarianship.

    For reference, the workshop document is as follows: The British Library Board Workshop on Curriculum Development in Librarianship and Information Science College of Librarianship, Wales, 1977. London: BLRD, 1978.

23. Example of an anti-core paper presented at the seminar includes: Needham, C. D., 'The Common Core. ' Paper given at the BLRD curriculum development project meeting: Curriculum change in the 80's. Windsor: Cumberlan Lodge 1980 (mimeo).

24. Dudley, E. P., 'Curriculum Change in the 80s: Time for Significant Developments,' *Library Association Record,* 83(7), 1981:333.

25. Eyre, J., 'Teaching Students in Schools of Librarianship and Information Science about Computers and their Applications,' London: British Library, Research & Development Department, 1979. (Report No. 5466).

26. Quoted in Dudley E. P., 'Curriculum Change' ... *op. cit.*: 334

27. *Ibid.* 334

28. *Ibid.*

29. Quoted in Dudley E. P., 'Curriculum Change' ... *op. cit.* 332.

30. Boll, J., 'A Basis for Library Education,' *Library Quarterly,* r542(1), 1972: 196-197. (Especially figure 5).

31. Asheim, L., 'The Core Curriculum,' *Journal of Education for Librarianship,* 19, Fall 1978: 153.

32. Bramley, G., 'Apprentice to Graduate' ... *op. cit.* : 92.

33. Williamson, C. G., 'Training for Library Service: A Report Prepared for the Carnegie Corporation of New York:' The Corporation, 1923: 21.

34. Reece, E. J., *The Curriculum in Library Schools*, New York: Columbia University Press, 1936:11.

35. Asheim, L. E., ed. *The Core of Education for Librarianship*: A Report of a workshop held under the auspices of the Graduate Library School of the University of Chicago, August 10-15, 1953, Chicago: American Library Association, 1954: 35-39.

36. Asheim, L. E., 'The Core Curriculum,' *Journal of Education for Librarianship* ... *op. cit.*: 154.

37. Marco, G. A., 'A Rationale for International Library Education,' *International Library Review*, 9, 1977: 358 - 359.

38. Horrocks, N., 'Pitt's Changed Approach,' *Journal of Education for Librarianship*, 9(1), 1968: 13-17.

39. Reed, S. R. , 'The Curriculum of Library Schools Today: A Historical Overview', In: Goldhor, H., ed. *Education for Librarianship: The Design of the Curriculum of Library Schools*, Urbana, Illinois: University of Illinois, Graduate School of Library Science, 1971:29 *et. seq.*

40. *Standards for Accreditation, 1972*: Adopted by the Council of the American Library Association, June 27, 1972. Effective from January 1, 1973, Chicago: A. L. A., Committee on Accreditation, (1972): 5.

41. Rees, A., 'Beyond the Basics,' *Wilson Library Bulletin*, 51, 1976: 333-336.

42. Asheim, L. E., 'The Core Curriculum.' *op. cit.*: 155.

43. Marco, G. A., 'Recent Advantages of the American Core Curriculum,' *UNESCO Bulletin for Libraries*, 32(4), 1978: 279-283.

44. *Ibid.* 283.

45. Wilson, M. L., ed. Papers presented at a workshop on the integrated core curriculum, University of North Carolina, March 6-8, 1977, *Journal of Education for Librarianship*, 19, Fall 1978: 151-183.

46. *Ibid,*: 152

47. Rees, A., 'Beyond the Basics' ... *op. cit.*: 334

48. Asheim, L., 'The Core Curriculum' ... *op. cit.*: 155

49. Asheim, L., 'The Core of Education for Librarianship' ... *op. cit.*: 1-2.

50. Dean, J., *Planning Library Education Programmes: A Study of the Problems Involved in the Management and Operation of Library Schools in the Developing Countries*. London: Andre Deutsch, 1972: 68.

51. *Ibid.*

52. Havard-Williams, P., 'Education for Library, Information and Archives Studies', Paper presented at the IFLA General Council Meeting (Section of Library Schools) Oslo, August 1975, *IFLA Journal*, 2(3), 1976: 139.

53. Ogunsheye, F. A., 'Formal Programme Development in Library Education in Nigeria,' *COMLA Newsletter*, 17, 1977: 19-24.

54. *Planning Information Manpower*, UNESCO Conference Document: COM 74/NATIS/REF.5.

55. *Ibid.*

56. General Information Programme, *UNISIST Newsletter*, 7(4), 1979:59.

57. Beraquet V. S. M., 'The Development and Significance of the Core Curriculum in Archives, Library and Information Studies'. (Ph.D Thesis) Loughborough University of Technology, 1981:142.

58. Ogunsheye, F. A., 'Formal Programme Development' *op. cit.*

59. Aboyade, B. O., 'Restructuring the Course Content of the Literature and Bibliography of the Humanities,' *International Library Review*, 11(1). 1979:125-130.

2

Literature Review on Curriculum Development

Objective and Scope of Review

As in any other profession, librarianship responds to changes in the society in which it exists. The changes which affect librarianship, especially in the last few decades have been phenomenal — the expanding frontiers of knowledge, the improvement in and application of modern technology and hardware, and the increased awareness and complexity in demand for information by the society the library exists to serve.

Education for librarianship is essentially concerned with transmitting knowledge and skills which are necessary for successful performance in the profession of librarianship. This function places library schools at the vortex of the profession, and whatever change is necessary naturally originates from curriculum renewal. The objective of the literature review in this section, is to trace developments in education for librarianship concerning aspects of curricula changes in response to the changing nature and practice of librarianship as viewed mainly from British, American, Nigerian and other countries' perspective — such as Australia and India.

No particular date limit is set, although, more attention is paid to events in the past two decades of curriculum development in librarianship. Matters of historical detail and other non-essentials have been left out in preference for an in-depth analysis of curriculum development activity in and outside the library schools.

In the field of educational studies, curriculum development is a rather broad area of activities which encompasses the orientation of institutional objectives and the form of knowledge required to bring about learning experiences in students. There exists various kinds of institutions, each with its own objectives, teaching strategies, and approach to selection of curriculum content — based mostly on historical, sociological , philological, and psychological perspectives. One fundamental point seem to emerge from a consideration of the literature on curriculum development, that it is generally accepted that students have many and complex needs, and that the curriculum should be sufficiently broad and varied to provide for as many as possible. But what kind of needs are they, and in what ways can the curriculum provide for them? The concept of 'need' is a difficult one.

In almost all kinds of professional organisations, few people would doubt that human beings have need of warmth, nourishment and security, without which they would perish.

But what, in the educational context, are a person's intellectual, social, psychological, aesthetic, emotional and physical needs? How are objectives determined and by whom? Too often in the educational literature, **needs** are assumed and prescribed rather than explained and justified, and curiously, library educators seem to follow this trend in their interpretation of educational needs of the librarian.

One explanation that may be advanced in respect of a determination of 'needs' is that, the primary **educational need** is for various kinds of knowledge and understanding. All human knowledge, according to this view, is the product of refined and systematic thought. The dimension of thought will vary from institution to institution as symbolised in the cadres of professions. For example, this school of thought justifies the difference that exists in the structure of the curriculum of professional schools, be it medicine, clergy, social works, management, library and other 'professional' bodies. The ability of professionals to work upon, and make sense of experience in any recorded form, results ultimately in a body of knowledge essential for growth and maturity in that profession. Thus, this form of organisation and refined experience has been classified into a number of public traditions of knowledge, modes of inquiry or what the educationists refer to as 'cognitive structures'.

Hirst[1] offers one possible list of logically distinct knowledge: Mathematics, the physical sciences, the human sciences, including history, literature ,fine arts, morals, religion and philosophy. Elsewhere in the literature, Hirst and Peters assert that:

> To educate a person significantly in some of these (form of knowledge) only is to limit the forms of his development which we are prepared systematically to pursue. The issue of breadth in education, as opposed to narrow specialization, is, if faced properly, surely the issue of whether or not a per-fundamentally different type of objective experience and knowledge are open to men.[2]

Reading through the literature, it is interesting to observe the varied influences of the author's view on some library educationists' work. In a similar manner, Phenix offers the possibility of an alternative way of classifying experience for the purpose of education. In his *Realms of Meaning*[3] he argues that man makes sense of his world in six fairly distinct spheres:

> Symbolics (verbal and non-verbal communication): Empirics (the controlled testing of hypotheses): Aesthetics (the exploration of form, as in the visual and plastic arts, music and drama): Synnoetics (insights into human identity and personal relationships: Ethics and Morality (involving standards and

values which legitimise human conduct): Synoptics (the study of man in some holistic or integrated fashion).

Phenix's approach to knowledge, as summarised above by the present writer, can be observed to provide a less clear curriculum blueprint than does Hirst's cognitive structures, which are somewhat closer to familiar subjects in the curriculum. Hirst, for example, calls specifically for religion and history, whereas Phenix's *Realms of Meaning,* though not excluding either in the curriculum, appear to permit their incorporation within broader categories of experience. But it is important not to exaggerate these differences since the elements of study in the disciplines tend to overlap, say in history and sociology, where one has the option of choosing either a simple classification or a complex one.

However, other schools of thoughts need to be taken into account. For instance, Pring argues that educators are centrally (but by no means exclusively) concerned with the development of knowledge and understanding.[4] According to Pring, it is important not to lose sight of practical knowledge partly because it is valuable in itself, and partly because practical knowledge is so often what theoretical knowledge is theorising about.[5] In spite of this assertion, Pring admits that there are many different kinds of knowledge, developed into various disciplined modes of inquiry, but he provides a counter-view that the major problem lies in the selection of particular subject matters from the vast range of possible ones especially with the limited amount of time allowed on the time-table. Although Pring's argument is child-oriented in the context of the school curriculum, nevertheless, it is generally agreed in the literature that the author's viewpoint bears relevance for practice in the higher education system. On balance, his argument would seem difficult to ignore in relation to those of Hirst and Phenix. Pring's submission that the principles of selection are many and thus any curriculum must be a compromise seems valid, since it is difficult to prescribe in detail what such content should be. That would have to be debated in particular schools, or school systems, in the light of principles which a teacher or school or authority finds defensible.

It is against the foregoing background of the basic tenets of educational theory that we now examine the concept of Curriculum Development and its interpretation and practice in librarianship.

Definition of Curriculum Development (CD)

The view of the curriculum, which is presented in the introduction and in the previous sub-sections of this chapter suggests that effective policies for an overall curriculum should embrace all of the following elements:

(a)   The aims, purposes or principles of the school;
(b)   The selection and arrangement of studies and activities;

(c)　The methods by which these studies and activities are to be mediated;

(d)　The availability of the curriculum to students and the principles governing availability;

(e)　The methods of curriculum planning and strategies for curriculum development;

(f)　The methods of assessment and evaluation in the school;

(g)　The local factors, and in particular, the claims of the community.

These elements (a-g) are co-ordinated into policies for the curriculum. Given such framework for an overall policy, the curriculum is always subject to debate because of its intimate relationship to social and political values.

The norm of socio-economic changes dictate a constant need to clarify and up-date teaching objectives and procedures.[6,7] Changes in the society are more or less reflected in a reappraisal of values and change in student attitudes.

In the literature on sociology of education, sociologists accept and view education as inevitably adaptive to economic and technological change, whereas educationists argue that education itself generates change in these areas. Both arguments have had a prodigious influence on the planning of curricula as a continuing process. The sequence of the theorist's planning, i.e. identifying the aims and objectives, selecting content, methods and organisations, and finally evaluating, may not represent the exact sequence the practitioner follows, but at some stage in the planning process, it can only be assumed that objectives need to be identified.

Consequently, in view of existing influences that may mitigate against successful implementation of any curriculum design, it is important to seek a working definition of curriculum development to aid in the application of the concept in planning library education programmes. Hirst's definition, as quoted by Ghuman in a recent paper, states that curriculum development is:

> A programme of activities designed so that pupils (students) will attain, as far as possible, certain educational ends or **objectives**[8] (my emphasis).

The objectives theme is taken up by Lawton who explains that the need for curriculum 'change' (or 'development' as the term is interchangeably used) seems firmly rooted in the objectives model. For example, what are to be the objectives of a given course? Usually for 'objectives' to be objective in the real sense, it must be the product of an agreed ᶜonsensus among the curriculum development project team in the educational establishment. In this context, objectives have to be specific, unlike 'aims' which can be very broad and general, thereby representing a main focus for clarifying fundamental questions for relevance, logics and contradictions as often occur in curriculum development processes.

However, in its educational context the varying use of the objectives model is borne out in studies by Bloom,[9] Kratwohl,[10] Musgrove,[11] Stake,[12]

Gribble,[13] Kratwohl *et al*,[14] Harien,[15] and Hogben[16] among others. These educational writers focused their attention almost exclusively on primary and secondary education with no appreciable implications for individual course development at the higher education sector. It can also be observed that, until recently, very little attention was paid to the problems arising from pre-specification of curriculum objectives. For example, Tyler[17] had earlier in 1949, offered a model of curriculum planning which commenced with the specification of objectives, but like the later work of Bloom in 1956 it failed to make an immediate impact on either the theory or practice of curriculum development. The situation changed in 1965 when in Kratwohl's work it was suggested that three or more levels of specificity be recognised, i.e.:

(a) The general statements of goals that will guide the planning of the curriculum as a whole;

(b) The behavioural objectives derived from these (statements) which will guide the planning of individual units or courses;

(c) A third level of objectives appropriate in some cases to guide the planning of specific subjects.

In retrospect, it is important to consider Bloom's offer of three clear domains in the range of objectives — the cognitive, the affective, and the psychomotor — the first two of which are fully worked out in the two volumes of the taxonomy. Bloom seems to suggest that in framing objectives, it is important for educators to be clear not only about the sequential nature of the activity but also about the different categories of behaviour that are of concern. The 'cognitive domain' is defined as comprising 'objectives which emphasise remembering or reproducing something' which has presumably been learnt; it also comprises objectives which involve the solving of some intellective task for which the individual has to determine the essential problem and combine it with ideas, methods or procedures previously learned.[18] Questionably, Bloom offers no criteria for the evaluation of objectives, i.e., no basis upon which a choice can be made concerning specific objectives in a given educational context.

Perhaps more important is the clear omission in the taxonomy of any account of the nature of knowledge — the premise on which the work is supposedly based. Furthermore, educational philosophers like Pring have noticed that the taxonomy has no clearly worked-out epistemological foundation. Pring[19] argues the need for such a foundation as being an essential prerequisite for any taxonomy of educational objectives, since whatever else education is concerned with, it is certainly concerned with cognitive development of many kinds, and with the acquisition of knowledge of many forms. But, in whatever perspective that curriculum development is viewed; as a 'process', or 'system', or 'activity' by its practitioners, the problem of finding a parameter for its definition within the context of professional education still persists.

In general, those responsible for professional development in all fields, have indirectly contributed towards providing a sound knowledge base relating to practice in the different spheres of professional activity in which they are engaged. The process through which such a base is achieved is largely dependent on factors such as; attendance at many meetings over the years; group seminars; writing; and a good deal of exchange of views about content and relative weighting of courses, not to mention the effects of the 'invisible college' on exchange of information and material. With the tenets of practice clearly developed, every profession depends upon its system of education to be the primary entry point for new professionals. It is in this vital role that professional schools are expected to sort out the aspirants, and to decide which of those who are admitted for professional training qualify for graduation. Curriculum development as an area of activity in the library school is therefore a vital element in the furtherance of aims and objectives, and content through learning experiences based on change in the circumstances of practice. Thus, for the purpose of this study, a working definition of curriculum development would be:

> The continuous review of course content and relationships undertaken as **needed**: such as, when the employment market, or professional thinking, or manpower forecasts, or the trend of research interests dictates that change is due.

This definition is all-embracing, including the elements of educational objectives. Curriculum development may thus be regarded as a cyclic process represented in a simple but effective model:

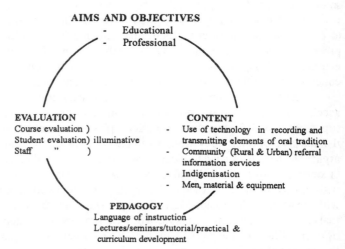

Figure 2.1: Curriculum Development as Cyclic Process in African Library Education

Education

It is immediately noticeable that the need for change seems firmly rooted in the objectives model since it serves as a focus for clarifying fundamental questions of relevance, logics and contradictions as often occur in curriculum development processes. In order to be satisfactorily related to changing circumstances in the profession, the pattern as set out in the Chart is now emerging although priorities would need to be determined in the subsections of each main heading.

In examining the literature on curriculum development it becomes apparent that much work remains to be done in relating the values pervading **professional** activity to the values pervading other parts of society, such as: economic, political, and religious. This is essentially because the core of the generally-accepted criteria on professionalism is itself under constant stress of change since the Industrial Revolution through the nineteenth and twentieth century. For the 21st century, the implications are quite enormous for educational practice in the professions which are already having more than their fair share of splinter group and elements. In this respect, one can understand the present confusion as to the undoubted distinction between those subjects which are considered as purely 'academic' and those (like library studies in the 50s and early 60s) which are considered as 'vocational'. In the case of the latter, there exists a peculiar problem arising from the need to work out, for educational purposes, a satisfactory relationship between theory and practice. Consequently, most of the professions include elements of academic study in the curriculum, either to enhance their status or improve the theoretical foundation of the intellectual content of professional practice.

The educational activities of library schools and establishments concerned with library education are examined in the following review of curriculum development literature in library and information studies. For convenience of thought, the review is conducted *in seriatim*, indicating British, American, Nigerian and other studies mainly from Australia and India.

British Studies

Contributions to the curriculum development literature in library and information studies in the United Kingdom have accumulated over the years in a rather unique fashion. Unique, in the sense that by the end of the eighteenth century the education of professional 'men' (unisex term) was almost entirely by the apprenticeship method. It was only in Britain that, by the end of the nineteenth century — a **professional** qualification granting chartered status was well-established. The holder of the (British) Library Association (LA) Diploma had chartered status as distinct, for example, from the American **pre-Due** (Dewey) years of apprenticeship and in-service library training classes designed to improve local services.

The 'Professional' Element

In the United Kingdom, an historical overview of the development trends in the library education scene is covered in detail in Gerald Bramley's *A History of Library Education,*[20] which not only sets out to complement the earlier work but also examined, (a) 'the results of the decision taken by the Library Association to assume the role of an examining and a qualifying body; and (b) the responses of the Association to **changing educational and social influences** (my emphasis) to the point where the Library Association relinquished its direct responsibility for the conduct of examinations in librarianship.'[21]

Bramley chronicles the pattern of the changing educational and social influences by tracing the metamorphosis of librarianship from a mechanistic function to a fully-fledged profession, i.e. from the introduction of competitive examinations in the nineteenth century to the predominantly graduate emphasis of modern times. He also showed the conflict of interests which occurred within the profession, the arguments about status, and what he uncharitably referred to as the 'withering' of the Library Association's examining function as independent library schools grew and began to flourish. In terms of content of courses, the Library Association used its monopoly of the register of chartered librarians to impose restrictions on the schools. For instance, the Library Association's policy at the time was that if academic subjects were introduced as stiffening elements at the expense of library study, then it might well refuse to recognise such courses as suitable preparation for admission to its register of professional librarians. The courses which were eventually introduced under C.N.A.A. auspices, at undergraduate level in librarianship, represented a compromise. Bramley submits that:

> The curriculum of the librarianship content, for the most part, closely followed the pattern of the syllabus introduced by the Library Association in 1964. The students were usually required to study the core subjects in their first year, covering library administration, cataloguing and classification and reference work.[22]

Apart from the specialised options made available in the second and third years, each library school had introduced one or more other subjects into the curriculum which would usually bear some relevance to the study and practice of librarianship. Davinson,[23] for example, reflects that languages were often accorded an important place in the curriculum, as well as sociology and economics. The subjects were usually taught by other departments in the college, sometimes quite independently of the study programmes in librarianship.

Despite the historical details contained in Bramley's work, it still provides a good background from which to have an in-depth view and understanding of curriculum development in British librarianship. The importance of the Library Association as a valuable contributor to what constitutes the professional context of the curriculum cannot be ignored. The Library Association has for several years provided the syllabus for professional examinations for the chartered status both at the associate and fellowship levels in Britain and many overseas countries. By mid-seventies, the educational trend in British librarianship was towards a graduate entry into the profession. Therefore, pressure naturally came to bear on the profession to restructure its system of education and pattern of recruitment. Most library schools were increasingly attached to higher education establishment at universities and polytechnics and their consequent expansion within the higher education system made curriculum renewal an absolute necessity. Besides this point, other professional bodies in U.K. were already re-examining and restructuring their system of education in view of changes in the field. There may appear on the surface little in common between, for example, accountants, civil engineers, medical practitioners, and librarians, but professional bodies in U.K. all have royal charters and are therefore all under the general supervision of the Privy Council. Thus, the Library Association Council in 1975, appointed a working party to investigate 'The future of professional qualifications'[24] with the following terms of reference:

(a) To determine appropriate levels of registration and certification in relation to the present and future needs of the profession;

(b) To consider and define thereof, and to identify the principles underlying professional education and registration and how these should be attained and regulated, in the light of available evidence;

(c) To assess the resources required from employers, training boards, educational institutions and the Association, and to determine priorities;

(d) To make recommendations.

The ensuing Report[25] took cognisance of developments in other chartered professional bodies and found that they too were reappraising their education and training policy. Perhaps of significance in the case of the Library Association is the fact that the working party worked in consultation with the influential Professional Development and Education Committee of the Library Association, an executive body through which the recommendations were forwarded to the council.

In all, seventeen recommendations were made, three of which are pertinent to mention here:

(i) That all students entering schools of librarianship in and after 1981 should be required to achieve graduate status before being admitted to professional membership of the association.

(ii) That a new membership structure be introduced with effect from 1981 as follows : Chartered Librarian, FLA — Fellow, after at least 5 years as Associate; ALA — Associate, after 3 years as Licentiate and completion of a professional report and interview; LLA — Licentiate, after one year of approved service and apprenticeship at graduate or postgraduate level.

(iii)   That the Library Association should take the initiative in establishing a standing committee with representative of the Library Profession Education and Development Committee, Association of British Library and Information Studies Schools, and other interested organisation to act as a focal point for communication between the schools and the rest of the profession, particularly in regard to **content of courses** (my emphasis).

Clearly, the implementation of the report is at present in progress with considerable scope for optimism as indicated in current trend. The proposed structure, would establish a solid base for the 'professional element' in curriculum level. Furthermore, attempts to widen the route to FLA status through professional qualifications such as Ph.D in library and information studies, have been restricted perhaps understandably in view of the fact that the fellowship is the highest accolade that can be conferred on a 'professional', and if he/she is not to lose that status, it ought to be awarded selectively, and more importantly, on presentation of professional contribution based on practical rather than theoretical experience. However, for the Library Association under the new regulations, it was 1986 before any new-style association was elected.

The Academic Element

With the advent of university and C.N.A.A. degrees in library and information science, considerable attention has been focused on their development at both undergraduate and postgraduate levels. It would seem that contributors to the literature on curriculum development in the U.K. chose specific area of practice in the disciplines. For example, in the international scene, Franz and Havard-Williams [26,27] have proposed the harmonisation of the core curriculum for the educational preparation of the librarian, archivist and documentalists. The paper came out fairly strongly on the notion of a 'harmonised' core curriculum for the three disciplines or as they put it, 'three aspects of a basic discipline; based on a general division of the curriculum into — foundations, materials, methods, management, mechanisation and men.' Another strand in the document is that of different levels of performance and therefore, for training similar to the division identified in earlier works by Schur on the Education and training of information scientist in the '70's[28], and the survey done by the British Government Department of Education and Science.

Elsewhere in the literature, Havard-Williams [29] argues that the connection between a core curriculum and the different levels of education and training were insufficiently worked out in the UNESCO paper, as each kind of professional should be thought of in three distinct ways of the curriculum:

(a)   General Education

(b)   Professional Education

(c)   Supervising training before/during and after the period of education.[30]

In expanding on the notion of training, the author cited the example of practice in the United Kingdom where the usual practice is to complete a three or four-year degree in the subject other than librarianship, information science, or archives study, to undertake a year's practice in a library, a documentation centre or an archive repository. The candidate then takes a year's master or diploma course, and for librarianship or information science needs a year's practice under (chartered) supervision before being admitted to full professional membership of the Library Association. It is this link, between curriculum development activity and professional manpower planning, which formed almost all the professional literature on the concept of library professionalism and this fact seems to have been largely ignored.

More fundamentally, those concerned with professional education have been pressurised into taking increasing account of the changing nature and needs of library and information work. And the consequent implications for professional education. The Council for National Academic Awards (C.N.A.A.), library and information studies degree curriculum owe immense debt to the Library Association syllabus but then began to break out in other directions so that innovation in the curriculum became a significant feature of the periodic five-year C.N.A.A. submission . The freedom enjoyed by individual institutions in preparing their own programmes led to a concern on the structure and content of degree courses in library and information studies. Technological change has invariably implied a change in professional and education objectives.

In terms of structure, a change which has been of considerable significance is that when the bachelor degree in librarianship started, the general opinion in the profession was that the library subjects had to be shored up by more respectable academic subjects which would give the degree much desired respectability. But as time went by, more articles and books have been written and more research done, and as Havard-Williams has observed, 'library studies has become a subject sufficiently respectable to stand on its own.'[31]

However, this situation far from 'shoring' up library studies as a subject, changed the direction from which pressure came to bear, i.e., the question as to whether postgraduate librarianship is effectively taught in the short space of nine months (PG Dip); and whether strictly as librarians, candidates with a B.A. degree are not better prepared than those with a postgraduate qualification in librarianship after taking a degree in another subject.

Next to experience change is the content, as the climate of educational qualification and professional practice became dominated by the whirlwind of the new technological age with which, in the future, librarianship is most likely to be associated. Again, it has been predicted on paper that curriculum development would take an effective account of technological innovations by providing in the curriculum similar schemes 'to professional education schemes found in other spheres of social and scientific activity' (mainly engineering, computer sciences, and acoustics).

Another unique proposition relating to structure and content of library studies is that an integrated master's degree of five years' duration might be a future alternative, on the model of the five-year degree in architecture. In proposing that these developments in the professional education of the future 'librarian' be incorporated in curriculum development, Professor Havard-Williams admits that it is 'not so easy to forecast the orientation of new objectives as the general emphasis on information, computer studies, community librarianship, and services to education is likely to continue'. The feasibility of a two-year master's programme and doctoral by course-work as proposed by Havard-Williams is already being explored by library schools in the developing countries of Africa.

Other British writers in contributing to the analysis of curriculum development in specific areas of library and information studies, have concentrated on comparable elements of the curriculum. For instance, Grogan[32] has examined in detail, the non-librarianship elements of degree courses in librarianship, and thus provided a valuable insight into their development; Wilson[33] has investigated the influence of research on the processes of design and development of librarianship curricula and found that the literature on curriculum development which indicates theoretical or descriptive models illustrating the influence of research, was almost non-existent. The available literature, according to Wilson, is chiefly American and concerned almost exclusively with primary and secondary education.[34] The author then examined the semantic difficulties usually associated with attempts to provide a working definition of curriculum development both in an educational context and in specific applications of usage. Although Wilson's contribution to curriculum development literature is a welcome addition in a field already starved of documentary evidence of practice, the scope of the paper was strictly limited to the writer's experience of the design of C.N.A.A. proposals, contribution to the design of the M.A. in Information Studies at Sheffield and earlier contributions to discussion on the Library Association syllabus. His conclusions show that research has only a marginal influence on curriculum development.

With regards to weighting and assessment, Holroyd,[35] Kaye and Wood[36] have related their findings to a general application of the assessment procedure in library and information studies, and specific application in terms of coursework, using the basic principles of educational theory and practice.

The development of thought on educational trends in the field of information studies (and 'science') have also proliferated. For instance, Foskett[37] has provided an in-depth review of the intellectual foundation of information 'science' as a discipline and argued the case for its development within the curriculum, based on the 'real needs of users'. Saunders[38] has conducted a review of the whole field of education for science information work with emphasis on the unity and the interrelated nature of librarianship and information work. In a UNESCO/UNISIST Report, Saunders[39] proposed guidelines for curriculum development in information: although it is apparent that the work is not original it still provides a useful confirmation of the status quo for the developing countries as it serves as a focus for standardisation in the provision of information studies programme in the library schools.

The opportunities and problems encountered in the process of developing the information science curriculum have been discussed in the work of Maguire.[40] In all these studies, the language and methodology of curriculum studies have been related practically to the formal processes of the library and information field, although such application of educational theory have not altogether escaped from criticism in the library profession. For example, Dudley observes, that the trend in curriculum development processes for undergraduate courses is not without its flaws:

> ...These (curriculum development language and methodology) seem little understood by many practitioners – not altogether surprising because the B.A., B.Sc, B.lib qualified librarian is still the exception, accounting for no more than one in ten of working qualified librarians.[41]

Despite this criticism, it is important to this study to closely consider contributions to the curriculum development literature as experienced in the process of design by British library educators.

Needham[42] refers to the undergraduate curricula of library schools in the U.K. as collective representations – 'images of reality' as perceived by planners. He points out that these 'images' are most clearly to be perceived in the **structure** of the curriculum i.e., in the general plan and sequence of study; the designation of core areas (and hence peripheral ones); the kinds of approach adopted, such as the relative degree of priority given to types of libraries as against processes and operations; the weighting of parts and the balance between theory and practice; and, the span of internal relations between elements.[43] The 'images' are reflected in three core areas: management, indexing, and bibliography. Arguably, this identification of the core areas cannot be generalised due to different interpretation in terminology, e.g., 'management' or library administration, and 'indexing' or cataloguing and classification. Whatever terminology is used the framework remains the same. For instance, the writer suggests that librarianship subjects can be studied in context of their intellectual environment. In the chart on 'Curriculum Development as a Cycle Process in African Library Education' (p.26) academic subject study through learning experiences is inscrutably attached to community studies, yet Needham does not see any justification in their inclusion in the curriculum. He concludes by proposing an integrated approach for developing elements in the curriculum as exemplified in the chart, but 'integration' is not mainly the basis for planning teaching strategy for the interdisciplinary parts of the curriculum.

Wilson,[44] in a related study identifies three categories of factors influencing curriculum development:

(a)   Preconditional factors — i.e. those factors that create the need for curriculum development, e.g. the creation of polytechnics and the establishment of the C.N.A.A.

(b)   External or 'environmental' factors, such as the needs of the market, the quality and background of potential students, general professional opinion, research trends, and overall time constraints.

(c)   Intra-organisational or internal factors, such as available teaching skills, internal competition for time and associated 'power' struggles, general knowledge of the field and trends within it, and research.

Clearly, an interaction of both the external and internal factors indicate a reliance on the objectives model in view of the stated preconditional and environmental factors – this vital link with the necessary statement of objectives is missing in Wilson's analysis, but the paper cannot be faulted on the value of its contribution to the understanding of the curriculum development process. In other instances, articles and theses have been written in aspects of curriculum development activity.

Davinson[45] traced the influence of computer and telecommunications technology on curriculum development in librarianship and found that the rate of change 'has transformed the face of librarianship in Britain'. The consequences for traditional forms of librarianship are that this rate of change will accumulate at an increasing pace until, within ten years or so, considerable amounts of present range of tasks carried out by librarians will be 'virtually dead' (*sic*). While this assertion may be true, for example, in the area of co-operative cataloguing services with the consequences for teaching, (as librarians may no longer require a high standard of competence as cataloguers) it is nevertheless unlikely that library traditional system will be 'virtually dead' either now or in the immediate future. Such exaggerations can be rather startling and counter-productive in the recruitment of new professionals

In a comparative study of degree courses in librarianship and information science in the U.K., Lawal[46] submits that:

(a)   There are different elements constituting degree programmes offered in British library schools, in terms of varying structure in course content. For example, different regulations govern course weightings and assessments thereby leading to obvious differences such as in the area of degree classification, supervised projects and dissertations, and fieldwork; the nature and period of library placements for students and the degree of success or failure thus achieved.

(b)   There is a common ground in the specialised options for the postgraduate diploma course content. For example, in **area studies,** each institution specialises in studies relevant to their locality, e.g. Wales (CLW): Welsh area studies in Bibliography; London: UCL's Palaeography and Archives; the former Polytechnic of North London (PNL) – music course combined with librarianship studies.

(c)   The separate institutional development of information science courses has led to no discernible pattern as regards what level the course ought to operate. The unique features of existing information science curriculum are analysed to show their comparability in the light of programmes being run at Leeds; City University, London; Sheffield; Loughborough; and Wales.[47]

The study presents a wide variety of evidence as regards curriculum development activity in the sixteen library schools examined.

Burrell[48] in a comprehensive two-volume work, investigated the systematic foundation for professional education and training in British librarianship and information 'service'. Burrell states that the system approach to curriculum development process consists of six phases:

(a)   The initial selection of aims, goals and objectives at successive levels of specificity, expressed in terms of desired behaviours.

(b)   The selection of such learning experiences as are likely to help students to attain the chosen aims, goals and objectives.

(c)   The selection of suitable subject-matter content as a vehicle for the chosen learning experiences.

(d)   The organisation and integration of learning experiences and subject-matter content to sustain the learning and teaching processes in the classroom, i.e. in all learning environments.

(e)   The planning of certain other elements of the educational process i.e.,
(i)   learning and teaching methods;
(ii)   assessment of student achievement;
(iii) selection or adaptation of plant and facilities;
(iv)   preparation, deployment and continuing education of staff;
(v)   recruitment of students;
(vi)   the follow-up of ex-students.

(f)   The planning and implementation of the continuous evaluation and modification of the whole system.[49]

Based on the above-mentioned system orientation of curriculum development as a process, the author hypothesised that current unsystematic methods of constructing programmes in education for librarianship in the U.K. lack simplicity, predictability and flexibility of structure; ease and economy of administration; relevance to professional life; and a basis of sound educational theory for teaching, learning and assessment.

Because of these deficiencies, students and teachers tend to be confused about the nature of the aims and goals of programmes, about the level, direction, pace and desirable content of studies and about the efficacy and relevance of the procedures. Burrell suggests that there is a common conviction that a curriculum is merely the sum of its content. For the same reasons, librarians in the field, as potential employers of the young people concerned, are unable to evaluate, influence or complement the programmes to the full. It was further suggested by the writer that there may well be a significant degree of under-achievement in all quarters as a further consequence of these deficiencies. In Burrell's study, the conclusions show that:

(a)   A vocational curriculum must be designed to produce, not a practitioner who merely retains a given body of knowledge, but one who is the right kind of person for the activity, possessing appropriate attitudes, behaviours and complex intellectual skills of a high order and who is eager to perform effectively as a librarian in any context.

(b)   These attributes may be enhanced and orientated, but not necessarily inculcated *ab initio*, by exposing the student to a carefully chosen set of experiences, presented through the medium of an appropriately integrated and smoothly unfolding body of subject content which is, itself, suitably structured and weighted and presented in an appropriate sequence.

(c)   Librarianship and information service do not constitute a traditional profession however, primarily because they lack any distinctive central philosophy, theory or principle.

(d)   The curriculum should not be confined, metaphorically or in reality, to the four walls of a library but should explore many aspects of the practical and intellectual life of the community, its institutions and records, with academic vigour.

(e)   Because the curriculum is based upon a close analysis of the tasks to be performed and upon the implications of these tasks for the 'life' of the society, particularly for its documentary and information needs, the curriculum is thus assured of 'relevance', a basic criterion of validity for an educational endeavour.

(f)   The library schools should teach 'what could and should be', not merely 'what is', the state of affairs of librarianship.

The curriculum is in effect a bridge reaching out towards 'what should be' but firmly anchored to 'what is'. The proposed curriculum is not a bland placebo but a prescription for basic professional skills, attitudes and knowledge, interpreted and delivered in a more realistic, systematic and flexible manner than has been attempted before, and thereby rendered adaptable to change so long as the profession regards changes in services as **opportunities** and new technologies as **tools** with which to exploit the opportunities.[50]

Burrell's recommendations reflect the growing trend towards relating the curriculum of library schools to the tasks and functions of professional library and information services, but the curriculum development process should also take cognisance of the manpower implications for all categories of library staff.

This requires that quantitative data will be required on the 'work characteristics' of library and information professionals in order to accurately determine the task analysis and relative educational innovation needed to bring about the desired factor of 'relevance' in the curriculum. Some of Burrell's conclusions along this line could not be tested nor evaluated since the work lacks the essential methodology for achieving any such objective. In this present work, this element of evaluating specific task items in library and information is examined in detail in the chapter on 'methodology'. However, this point should not detract from the rather high qualities of Burrell's work. The work is certainly the most substantial literature on U.K. curriculum development process for some time, using appropriate educational theory to illumine the system approach to modes of education for librarianship and information service through in-depth analysis of: 'objectives', content, learning and teaching modes, plant and facilities, deployment of staff, recruitment of students, and follow-up of students (including career counselling and placement).

In May, 1978, the British Library Research and Development Department's Curriculum Development Project was commissioned to:[51]

(a) Study the development of the professional curriculum, particularly the nature of the 'common core', its relevance to other and newer aspects of the curriculum and to the changing activities of libraries and information units.

(b) Attempt to identify lines of needed and fruitful development.

(c) To give some consideration to the nature of constraints on curriculum change.

(d) Generate discussion of the topic among teachers in the schools and practising librarians.

(e) Organise a workshop on the subject.

A main focus of the enquiry would be the so-called 'common core' of the professional curriculum, seen both as a foundation of the curriculum and as preparation for professional work. There is little doubt that indexing, bibliography and management are, however labelled, regarded as the three basic areas of study in most, if not all, British schools. It is also fairly certain that this core based as it is on a traditional view of librarianship, is increasingly the subject of criticism. It would be widely accepted that as a structure, it leads to disintegration: relationships between the elements of the common core necessary to adequate study and professional practice are not visible. Moreover, given this core, professional concerns tend to be reduced to technicalities because context is secondary. Nevertheless, most schools have introduced a wide range of contextual studies during the last ten years: again they tend to remain isolated. It would be fruitful therefore, to enquire into the internal core relationships and the relationships between the core and contextual studies.

The scope of the enquiry would be primarily but not exclusively concerned with first professional qualification courses: undergraduate, postgraduate diploma and master's degree.

Methods. The nature of curriculum development and innovation does not easily lend itself to statistical analysis and easily quantifiable date. Questionnaires will have a small and useful part, but only discussions and interviews are likely to reveal information and important shades of opinion and the motivation of teachers and students. Accordingly, the approach will be by means of visits to schools and to some libraries and will employ what educationists. Sometimes term 'illuminative evaluation'....

It was decided not to make a close survey of the current curricula at the various schools in the hope that they might be reduced to some comparative evaluation, nor to send detailed questionnaires to each institution but rather to visit employers of librarians and information workers as well as schools of librarianship and information studies and by personal discussion attempt to obtain more significant information... we are hoping to focus attention on new developments in the belief that many of them would turn out to be stimulated by some major dissatisfaction with a previously existing state of affairs.... Consideration has also been given to an evaluation of students' opinions of the curriculum.

The summaries of interviews were analysed under headings which give some idea of the scope of the work, i.e.:

— changes in the curriculum; the common core; computer studies; the future; the gap between the teaching and practising profession; joint honours degrees; librarians and information officers; the over-production of librarians; the (field work) placement of students; postgraduate courses; the role of the curriculum; the selection of students; the teaching of management; user studies; and some additional topics such as the education of the specialist and generalist; over-high expectations of students; community information; teaching of bibliography; post-qualification courses; job opportunities; the teaching library; the teaching of statistics; speaking and report writing; research; training; school librarianship; job descriptions; short courses; audio-visual materials; commercial and technical information. (These are presumably reduced to order in the Final Report.)

From the foregoing quotation on the scope, methods and purpose of the Curriculum Development Project, it becomes clear that the 'common' core in British library schools is traditionally composed of three areas of study (which have been identified in an earlier paper by Needham[52] at the Wales workshop on Curriculum Development in 1977): 'bibliography', 'indexing' and 'management'. In another paper delivered at the Cumberland Lodge Seminar on the Curriculum Development Project in 1980, Needham again examined 'The common core'[53], and in an observation of the core trivium — 'bibliography', 'indexing' and 'management', he commented:

> Continuing espousal of this trinity prevents the proper recognition of people and requirement. Inevitably, the needs of those served by the systems of indexing, bibliography and management are viewed obliquely (in so far as they are viewed at all), professional education thus fails to promote a sense of service — a fact too attested when service is sought.[54]

This view seems to reflect an 'anti-core' stance in favour of an integrated approach to the curriculum. When evaluated in context of the curriculum, 'bibliography' contains two elements that are of minor consequence, i.e. the physical bibliography of printing and book binding, and the physical attributes of tape and film are fascinating concepts broadly refined by experience, but need they be allowed to further side-track potential librarians since they can display ability to talk intelligently with the trade and draw up sensible specifications? Historical bibliography though of considerable value has limited opportunities for application by potential librarians taking up their first duties in libraries, how then can it justify its time allocation on a tightly scheduled programme?

These questions have wider connotations in that they invoke curious examination of the other parts (subjects) constituting the curriculum in order to determine the range of priorities. In context of developing countries such as Nigeria, for example, aspects of historical and physical bibliography are treated as optional courses, thereby, implying that there may be many library school graduates without knowledge in this area.

'Indexing', in its broadest sense, may very well include traditional classification and cataloguing, but in the narrower interpretation of the concept, one may argue that it has little in the way of a direct 'public service' content and its products are not understood or used by the public to the extent that its practitioners would wish. This observation is backed up in the findings of numerous 'catalogue use surveys,'[55] but even more significant is the probability that practitioners lack initiative in educating or training their clients in the use of classification schemes, catalogues, indexes and data-bases.

'Management' is more inherently accepted as a component of the 'core', as it is usually envisaged and sometimes extended to include a substantial element of the social context of librarianship with which there may be little in common. This pragmation lends itself to the theory that 'management' is utilitarian in a subject-departmentalised school organisation. One may relate this to Needham's suggestion about the common core:

> Three steps seem to be called for. First, people and their requirements must somehow be made real to students. Second, means must be found for ensuring that students undertake the creation and analysis of systems in the light of that reality. Third, existing systems must be presented not as the

absolutes they so often become when they themselves are the core, but, on the contrary, as human responses to particular and often complex situations, always bound to their historical context and therefore provisional.[56]

The core therefore becomes a matter of aim and method rather than of content, thus, it is susceptible to change. Dudley observes that where the common core is concerned, there has been 'the most extensive change in our (British) courses, most of it unrecorded outside the official documents of each school.[57] Dudley also reveals, in relation to management of example, that discussions during the Curriculum Development Project indicate that an area where courses can possibly be in advance of practice (as some were with the computer in the 1960s) is indeed the 'management' of the new technologies if that is taken to mean the possible changes in the nature of library and information work, of library staffing and the use of libraries and information which technology will bring about — changes often not planned.[58] This implies that while traditional library skills and practices will in future still be required, areas of certain growth lie outside them. This has wide implications for curriculum development in library and information studies.

The British curriculum development scene in librarianship and information science may from the foregoing be observed to be actively in the forefront of world trends in the field. In terms of the impact of computer and its role in the curriculum for library and information studies, Eyre,[59] has reported recently under the aegis of the British Library, thus, developments in this area are closely followed. Similarly, the visionary Library Association has instituted a working team on the new technologies. The prediction, with regards to professional education in this respect, is that emphasis will be placed upon the need for post-qualification retraining in information technology but the impact on courses and curriculum development as a whole still remains obscure in terms of the response needed by the library schools to meet the new challenge.

American Studies

The 'Apprenticeship' Approach

In the United States of America as well as in other parts of the American continent, vast amounts of literature have emerged on curriculum development in the form of articles, papers, reports, monographs and theses. In the field of librarianship, the earliest publication that is of pertinence to this present study is Churchwell's[60] doctoral thesis of 1966, 'Education for Librarianship in the United States: Some Factors which Influenced its Development between 1919 and 1939'. The study itself is full of stodgy details which contributed to knowledge only in the historical sense. In the study, the author accords incidental treatment to curricula issues 'not because they are unimportant aspects of the development of library education, but rather because of the necessity to limit the study, and because they have already been the subjects of several studies.'[61] However, if one considers the relative importance of library education development trends in the period under study by Churchwell then clearly his omission of curriculum issues creates a serious gap indeed in the understanding of the curriculum development process.

As historical studies show, learning how to do the job (apprenticeship) gave way to learning the elements of each operation, e.g., courses in 'reference', 'bibliography', and the 'selection of books' were well lodged in the curriculum shortly after 1900. Reed, in a background paper focusing on a historical overview of curriculum development, gives a brief summary of the history of American library education – *vide* the pre-Dui (Dewey) years 'apprenticeship' and in-service library training classes designed to improve local services: 1887 — Dewey and his rationalisation leading to a common avenue of library training and his Columbia School of Library Economy; 1923 — Williamson, the A.L.A. Board of Education for Librarianship and initial accreditation of professional library education; and the 1933 standards.[62] Reed emphasised that in the early schools the curricula stressed cataloguing, classification (according to Dewey), library techniques including the 'library hand', and an extensive practicum frequently reported to have been of more benefit to the library served than to the student. In the Dewey years (1887-1920) the 'proper professional preparation' (still apprentice in outlook) are as follows:

(a)   A college course;
(b)   The three months' course as designed for the Columbia College School of Library Economy;
(c)   The completion of one or two years' actual experience in various kinds of library work;
(d)   A return to the Columbia College School for the three months' course taken again in review.[63]

Faithful though they were, no record exist to indicate that any of Dewey's portages returned after two years to repeat the initial course. Elsewhere in the literature, White lends weight to the 'apprenticeship approach' when as a result of observation   of the 1887 programme at Columbia, it was found that the programme consisted of lectures late in the afternoon twice a week followed by discussions of what students were doing in their various libraries,[64] By 1923 the waning of the apprenticeship method was becoming obvious as revealed in Williamson's report of library schools:

(a)   There is little agreement among the schools at the relative importance of the different subjects in the curriculum. About half the student's time is devoted to four subjects — cataloguing, book selection, reference work, and classification.
(b)   The content of the curriculum should be determined by first-hand

acquaintance with the most progressive library service rather by tradition and imitation.

(c)   A composite statement of the scope and content of the twenty-five or more distinct subjects included in the curricula of the library schools reveals the necessity of a broad, general education of collegiate grade as a basis for library school instruction.[65]

The first twenty-five years of this century have therefore witnessed the character of library school curricula in the USA, substantially influenced by the pragmatic approaches of practitioners. Many library schools originated in librarians, and even those located in universities existed in splendid isolation rather than entering into the mainstream of university life. Besides, many courses were taught on a part-time basis by retired librarians, and large share of the student's time was spent in **field work,** often never evaluated by librarian or library educator, hence the status quo syndrome prevailed. This then was the nature of 'the apprenticeship approach' to curriculum development at that time.

During the 1940s, at least four important surveys of library education were made. One of them of pertinence here is the survey by Metcalf, Osborn and Russell, who in 1942 pointed out the inadequate educational qualifications of many library school instructors, the elementary nature of much of the curriculum, and the fact that there was no philosophy of librarianship to give point and depth to the programme. They found that, for the most part, Dewey's idea of apprenticeship had largely disappeared from the programme, but that despite this, the topics studied remained close to the practical matter of running a library. A frank and reasonable approach to the survey earned them a measure of authority and acceptability among library educators, and the survey can be said to have a decisive effect on the direction library education (in particular curriculum development)was to take in the nineteen fifties.

Graduatisation

Taken literally, 'graduatisation' in the context of this present work, is taken to mean a decisive trend in professional education, towards graduate level of entry, teaching and research in an educational establishment and/or professional organisation.

In the U.S.A., following the apprenticeship period, there was a perceptible movement towards graduatisation in the American library scene. Specialised schools emerged to prepare students for various library types, with each school identifying itself with: cataloguing; library administration; public university; and special libraries. But this was short-lived as in 1951, the *Standards for Accreditation* was published stating that schools were free to specialise but only after meeting the basic requirements of preparing general librarians through a 'study of professional principles and methods common to the several kinds of librarians and of library service.'[66] This move practically halted an era of specialised library schools because as a result of the *Standards*, the Committee on Accreditation has consistently refused to accredit schools specialising in specific types or levels of librarianship.

However, by the mid-sixties the need arose for an additional degree, between the master's degree and the doctorate, which would make it possible to qualify as a specialist in school libraries, or public or university libraries. The library schools' response to this need was to establish Advanced Certificate courses in library science to cater for the experienced professional, who already has a master's degree but does not require a doctorate as a further advanced degree. A study of such specialist programmes has been made by Danton[67] under the auspices of the American Library Association. Again, Swank[68] observes that there are four important roles for such an intermediate curriculum: a sixth-year specialised curriculum; an internship; an opportunity for continuing education; and an alternative curriculum in information science. Fryden,[69] in a survey of the so-called 'post-master' programmes, found that they now exist in a number of schools accredited by the A.L.A. with at least eleven schools offering such courses. Three main course objectives were identified in Fryden's survey, i.e.:

(a)   To prepare teachers **in** (my emphasis) undergraduate or graduate library school;

(b)   To prepare additional librarians to advance into administrative or specialised positions; and,

(c)   To provide additional knowledge and training that would permit practising librarians to improve their performance in their existing positions.

In most of the schools, the degree is terminal, although in three it was the first step toward the doctorate and one would like to think that objective (a) above would be aptly suited to those wishing to obtain the doctorate since they have to be highly qualified to teach in the library schools.

Computers and the technologies have also had their impact on curriculum development in U.S. library and information studies. In particular, the influence of the technologies on information education and the consequent future role of the library has been examined in studies by Licklider,[70] Becker,[71] Goehlert and Snowdon.[72] In the related field of information science the impact on the curriculum development process has been marked.

Rees and Riccio[73] in their (1967) survey showed that twenty-five of the A.L.A. – accredited library schools offered one or more courses in information science. Two years after the survey (1969), thirty-five of the forty-four accredited schools offered at least one course in information science, indicating an increase in the number of schools offering more than one course in the subject.

In another article, Rees[74] reported the difficulty existing in correlating course titles with course content. According to Rees, this difficulty arises due to the lack of common agreement as to the definition of documentation, information retrieval, information science and library automation – titles commonly in use in U.S. librarianship curriculum. Rees submits, in the article, that analysis of course descriptions and outlines reveals three major areas of emphasis as follows:

Area I: Library Automation — Systems analysis, computer and allied hardware, theory and application of automation to library processes and procedures such as acquisition, serials, circulation control, catalogue production.

Area II: Documentation and Information Storage and Retrieval Systems — Design of retrieval systems, subject analysis, abstracting and indexing, structure of index languages, file organisation, question analysis, search strategy, dissemination, translation, testing and evaluation.

Area III: Information Science Research Methodology — Basic principles and tools of mathematics, logic, linguistics, statistics, psychology and other disciplines, and their application to the investigation of library-based and communication-related phenomena.[75]

In the 1967 study, seventeen schools offered twenty-five courses in Area I, nineteen schools offered thirty-nine courses in Area II, six schools offered thirteen courses in Area III. According to the three areas as set out above, Area I (Library automation) represents the application of computers and related hardware to the task of improving the efficiency of library housekeeping functions such as acquisitions, serials, catalogue production and circulation control. These are processes and procedures which Rees regards as comparatively easy, formalised, structured and controlled by computer routines. Furthermore, it can be observed from the given areas that the distinction between Areas II and III reflects the relationship between a science and its related technologies, both of which Hayes[76] in his study, found to be unidentical and therefore different in application.

Based on the three 'Area' classifications, Rees offers a definition of 'information science' as, a theoretical discipline concerned with the application of scientific research methodology to the investigation of communication and to the properties of systems of communication. It is concerned with the behaviour, properties and transfer of information; the processes involved in communication; and the tools involved in the design, implementation and evaluation of communication systems.[77]

The differentiation of 'information science' from 'information technology' i.e., documentation as opposed to information storage and retrieval systems is not new. For instance Borko[78] notes that information science has "both a basic science component which inquires into the subject without regard to its application, and an applied science component, which develops services and products.'

However, Hayes[79] states that 'information science is a theoretical discipline

... concerned with information technology but is in no sense identical with it ... the tendency to identify the two is an unfortunate one'. Given the foregoing reasoning, the response of library schools in the U.S. to the growth of communication technology has been to add courses in information science, information retrieval, documentation and library automation. In assessing this situation in library schools, Reed[80] suggests that although the schools are educating persons able to understand the rudiments of computer technology and their application to library procedures, library education is not producing persons capable of undertaking formalised analysis of library systems.

In an apparent appeal for a unified approach to curriculum development in the field of librarianship, Harlow[81] suggests four sub-systems within the scope and activity of librarianship in the curriculum development process.

(a)   Acquisition – organisation
(b)   Interface between record-user
(c)   ⁄Retrieval – transmission
(d)   Evaluation-feedback

Each of the sub-systems impinges upon the others, and all of the other influences and systems have reciprocal effects, such as exemplified in the 'literature' of the subject areas (which vary in their organisation as well as in form and content, some being cumulative and others additive with varying amounts of access built in). Harlow therefore contends that the actions and functions of librarianship will be ineffectual if carried on in isolation, hence, the need for a unified approach to curriculum development.[82]

In September 1970, the University of Illinois Graduate School of library science hosted a conference on the design of the curriculum of library schools. The papers presented at the conference were published as a monograph a year later.[83]

Reed reported on a study of the most recent bulletin available from 50 of 52 A.L.A. accredited library schools, so as to determine the general pattern of curricula, core courses, and elective offerings.[84] Reed found that the distribution of core courses by number and percentage of schools shows a maximisation of points, with four courses scoring 100% among the 10 examined. The subject areas scoring a complete 100% include: Reference and bibliography; cataloguing and classification; administration, management and systems analysis; and information science. History of books and libraries, selection and acquisition, came a close second and third scoring 96% and 92% respectively. Reed notes that in spite of the tendency to retain a core of introductory professional courses, Williamson's comments of some fifty years back at the time, still held true by 1971. Of course, there are marked differences among the schools as to the relative amount of time devoted to the different major areas of the curriculum, with the persistent problem of how to provide thorough teaching in one year in the entire field of library and information work.

Similarly, Asheim in a survey of the current trends in library school curricula, observes that there is an in-depth activity relating to curriculum structure and content in the library schools. His findings show that much of this activity was dictated by considerations other than that of providing the most desirable learning experiences.[85] It was also observed that there was a growing trend extending the length of M.L.S. degrees from one to two years.

Another important observation by Asheim is the relation of the curriculum content to information science and the 'new technology' in forming traditional courses as well as introducing new ones. In the demand for change in curriculum provision, the challenge to traditional values usually is based on the claim that they do not have current relevance. The attacks on education in general, and library education in particular, often feel obliged to make no more specific indictment than that. Asheim, as do many of his peer, regards the new relevance as frequently utilitarian in its aims: i.e. learning only that which one needs to know to handle the specific task confronting him. If Asheim's proposition is accepted that charges in relation to traditional values also reflect the concern with relevance, then the proposition has wide implications for current concerns in library education.

A classic work, that is a favourite in most library schools, is the text by Shera[86] in which he explored the role of the library as a contributor to the total communication system in society, and the meaning of that role for the library profession. Having determined the requirements of that role the author proceeds to identify those (requirements) which are 'appropriately' (*sic*) met by graduate professional education. Thus, Shera suggests that there are four objectives by which the professional programme of study is to be judged, they are:

(a)   It must represent a well-developed theory of the social function of the library;

(b)   It must extract from the totality of the librarian's knowledge and skills those which are professional;

(c)   It must represent librarianship as a unified cluster of specialisations as opposed to the earlier concept of a 'universal' librarian; and

(d)   It must be directed toward the training of the intellect.[87]

Based on these four cardinal points, Shera argues that the criteria for preparing the student professional to undertake graduate professional study, rest on the following:

(i)   A fundamental understanding of the role of the library in the communication process of society together with the historical development of the library and of library materials as social instrumentalities shaped by and responding to their coeval culture.

(ii)   A comprehension of the basic theory and the appropriate system for the organisation and interpretation of library materials, and in particular the intellectual content of those materials, together with the necessary skill to deal practically with the techniques and routines relating to library organisation and use.

(iii) A knowledge of the principles and methods or research as applied to the investigation of library problems, together with the ability to evaluate research results, especially research in librarianship in terms of the appropriateness and reliability of the methods used and the validity of the results obtained.

(iv) An understanding of the basic principles of administration and their application to librarians as organisations of people working together to achieve specific goals, with special emphasis upon the administration of libraries serving the field of the student's special interests.

(v) A mastery of the basic elements of a library specialist or cluster of specialists (e.g. children's work, school libraries and educational media).

(vi) Exposure to practical library experience, when the student has not previously had such experience, as exemplified by a well-supervised work-study programme or internship which makes possible controlled experience...

(vii) Contract with the professional field of librarianship through lectures, discussions and other special events which will bring the student into contact with a variety of libraries outside the academic setting.

(viii) Encouragement of contacts, either formal, of the student with other departments and schools of the university to ensure that he does not lead his academic life in a sterile library vacuum.

Shera suggested that if these criteria are to be fully and successfully met there must be a continuous review of the curriculum both with respect to keeping it up-to-date with current developments and trends in librarianship and related area of knowledge, and to utilise new methods of instruction. However, it should be borne in mind that a total fulfilment of Shera's criteria as outlined above would incur a 'world of perfection' but this hardly occurs in the process of curriculum development. In addition to the disequilibrium effects a 'world of imperfection', there is a limited time available to both faculty and students in satisfactorily fulfilling, for examples criteria (iv), (vi) , (vii) and (viii) and above all, the nature of the duration of courses which in most cases are still one year oriented for postgraduate study. However, despite these difficulties in planning of educational programmes for graduate professional study, the key element to future success in planning an effective curriculum lies in an extension of the duration of study for the master's degree programme, say a two-year duration. Most M.L.S. programmes are currently run for two-year period, although, in Nigeria this may be a little longer due to closure of universities, etc.

Another contribution to the analysis of curriculum development in

American librarianship was made when in 1973 a collection of studies was published, edited by Harold Borko.[88] For example, Jahoda [89] wrote a review on the literature on teaching library automation and information science. The author found that although to a 'certain extent' (*sic*) approaches become mixed in order to make teaching responsive to the interests of the student in the classroom, governing attitudes do prevail, Jahoda argues that these should be isolated in order to perceive their implications. If, as it seems likely, graduates of the library school programme (on information science) are being prepared for beginning positions, then the beginning librarian will be a practitioner rather than a theoretician. Thus, the emphasis in teaching the topics on information science should be on applications, i.e., equipment, abstracting, indexing and system studies. As users, tools and techniques subjects that might be included in the curriculum are library retrieval systems, and information science research methodology. The selection of the topics itself is theoretical in approach and the extent of their coverage will have to depend on the state of both the technology and librarianship fields at the time. In this respect, Jahoda's contribution seems consistent with similar findings from previous studies[90,91,92,93,94]— the results of which show and confirm the integration of information science subjects in the librarianship curriculum.

'Integration' of courses in the curriculum development process in library and information studies is always a radical departure from the status quo. A workshop[95] on 'the integrated core curriculum' was held at Chapel Hill, University of North Carolina March 6-8, 1977, in which attempts were made to sample professional library educators' view on the subject. However, it is important to point out here the results of the survey conducted on the views of participants at the workshop, regarding the concept of the 'integrated core' as it is practiced in their various institutions. The workshop proved that there was universal enthusiasm in the acceptance of 'integrated core.' However, the results of the survey conducted show the following variables: for instance, when an integrated core curriculum might be considered for the school, 32% (for 71 participants) said YES; 16% — MAYBE, and 45% — NO.[96] The percentage of rejection seems rather high compared with others. This may very well be for reasons of tradition, faculty, resistance, financial considerations and presence of the part-time students in the school's programmes. Some of the library educators participating in the workshop were dissatisfied with their programme as existing at the time, but they were not convinced that an integrated core curriculum was the solution.

The importance and role of an integrated approach to the core has been stressed in Asheim's paper. In it, he observes that:

> ...the instructor of the elective courses can build upon the assumption that all of his or her students do have a commonly shared background in the basic substance of librarianship. The key characteristics of the integrate core is that it attempts to put into practice a long-standing tenet of good educational theory: that learning is an assertive process, and that it is most

effective when that student proceeds in a logical fashion from basic ideas to their expansion and adaptation to increasingly complex situations. The integrated core tries to identify what aspects of the total learning process should come first, and then arrange that they indeed do so.[97]

However, as the author himself admits, a great weakness in many core programmes of the traditional types is the looseness of their sequencing. Prerequisites are identified and then ignored in their priority order, so that students frequently find themselves in an introductory course after they have had the content to which it is meant to be an introduction. Thus, there is a great need to demonstrate logic in the structure of the curriculum, since an important aspect of professional education is firmly rooted in the objective of stimulating logical thinking in students. Therefore, it may not altogether be surprising to find that a majority of the participants at the Chapel Hill Workshop chose **not** to consider the application of the concept of an 'integrated core' in their library schools. In expressing influential views along this line, Garrison has cautioned that experiment with format and with packing core courses have really to date integrated the **courses**, not the **content**.

Garrison submits that it is not enough to integrate the format unless the content is right. He adds:

I am more convinced now that in 1970, when we began our integrated core course at Drexel, that the future lies in breaking out of this institutional mold. Already, 20% of our graduates at Drexel do not find employment in libraries as such but in the broader information profession. I do not feel that this is merely a reflection of a tight job market in traditional libraries, but rather of a major shift in our field.[98]

Perhaps a most pungent observation yet by Garrison is in relation to joint degree programmes — a reflection of experimentation in the integrated approach. He notes that:

Despite these and other experiments at broadening the curriculum there are other less positive signs of stress all around us. I am particularly alarmed at the hasty marriages evident in the proliferation of joint degree programmes. These sound like a good thing until you look closely at the structure and realize that, in many cases, the library science content is sacrificed and the programs seem more directed at finding job for surplus humanities and social science graduates than toward preparing information specialists.[99]

In an interdisciplinary discipline such as librarianship, there can be no more indictment than that contained in the above quotation as regards the selection of content in the curriculum development process. For example, in terms of current trends in the employment situation, the library schools need to (but do not have to) respond in some measure to the need for science information specialists by integrating documentation plus other information science content into their curricula to a degree that makes them credible and thereby attract people with technical backgrounds to meet market demands.

A general observation that could be made about the whole exercise of 'integration' at the workshop resides in the fact that there was a lack of cohesiveness in the pattern of approach to the core as reported by the library schools. This point is further buttressed by the fact that curriculum revision seems to continue to be handled as strictly a local matter, adjusting to local needs rather than coming as part of any generally planned change. The schools are still dominated by independent programme revision without any binding professional education guidelines. It remains to be seen if current thinking amongst the participants at the 1977 Workshop reflects their earlier views even in the new millennium.

Another aspect of the literature on curriculum development in librarianship in the U.S. is its reflection on the role and significance of foreign language study as an element in library education. That foreign language study should be one of the librarian's tools of the trade was repeatedly stressed by early educators in the field. Dewey in 1887, prepared a proposal which suggests, that the 'better' library and information science students should spend almost three years on their professional preparation. The latter would include, in addition to the library-oriented courses, 'considerable work in languages and comparative literature.'[100] Also among the recommendations made in Williamson Report (1923) is the Statement, 'languages and general information are of fundamental importance for all professional library work.'[101] Theoretically, these two citations (Dewey/Williamson) reflect age-long tradition in academics, whereas, it was not quite the fashion of insistence in areas of professional education except in Law where the study of Latin is *sine qua non*.

Thus, the foreign language requirement becomes slightly more complex at the undergraduate level, since it is inextricably tied to the tradition of general education and to the question of whether or not students should be allowed complete freedom of choice in planning their coursework. The main principle behind general education, like the defence of foreign language study because of its cultural values, tend to be slated in rather broad, general and vague terms. It becomes increasingly difficult to defend such principles in this era of pragmatism and professionalism in education. Indeed, the literature in this respect reveals that various authors identify the main goal of both general education and foreign language study — that of 'producing the truly educated man' — as being the same.[102,103]

Similarly, as McGrath has shown, no particular curricula pattern exists any longer that can be exclusively identified as liberal education.[104] McGlothlin[105] too argues that the resultant effect of a changing pattern in the form of liberal education is a loss of a definite educational objective, which to many educators means that most of the purposes of a general arts education can be just as well met by professional education. Questionably, this implies that the professional school, by focusing on competence to practice, will produce 'trained robots who can perform set tasks with skill, but who will have little understanding of the significance or relationships of their efforts to human welfare'.[106]

Recently, however, Fisher and Beck[107] have reported that despite the emphasis on a liberal arts background, including foreign languages, most library schools have in fact eliminated the language requirement for either admission to, or graduation from their programmes. The 1972 'Statistics of the Library Education Division of A.L.A.' also showed non-English materials actually increasing. Consequently, research libraries will be requiring the services of individuals with linguistic skills as well as training in librarianship.[108]

The aspect of specialised subject study in curriculum development in library and information studies is another area which has drawn the attention of American writers. The Americans regard subject specialisation as an essential factor in the needs of both the faculty and services. In the library schools, the courses with subject specialisations are designed to link library and information science course of graduates with specific professions such as law, arts and medicine. Library educators believe that these developments contribute to a higher calibre of graduates, and to a widening of the career spectrum especially in view of competition for job places after graduation.[109, 113]

In his fascinating study, Lemke[114] examines in detail the form of subject specialisation in library education, and categorised the findings under the heading 'alternative specialities'. In order to obtain information on the current situation of subject study in the library schools, Lemke administered a brief questionnaire and a request for bulletins of all 59 accredited library schools in the U.S. 54 replied and the data, as analysed in the article, was based on all these schools listed in the October 1977 A.L.A. roster of accredited programmes. The term 'alternative specialities' was defined below:
Included in the definition are:
(a)   Courses designed for specific information needs outside of the immediate library/information/communication professions, e.g. music, art.
(b)   Fields within the broader library/information/communication professions, for which no formal academic programme exists, e.g. archives, publishing.
(c)   Courses related to current social concerns, for which formal programmes are emerging, and where teaching research and library information service programs develop in many instances in close exchange, e.g. garoutology, and new urban service programmes.[115]

Excluded from the definition are:
(a)   Courses on special librarianship because they are considered 'type of library' courses, as those dealing with public or school librarianship. They may include but do not focus on, discrete subjects or professions.[116]

(b)   Media courses (film, T.V., etc) because this constitute part of the librarian's basic education.

In the schools' bulletin, it was noted that programmes in co-operation with academic disciplines are also on the increase, such as in the fields of History and English. Clearly, there seems to be some inherent factors influencing curriculum development along these lines. Lemke suggests that such factors may be identified as:

(a)   *The university,* i.e. strong (well-established) departments, special programmes, campus and museum are essential in any consideration of alternative specialities.

(b)   *The community,* i.e. in larger communities, other academic institutions, governmental and private agencies often provide ideal partners for co-operative programmes, e.g. the Washington and New York City library schools have the unique opportunity to project this partnership in courses opened e.g. 'Federal Library Administration'.

(c)   *Interest of faculty members and deans,* is a strong factor in the decision to implement new courses, and the professional background and motivation of those in charge are essential to the quality of the programme.[117]

The work of Lemke, in respect of the above, is a valuable contribution to the literature of curriculum development in American library and information studies since it is very informative on the trend showing the schools' response to the stimuli of change in the community. In a related study, Dresang[118] provides further application of the study to the specialised course on Library Service to the Handicapped, although, according to Lemke's classification this would rank as a 'library type course'.

There have also been recent developments in the cognitive approach to curriculum development in librarianship. For instance, in a project at the University of Maryland, researchers have been actively involved in determining the cognitive styles of information professionals, and relating cognitive style to task performance. The report, written by Johnson and White indicates the usefulness of cognitive style as a means of analysing problem-solving or decision-making behaviour. Practically, the report discusses some cognitive style dimensions and models which are pertinent to the analysis of information science professionals within the context of their training needs in a field as wide and varied as library and information science.

The report posits that the idea of matching cognitive styles and learning situations, assumes the ability to recognise 'cognitive styles' and the ability to structure the learning or task environment to create specific conditions. Even by modern day standards, the effective implementation of such a tall order seems questionable in a busy library school's programme schedule, as the variables surrounding such concept dictate and perhaps, more importantly emphasise the existing basic differences and variety of courses in each library school, i.e., the number of 'required' courses is usually limited even if the lecturer's cognitive style introduces another variable. On the face value, a course's subject-matter is not monolithic, as within it, students may still have to address problems and tasks which are incompatible with their cognitive style. At best, in the present writer's view, such proposition seems impractical and may prove too empirical and expensive in terms of valuable administrative time of the library educator.

Another element, perhaps of more practical application in curriculum development literature is the influence of 'field experience' on curriculum planning. Monroe[119] has surveyed the literature on library education's use of the concept as an element in the master's degree curriculum. Monroe focused on the use of 'field experience' in its contribution to the learning situation. The professional fields of medicine, public administration, education and social work have regularly relied upon field experience as an essential ingredient in preparing practitioners and their rationales are available to library educators. According to Sexton and Ungerer, the other professions have looked to field experience and its alternatives in experiential learning for fulfilment of needs:

(a)   Skills development;
(b)   Developing a 'feel' for the situation and seeing how people behave;
(c)   Socialisation into the profession in terms of values, behaviours with colleagues and with those served;
(d)   Problem identification, analysis and solution; and
(e)   Facilitating social change in the profession.[120]

Based on the experimental needs as outlined above, Monroe points to the limitations and problems of the learning theory in relation to course work, analysis of tasks for learning, assessment of individual students' needs and interests and suitable host library situations which need to be identified for their (students') placement. Clearly, these are not new premises on which to base a 'revolutionary' innovation to the existing pattern of student placement (by library schools) in libraries, although one must acknowledge Monroe's hypothesis that 'graduate school acceptance of field experience for academic credits has no means become general. The conclusion seems inevitable, that it will be difficult to institute field experience programmes in librarianship **comparable** to those in medical, law, social work and education.

In general, the structure of library school's programmes in United States of America has also come under close security recently. An evaluation of library education was initiated by the Advisory Committee to the office for Library Education of the American Library Association (A.L.A.) with fieldwork starting in 1972 and the project finally getting published as the Conant Report in 1980.[121] Pertinent to this present study is the recognition of the need to restructure the duration of the masters' degree to two years instead of one. Dr. Conant submits that:

Librarianship is one of the last of the demanding professions to require only one year of professional training. It is the only one to discourage basic or introductory course at the undergraduate level. The one year programme have come to crowed graduate training with elementary material, to limit the opportunity for specialization, to preclude in most schools an internship or work-study programme, to limit the influence of the faculty on their students, and not the least, to provide for a 'quikie' professional degree that reflects badly on the reputation of profession.[122]

In the literature on curriculum development, many educators already recognise the need to restructure one-year masters' degree programme in library schools especially first professional courses. However, elsewhere in the Report, Dr. Conant seems a little more realistic as he observes, that:

The faculty of the graduate library schools.... Faced with the practical consideration that a change in the length of the programmes **might** reduce enrolment below a level that their institutions could tolerate. The uncertainty of the effect on enrolments has caused library educators to be wary of a shift to longer programmes, even though many of them recognize that there would be educational advantages in doing so.[123]

In a one-year programme, there is hardly time to put across the basics of librarianship and at the same time bring students to the point in their knowledge, where they can understand the complexities of theoretical problems of libraries and library resources. In a sample of opinion amongst faculty members in library schools, the question was put on the adequacy of the one-year programme. Of the 84 respondents 26 (31%) said that one year was sufficient for professional education in librarianship; 46 (55%) said that the programmes should be longer than one; and 12 (14%) gave answers that indicated indecision. 'Most' students interviewed on the question expressed their reluctance to invest more than a year in librarianship training, considering the low salaried status of the profession. However, one would have wished that such respondents were quantified as the others.

As regards **content** of courses, Conant provides what he terms 'a comprehensive curriculum' model, derived from an examination and analysis of the curricula of the 60 accredited programmes in the U.S. It was found that none of the accredited programmes offered **all** of the topics listed. Conant therefore proposed a scope for a comprehensive curriculum. According to the Report under discussion, none of the accredited programmes was found to reach the scope of the curriculum as provided. Conant relates some of his findings on professional education to the overall concept of professionalism thereby bearing a semblance to the objectives of this present work. For example, his conclusions show that the library profession needs to develop a coherent basis for its claim to professionalism. He suggests that one way of achieving such coherence is to separate professional from non-professional 'training' (*sic*) in its system of education and to improve the quality and content of the master's programmes, although how this could be done was not stipulated. It was further suggested that there is an inherent need:

(a)   To establish a common educational format (a curriculum) for the first professional degree (the Master's programs). The format should be comprehensive as set out (in Table 6,p.), and should define what knowledge and training is deemed the appropriate basis of **professional** competence in the field.

(b)   To provide additional opportunities for specialisation and career education that are clearly articulated with the master programs.

(c)   For library educators to make every practical effort to liaise with working librarians and thereby close the gap between them. Experienced professionals should be invited to teach in greater numbers in the library schools and the educators should utilise libraries as training laboratories and as research sites. Joint research projects between library educators and librarians should be a regular activity of the profession.[124]

There was an understandable reaction of severe criticisms of the Report by library educators who argued that the Report has been based on 'uncritical selection of the opinions of faculty, students, alumni, and practitioners, as gathered from interviews and questionnaires.'[125]

Whatever may be the justification for these criticisms, it would seem that the Conant Report is a substantial contribution to the literature on American professional education in library and information studies.

Nigerian Studies

Scope of the Problem of Literature Output

Unlike other aspects of professional education and training which have drawn the attention of librarians and library educators over the years, curriculum studies is still bourgeoning when compared with world trends on the subject. This is due, in part, to the considerable foreign influence on the library schools' curricula (mainly British and American), and to the lack of documented literature on the subject from indigenous writers. As a result, the literature on curriculum development in Nigerian librarianship exists in a sparse form – mostly as unpublished papers; documents originating from the library schools and therefore privately restricted in distribution; conference papers; and theses work both in foreign and local universities with topics based on Nigerian library education practice.

It becomes clear that one element of disadvantage in the situation as described above, is the handicap suffered in promoting indigenous publishing. Consequently, both the library schools and the profession at large are starved of valuable record of professional thinking, latest trends arising from intra- and extra-mural teaching, and the dissemination of ideas relating to new techniques and developments in library and information studies.

The kind of material which emanates from the library schools include research reports, statistical tabulations on library education, surveys, observations on the current library scene and practice, conference (including seminars, workshops and colloquia) proceedings, textbooks (although this is rarely the case in Nigerian library schools), annual reports and prospectuses, and the usual promotional literature. The publications that emerge from these quoted format appear as monographs, pamphlets or articles, depending on their depth and coverage, and are published under a variety of imprints including the library school's own.

However, the lack of vital publications in curriculum development in library and information studies has undoubtedly caused great difficulties in the efficient implementation of curriculum design as a survey of the literature would seem to indicate. Indeed, many writers on the subject agree that the lack of promptness in issuing situation reports on conferences, seminars, colloquia and other similar proceedings lead to events being overtaken by new offshoot of problems. The result is often 'chaos and mistrust' among educators and professionals rather than mutual understanding of the different practicalities in the curriculum development process. For example, textbooks on librarianship from African perspective. Similarly, materials that are African-oriented are merely incorporated in foreign-sponsored texts and are therefore lacking in in-depth analysis of African problems and the necessity to a strictly traditional approach to conventional library methods as viable alternatives to the European models. This leads to the element of 'bias' in foreign texts and the 'relevance' of using such texts in library schools in preparing professionals for local community services in the library and information field.

One should not be under the pretext of displaying ingratitude for the valuable contributions foreigners have made to Nigerian librarianship – especially the influence of British, American, New Zealand, Australian, Canadian and recently Asian library experts and educators. But the cogent point is that despite these contributions by foreigners, Nigerian librarians and educators seem to retain many aspects of conventional library provision including its system of education and training without reference to the urgent need of making professional education and services **relevant** to national objectives and development.

The over-worked professors and lecturers in the library schools are not to be blamed, but then attention needs to be drawn to present initiatives in the field of indigenous publishing and how the library profession in general could benefit from its participation. For example, indigenous publishing did not achieve its present rate of success in a vacuum, it had its teething problems as indicated in recent surveys by Barrett[126] and Hans Zell.[127] They suggest that the development of indigenous publishing on a scale that can handle internal distribution effectively is still in the primary stages; that the trend must be seen and interpreted against a background of several social and infrastructural elements, such as: a small per-capita income, a diversity of languages, a low rate of literacy, an emphasis on achievement rather than enjoyment reading, an insufficient number of retail outlets, frequently high custom tariff on essential printing equipment and supplies, and many other obstacles, some of near impossible dimensions.

However, despite all the stated 'obstacles', Zell reckons that the total output of indigenous literature has actually increased as much as 50% annually.[128] The library profession and library schools in particular can take advantage of this latest trend especially in scholarly output for it is in the exchange of knowledge and information can there be real progress in formally establishing the foundation of library and information practice for the next half century. The signs are there in Europe and America of the changing nature of the library profession in an information conscious society, but the theoretical foundation is constantly reinforced through an active publications programme. In terms of curriculum development an active publications programme is *sine qua non* for development activities such as course renewals, innovations, and evaluation of programmes. Researchers in the field are at present having to supplement the limited published sources with private documentation by institutions and individuals, hence, the need for objectivity not only in their selection but also in the analysis of the materials available for us.

Structure and Content of Courses: Historical and Current Review

One of the earliest articles to be written on the structure and content of library education in Nigeria was published in *Nigerian Libraries* in 1972. In the article, Akinyotu[129] examined the objectives and content of library education at all levels in Nigeria. In terms of structure, he observed that the establishment of library schools was preceded by an urgent need to fill the dearth of indigenous 'professional' librarians needed in response to national development and growth. He also noted that as there was no time to study critically the special needs of Nigerian librarianship with a view to drawing up an 'appropriate' (sic) local syllabus, it was expedient to adopt the syllabus of the British Library Association and to prepare candidates for the American Library Association at least for the first three years (1960-1963). In this way, library education developed at an unspecified level. In the 1963/64 session a new syllabus was introduced and the local Diploma (set at postgraduate level) of the University of Ibadan replaced the American Library Association.

The objective of the change centred on a shift of emphasis to the 'special requirement of African readers, on the problems peculiar to libraries in the topics and on the techniques required to organise collection ....' As events later proved, the change over to the Diploma of nomenclature rather than substance as the stated objective did not seem to be realised. According to Akinyotu, there was considerable doubt as to whether the philosophy of librarianship on which the syllabus was based and implemented for almost ten years, was sufficient board to make provision for both the immediate and further roles of libraries in Nigeria.

The validity of the author's statement becomes clear as one examines the content of 'sub-professional' and 'professional' courses at both Ibadan and Zaria, 1972, Akinyotu's observation is pertinent in this case, even though Ibadan was offering its one-year course at the Certificate level while Zaria's is the two-year Diploma, the course structure of both course is basically the same. Although not included in Akinyotu's outline, Ibadan students are also required to write an assessed long essay – typewritten, bound and submitted at the end of the year in duplicate. The 'research method' or a form of it as it exists on the Ibadan course is missing from the Zaria course. Thus, the long essay is the only element of difference in the structure of the sub-professional's courses.

The 'professional' courses as tabulated identifies 'professional' as being degree and postgraduate courses. Here, Akinyotu also observed that there are no significant feature of content distinguishing the courses from one another. In terms of academic subject study on the B.L.S. courses, Akinyotu noted that two subjects required are only taken in parts 1 and 2 and can even be dropped entirely at the end of the second year. This, he regarded as a weakening of the position of advocates for specialised knowledge provided through academic options.

B.L.S. Subsidiary Weightings, 1972

PART II:
Library Science
% age   15%   1ˢᵗ Subsidiary
                     5%   2ⁿᵈ Subsidiary
                     5%

PART III: a)   In the case of students with no subsidiary subjects:
                Library Science 75%
           b)   In the case of students with a subsidiary subject:
                Library Science 70%
                Subsidiary 5%

The weightings allotted to 'Library Science' induced Akinyotu to comment that the programmes are 'technique-oriented'. Similarly, one does not seem to share the author's argument (even at the time of writing the article) that the objective of education at the 'non-professional' education level should be to produce only library assistants who would be skilled in carrying out all library routines with minimum supervision. For instance, that:

> ... it is necessary to teach cataloguing and classification only to the extent that the students will know how to shelve and retrieve books, how to file catalogue cards and how to use the different kinds of library catalogues.[130]

The argument above is an over-simplification of the role of middle-level staff in libraries, especially in university, college and other academic type libraries. The skills described in the quotation above can be acquired through experience but the rationale for 'education' goes far beyond 'training' basics.

The 'Colloquium on Library Education and Training in Nigeria', held at the University of Ibadan 15-19 March, 1974, is a familiar source for discussion in the literature on curriculum development in Nigerian library and information studies. For the first time in Nigerian library education history, the academic staff of the two library schools at Ibadan and Zaria, the Heads of all the major libraries in the country, as well as many other librarians attended the Colloquium. With 49 participants and 20 observers, a total of sixteen papers was presented, spread through seven sessions conducted in a way to allow for full discussion of each paper presented. A vignette of the proceedings has been provided in the literature by Bankole[131] (representing the Nigerian Library Association, and the Department of Library Studies, University of Ibadan [132] as the organisers of the Colloquium). Some of the papers presented are of pertinence to this study and shall be examined as such.

Benge[133] in his contribution, observed world trends in library education and proposed that any theory on Nigerian library education must relate to social relevance without which, there are no foundations for right social action other than to nurse what he described as 'a kind of cultural imperialism'. Although Benge did not point any accusing fingers, he was indirectly referring to curriculum development activities in the pioneering library school at Ibadan where the curriculum was designed to conform with 'international standards' based primarily on the influence of Europe and American developments in library education. For example, Ibadan concentrated for some time on postgraduate studies in librarianship in pursuance of its 'leadership' objective, whereas the staffing needs of Nigerian libraries dictate priorities to the contrary.

Furthermore, attempts at standardisation have had varying effects on curriculum development as will be examined in other papers presented. In terms of 'cultural imperialism' the implications for libraries and library schools are clear although no one is under illusions as to the mounting difficulties posed in dismantling an educational system deriving its origins from the colonial administration period. From education and training viewpoint, Chan[134] reflects on 'cultural imperialism' as implying library schools teaching what is desirable rather than what is necessary in the developing countries. The 'desirable', Chan argues, is usually an impossible dream, while the 'reality' is a nightmare for which the student librarian may be unprepared and largely untrained. Consequently, 'the student may learn about O & M, MBO, and PPBS, but he will not learn what to do when the library is infested with mice'. According to Benge, while professional education should move away from mere techniques, care should also be taken to avoid laying to much emphasis on academic subjects.

However, Dipeolu[135] disagrees on the issue of the academic content of a librarian's education. In his paper Dipeolu urged that library schools' curricula should be based on a level of liberal education which is guided by the functions and activities performed by librarians and the library needs *per se*. As revealed in the comparative study of the two schools at Ibadan and Zaria, Dipeolu concludes:

(a)   That the content of the B.L.S./M.L.S. degrees at A.B.U., Zaria, and the PG Dip. at Ibadan are 'substantially similar'.

(b)   That the academic subject content of the BLS degree at A.B.U., Zaria, seems inadequate for employment in academic and university libraries.

(c)   That the B.L.S holders are inadequately prepared for acquisition, reference and assistance to readers services in the academic subjects.

(d)   That the trend is towards making librarianship a graduate profession all over the world.

This 'hard-line' approach towards middle-level management in libraries arises from a consideration of the content of the B.L.S degree course without formal educational evaluation procedure being applied in anyway other than a personal view of the trend. This fact alone makes most of Dipeolu's conclusions suspect, although, one may not contend with some of his observations especially as regards professional employment in academic libraries.

Ogunsheye[136] in her paper, traced curriculum development trends to the growth of information as an essential characteristic of communication using the fields of science and technology management, with the emergence of other medium, other than book, being fully integrated with conventional library services. Ogunsheye therefore proposed that curriculum development in librarianship should take account of the following:

(a)   The need for a grade for higher professionals (librarian/specialist) made up of people with a good first degree and postgraduate qualification in librarianship. The Postgraduate Diploma holders are included in this category.

(b)   The need for professionals (Associate Librarians/Specialist Technicians) made up of B.L.S. degree holders and A.L.A. with three years experience.

(c)   The need for an acceptance of the 'growing single professional theory' with a large core and longer duration to make room for specialisation. Thus, two-year master's degree by course-work, to be introduced as a prerequisite for achieving such specialisation.

(d)   The offering of degree courses with library science components should be discouraged (as agreed at the Dakar Conference, 1974).

In essence, Ogunsheye advocates a five-year professional education structure, with the master's degree as the basis for first professional qualification. The relationship of libraries to technological application is an innovation which would genuinely ease information dissemination problems especially in the rural areas; the factor of illiteracy and oral tradition also contribute to how professional education can be oriented to the relevant needs of the community served.

Moid[137] in his paper, presents a slightly different view from the others on the status of the B.L.S. degree. He proposed *inter alia:*

(a)   A discontinuation of the PG Dip. in favour of the two-year master's degree.

(b)   Acceptance of the B.L.S. as a three-year **first professional** (my emphasis) course after Diploma in Library Science or 'A' Level.

(c)   M.L.S. as a two-year degree after the B.L.S. could be of two types:

(i)   for B.L.S. holders, and

(ii)   'ordinary' (sic) i.e. subject graduates.

It can be observed from Moid's proposals that the two-tier master's degree was indeed both radical and innovative at the time it was being proposed, considering that in 1974 similar moves were made at Sheffield and Loughborough universities in the U.K. — both universities offering master's degree for degree and A.L.A. candidates. However, for the first time in the discussion the B.L.S. holder is recognised as a 'first professional'. In viewing this proposal objectivity one may even go further and compare with trends in other professions such as B.Ed. (Education), LLB (Law), B.Mus (Music), M.B.B.S. or Ch.B (Medicine), and B.D. (Religion). The conclusion seems to be that an illuminative evaluation of a librarian's qualification along this line may be long overdue.

The following recommendations emerged from the 1974 Colloquium:

(i)   That library school courses should include special courses to meet specialist interests;

(ii)   That the facilities for the training of library technicians might be better provided for in a technical college situation than in a university situation as at present;

(iii)   That an active policy of continuing education be adopted by libraries;

(iv)   That library schools should organise continuing education programmes on a regular basis;

(v)   There is a need for a survey to determine job descriptions for various levels of personnel in different kinds of libraries in Nigeria;

(vi)   That the profession should develop a career structure and appropriate remuneration for library technicians as supportive staff;

(vii)   That the profession should aim at a school library service in each state manned by fully-qualified librarians;

(viii) That library school teachers should avail themselves of opportunities to improve the effectiveness of their teaching;

(ix)   That there should be mobility between the teaching and practising sides of the library profession;

(x)   That librarianship in Nigeria must move towards a postgraduate profession;

(xi)   That curriculum development must reflect the needs of the Nigerian society;

(xii)   That note should be taken of the termination of the British A.L.A. course in 1980 and that attention should be drawn to opportunities offered by the external degree programmes of Nigerian universities;

(xiii) That Nigerian library schools should investigate the possibility of starting courses for experienced librarians who hold only the British A.L.A. or F.L.A.qualifications to enable them to acquire Master's degree in librarianship.

(xiv)   That library schools should investigate the possibilities and avenues for co-operation among themselves;

(xv)   That library schools should maintain relevant statistics on library education and these should be comparable;

(xvi)   That the papers and recommendations of this Colloquium be passed on to the Nigerian Library Association for information and further action.

From the above list, the recommendations seemed to have touched upon virtually all problem areas in Nigerian librarianship and some of the far-reaching proposals such as items (ii), (x), (xii) and (xiii) were significant in view of the existing needs of the profession. Some aspects of the recommendations such as items v and vi are still largely unattended and certainly the 'aims' of such recommendations bear some similarity to the 'objectives' of this present research, namely the need to survey and determine 'professional' and 'non-professional' job characteristics in Nigerian libraries as a periphery of curriculum development in the identification of aims and objectives; and the consequent career structure and appropriate remuneration likely to emerge as a direct result of such survey.

Thus, the Colloquium, by addressing itself to urgent problems in the profession in a topical way, provided the opportunity for the two library schools (Ibadan and Zaria) to exchange views on their programmes for the first time in the country's library education history, it also enabled library educators, employers of librarians, and the professional association to exchange views on education and training programmes and needs, and to establish broad guidelines for a structure of education for librarianship in Nigeria.

Obi[138] (1975) examined the content of courses offered at both Ibadan and Zaria library schools, and came to the conclusion that a three-tier educational structure exists, represented by 'para-professional', 'first professional', and 'specialist professional', which affords both similarities and differences. This view contrasts with findings in previous studies indicating that curricula provision in both schools are the same (Akinyotu, 1972; Dipeolu, 1974).

According to Obi, the similarities are reflected in the close adherence of the programmes to the 'core' as laid out in the Ibadan seminar of 1953:

(a)   Library organisation and administration

(b)   Selection and acquisition

(c)   Cataloguing and classification
(d)   Reference and bibliography
(e)   Special types of libraries:
    (i)   Public
    (ii) School
    (iii) University
    (iv) Special

These 'core' elements of the library schools' programmes are said by Obi to have shown remarkable resilience to change for more than a decade up to 1975. The core courses are taught in a comparative manner 'with the libraries of Great Britain and America forming the background while libraries and librarianship in Africa are used as examples.'[139] The differences are observable in the duration of courses, entrance qualifications and weighting. For example, according to the tabulation on the three-tier structure, the M.L.S programme at Zaria (in the 'specialist-professional' category) is dual in nature comprising:

    (i)   A full-time two-year programme for graduates who have a professional qualification (B.L.S. or the equivalent) which comprises coursework for one year followed by a thesis to be presented at the end of the second year;

    (ii) A full-time two-year programme for graduates without prior courses in library science also to comprise of one year of course work followed by a thesis.

Additionally, there is a part-time programme for graduates, whether or not they have a B.L.S., who work on the A.B.U. Campus or in Zaria as a whole. Furthermore, there is a fundamental difference in the entrance qualifications and admission policy for the 'para-professional' category with Ibadan requiring a minimum period of one-year full library employment **plus** success in the entrance examination, whereas Zaria's policy along these lines are less rigid in view of the shortage of candidates of the right calibre in the Northern part of the country.

In the 'first-professional' tier one noticeable difference is that the postgraduate diploma of Ibadan lasts for only one academic year while the Zaria B.L.S. is undergraduate in nature and contains the equivalent of two years of professional study. This implies that Ibadan's first professionals (graduates) have had, at completion of the PG Dip., a longer period of academic study and a shorter period of professional study than the graduates with B.L.S. from Zaria.

Attention must now be focused on specific items of curriculum development as practiced in the library schools, having reviewed the literature on the varying degrees of structure, Nzotta's[140] survey to find out how the seven library schools in sub-Saharan black Africa taught management comes immediately into mind. Four schools returned the questionnaire sent to them, i.e., those situated at Ibadan, Zaria, Legon (Ghana) and Zambia. Nzotta[141] found that the management syllabuses in these schools covered most of the topics expected to be treated in such courses and that the teachers possessed most of the requisite qualifications for their job, but some necessary teaching aids were unavailable. On the method of teaching, it was discovered that while lecturing was the prevailing method, a few other methods were being tried out and that this situation was found to be similar to those in Britain and the USA. Nzotta argues that the course outlines in management offered no scope for discovering whether the courses touched on the differences between management as practised in Africa and management elsewhere. When compared with guidelines on the 'core' (Chicago Workshop, 1953),[142] only three of the eight topics recommended by the Workshop are covered by all of the four library schools: these are, general principles of administration, organisation, and management; personnel management; and financing and budgeting.

In a paper presented to the Standing Conference of African Library Schools (SCALS) in 1978, Mohammed and Otim [143] traced the trend towards the 'indigenisation' of the curriculum as practised in A.B.U., Zaria. Special emphasis was placed upon study in the area of 'Library and the community' as a core course:

(a)   Sociology of Library Science
(b)   History of Books and Libraries

These two courses are taught at first degree level in the context of Nigeria's social setting. Details of the course development in these two specific areas are evaluated in this present work. The value of the contribution of the authors to the study of curriculum development process in Nigerian librarianship is inherent in the positive indigenous approach to the curriculum and how this reflects in the total curriculum process.

However, Benge[144] suggests elsewhere in the literature, that the Departments of Library Studies have failed to make their programmes relevant to African circumstances. He argues further that all previous efforts to indigenise the curriculum have been implemented only to a superficial degree. He contends that basic theory is international whereas its interpretation is not. Thus, for example, 'The principles of classification are universal but the Dewey classification system is inevitably ethnocentric as it reflects the attitudes and characteristic of an American in the late nineteenth century.'[145] Furthermore, as Benge visualises, in subjects like the 'History of Libraries' the indigenous requirements are more obvious but not easy to fulfill, considering that the exclusion of the study of e.g. ancient Greece and Rome or the European Middle Ages is not necessarily the answer to a full-fledged curriculum that is strictly indigenous. Persuasive as Benge's argument may seem, it contributes nothing to developments in this aspect of curriculum development other than to reject the basic principles (rather than practise) of 'indigenisation' in the curriculum. However, 'indigenisation' of the curriculum is truly reflective of national development objectives and community needs for information and library services.

In more formal comparative review of the elements in programmes offered by both Ibadan and Zaria; Ogunsheye[146] has shown evidence of a unified approach to curriculum development with library science, documentation and archive courses formally represented in the syllabuses. The author observes that the development of the parts into a unified whole is not yet complete:

> ... the courses for the archivists programme are still to be initiated. Although an archives management course is offered in the Ibadan syllabus, no student has enrolled in it. Likewise information science courses are not fully developed. Although computer applications to libraries are offered, a programme for the training of information scientists in the M.Phil. specialist programme is in the planning stages.[147]

In countries like Britain and the U.S.A information science has developed as a discipline in its own right backed-up with the necessary framework for its curriculum. For the same level of attainment to be achieved in the Nigerian curriculum development process, the information requirements and needs of the various library users will require definition and detailed study to make such curriculum relevant to local needs. The level at which the curriculum for information science is planned will also need to be determined, i.e., either at undergraduate or postgraduate level. For example, Ibadan was reportedly planning the curricula 'for users of information' at all levels – primary, secondary, and teacher training colleges, with additional recommendation that library science becomes a programme in the curriculum of schools, colleges, and universities.

In the area of special library types such as 'school libraries', Fayose[148] made proposals for a one-year postgraduate education for school librarians in Nigeria. The proposed programme will prepare the school librarian for his dual function as teacher and librarian, and is set at the one-year PG Dip level, with possible adaptation for the two-year non-graduate (Diploma) students 'who wish to go into primary school libraries'. The author proposed six compulsory courses to form the core of the programme:

(a)   Educational psychology
(b)   Curriculum development
(c)   Materials for children and young adults
(d)   Cataloguing, classification, indexing, bibliographic compilation
(e)   Library administration
(f)   Educational technology; and one optional course styled 'one special subject' — from which the students can choose. It should be a subject that the school librarian can teach in the school after the completion of his course.

However, on the basis of Fayose's article, a definition of the needs of the school community is lacking, thereby making the proposals seem empirical when this should not be so as previous studies tend to justify.[149-152] In Ogunsheye's work for example, a theory was advanced that the educational needs of the school population in terms of supplementary information required as back-up to formal classroom studies are not yet met by books and these (needs) now require the availability of audio-visual materials, if the new education with cultural content is to become a reality: Ogunsheye submits that the school population as well as adult illiterates in rural and urban industrial communities, form the majority of the citizenry in Nigeria and therefore their educational needs for information should no longer be neglected. If tested, this theory could have been of added significance as prerequisites to Fayose's proposals. Again the author could have used available information in the literature to advantage if she had considered current research in the field of school librarianship. For instance, at both Ibadan and ABU, Zaria, there is a current investigation on the needs of the school population even at the time of Fayose's article. The Abadina Media Resource Centre Research Project under the direction and supervision of Professor Ogunsheye, is centred around service and research in five primary schools within the vicinity and there is a similar project at the Samaru Public and Children's Library under the direction of the Department of Library Science, A.B.U, Zaria. It would be useful to consider, *in situ,* what pattern of users' needs has emerged from these projects before curriculum decisions could be made based on learning experiences and the level at which such professional education could be offered.

The nature of assessment techniques in education with emphasis on the character of professional education in library and information studies has been examined in papers by Aiyepeku[153] and Edoka.[154] The library school has been highlighted as an academic unit of the university, thus, being naturally tied to the apron strings of university regulations in assessment of university students. Overall on the issue of assessment, there is the general tendency amongst library educators to apply the use of the concept broadly from education viewpoint. For instance, Ogunsheye defines assessment as 'the means by which we ascertain whether behaviour and attitudinal changes required have taken place in the candidates.'[155]

In a professional library programme education is the function of 'transmitting knowledge and skills which are necessary for successful performance in the profession of librarianship.'[156] This function places library schools at the vortex of the profession. Employers of librarians invariably depend on the judgement of library schools in choosing new entrants to the work force. Examinations as major assessment techniques are taken by the profession and the society at large, as having predictive value for future performance as, '...success in the examination is held to be *prima facie* evidence of fitness to higher studies or to exercise a profession.'[157] The methods of assessment in Nigeria library and information studies therefore encompass, in addition to evaluating students, course objectives and course content, through essay-type examination, continuous assessment, oral examination, objective testing and project work.

Other writers have focused on individual aspects of curriculum development in librarianship. One such writer highlighted the administrative aspects, i.e. the library school's role in curriculum development – Olden[158] in a descriptive survey of the Department of Library Science, A.B.U., Zaria, considered some elements of curriculum activity. For instance, Olden found that:

(a) The foreign language requirement as a compulsory element of the curriculum from 1968/69 to 1972/73 had to be dropped because most of the students did not have 'O' level French. This presented considerable difficulties to both faculty and students. At the Faculty Board of Education meeting of May 1973 it was adopted that the foreign language be recommended still, but not made compulsory. As a result of this regulation many students opted for other courses such as Education and Sociology at the expense of foreign language option.

(b) There exists inter-departmental co-operation in which courses in library management have been taught by lecturers from the Department of Business Administration.

(c) Students actively participate as members of the Curriculum Review Committee which was set up in 1978/79. Some of the Committee's recommendations as implemented in 1979/80, streamlined the B.L.S. syllabus and removed some overlapping of courses.[159]

Olden furthermore shed light on the structure of the new M.L.S. curriculum which has been designed on the same pattern as those for other master programmes within the faculty of education. The M.L.S. degree offers a choice between coursework (7 courses) plus thesis, and coursework (11 courses) plus an 'independent study' of not less than 6,000 words. The seven-course programme is for students without a previous librarianship qualification and they have to pursue four compulsory subjects, i.e. reference and bibliography; organisation of knowledge; collection development; and library management.

However, the eleven-course programme for students with librarianship qualification includes seven Library Science courses and four from the range offered by other Departments. For instance, **all** M.L.S. courses are to last one term (3 hours a week amounting to 30 hours), with an examination at the end of each term. This arrangement is different from the previous MLS module under which courses extend from October to May with fewer lecture periods a week per course. All the elements of the content of courses run by A.B.U., Zaria, are evaluated in Section 4.2 on Evaluation. Other writers such as Aboyade,[160] Mohammed and Afolabi[161] have also contributed to the literature on curriculum development in comparative studies published in *Nigerian Libraries*.

Aboyade, for example, has drawn attention to curriculum development activity at Ibadan library school where in the basic professional curriculum for one calendar year (M.L.S) , new introductory courses have been designed in information science, library automation, and archives and historical manuscripts collections as optional courses for students. In addition, some aspects of modern information handling techniques have been incorporated into existing courses. For instance, this is evident most especially in courses on, 'Special Libraries and the Literature and References Sources for Science and Technology, Classification and Cataloguing, and a bit of documentation processes in courses on Literature and Reference Sources in the Humanities and the Social Sciences.'[162]

For their part, Mohammed and Afolabi argue that curriculum development is a problem area of Nigerian library schools as 'an examination of the curricula reveals a preponderance in the traditional areas' (unspecified).[163] The authors suggest an orientation of the curricula, such that they would bear social relevance to the community. According to the authors, this can be achieved through adoption of a dynamic curriculum as proposed in the seminal work of Havard-Williams on the *Harmonisation of the Core Curriculum* and Saunder's *Guidelines for Curriculum Development in Information Studies*.

Some international aspects of curriculum development in Nigerian library schools deserve mention in this section, if only to illumine the library schools' efforts to indigenise the curriculum through the curriculum development process. In May 1981 a Meeting sponsored by the *Federation Internationale de Documentation* (FID), Education and Training (ET) was held at Ibadan University to discuss technical problems of identifying 'training' needs for library and information services in a predominantly non-literate society, with particular reference to agricultural and rural development.[164]

Most of the papers presented at the Conference, which was presided over by Professor Paul Wasserman, reflect the growing importance and recognition of information as supportive input for specific development programmes of which agricultural and rural development is a significant part. The large majority of the people living and working in rural areas are 'illiterate' and have thus been neglected, both in library provision and the required training necessary for personnel who find themselves working in such locality at one stage or another of their career. In view of this current awareness of the need to revitalise services to the rural community, it is gratifying to note the Conference's decisions as follows:

(a) Those responsible for formal education programmes in library and information science should take into consideration the need to prepare library and information personnel for service to the rural and non-literate communities;

(b) Continuing education programmes including short courses for library and information workers engaged in service to the rural and non-literate communities;

(c) Colloquia should be convened for library educators, adult literacy and agriculture extension specialists and other experts involved in rural development to plan for co-operative educational efforts;

(d) Schools of library and information studies in Africa such as the Department of Library Studies at the University of Ibadan, should be given adequate support by their governments and international organisations to prepare information personnel for service in rural areas in their country. (Summarised by present writer).

Perhaps at this juncture one should reflect on Ogunsheye's[165] paper presented at the Conference. In the paper, the author posits that:

(a) Rural non-literates have information needs which can be identified and categorised;

(b) A new concept of service and practice are required to meet those needs;

(c) Library and information services that can promote education, increase productivity and quality of life are feasible in non-literate rural communities;

(d) Rural society can be structured and organised to be receptive to information transfer from formal agencies like libraries;

(e) The relationship established between information flow and development is pertinent to developing countries;

(f) Special training programmes and curriculum are required for a new type of information counsellor librarian and 'para-professional' *(sic)* assistant to give this service.

Thus, an evolving hypothesis from the above outline is that the conventional library service has not succeeded in meeting the information needs of predominantly non-literate communities. This implied that for libraries to fulfill their roles effectively, a new dynamism is required in providing essential service to promote literacy; to educate for change, to articulate wants of rural communities, perhaps even to increase productivity and improve the general quality of life at the grass roots level commonly present in rural area life.

Given such a situation, it would seem positive to consider Ogunsheye's suggestion, that the personnel envisaged to implement rural library and information service be educated in two categories:

(a) *Professional cadre* — termed as Extension Librarian or Information Counsellor Librarian. According to Ogunsheye, the 'professionals' are individuals with first degrees in a discipline with training at postgraduate level for rural agricultural library and information service. The possession of a subject background such as science, sociology, or humanities is of distinct advantage. The structure of the 'professional' programmes should be either a two-year programme for an M.L.S. including an additional certification for rural librarianship, or a sandwich programme in two parts, consisting of a first professional M.L.S., with a continuing education programme for specialisation in rural librarianship after a period of practice.

(b) *Para–professional cadre* — styled by Ogunsheye as Extension Information Library Officers. These are individuals with a secondary education and a two–year diploma, with additional specialisation for rural librarianship. These will function as information officers executing services, working with agricultural extension team, health services team, functional literacy team and others in an outreach programme or at the information referral desk under the supervision of the professional extension librarian.

It follows that a curriculum requires to be worked out for both categories of library workers with guidelines as follows:

	Level	Orientation
(a)	M.L.S.	Theory, practice and decision-making
(b)	B.L.S.	Theory and practices
(c)	D.L.S.	Operational executive function.

The core curriculum for the various level — M.L.S. – PG Dip, B.L.S., and D.L.S. is as proposed by Ogunsheye.[166] The curriculum as proposed by Ogunsheye cannot be faulted on *a priori* basis, for it was based on sound theory and previous related studies on the subject. For example, in addition to using her own comparative methodology from an earlier work, [167] the author also consulted other works of importance such as report of decisions taken by Directors of African Library Schools at the Dakar meetings of 1974 [168] and 1978[169] which persuasively advocated for the 'Africanisation of the curriculum programmes from other parts of the world.' Of particular relevance are the programme for information specialist for various specialised services by INSDOC[170] (and the special documentation centres in Delhi, India), and the School of Library and Information Studies, Pittsburgh's newly planned 'Agricultural Information Specialist Programme' for candidates from developing countries. The latter is, however, considered as offering at bachelor and master's level, courses which are related to conventional library and information services for agricultural establishment rather than for the whole spectrum of rural development.

A general observation on the papers which have been surveyed here under 'Nigerian Studies' shows that the current trend of thought in professional education relates to developing the curriculum on the basis of extended duration of programmes especially at the master's level. This is due in part to the current expansion in the frontiers of knowledge in professional library and information services.

Other Studies

Australia

In 1974, Colloquium on Education for Librarianship was held at the Western Australian Institute of Technology (W.A.I.T.) August 28-30, 1973.[171] The Colloquium compares in similarity with colloquia held elsewhere such as, the Illinois Graduate Library School Conference of 1970 in the U.S.A., the Ibadan University Colloquium on Education for Librarianship in Nigeria, 1974, the U.K. British Library Research and Development in Library and Information Science, 1977, and the Cumberland Lodge Curriculum Development Seminar, 1980. An internationalist approach to curriculum development problems is particularly evident in the 1973 Australian Colloquium. While other similar colloquia have concentrated on national curriculum development problems the W.A.I.T. Colloquium examined problems of curriculum design overseas, more especially in the developing countries. Some of the resolutions of the colloquium bear salutary inference to library education as practised elsewhere in the world. For example:

(a) That further investigation is required into the future role of the professional;
(b) That curriculum design is dynamic in concept and essentially related to the future;
(c) That the curriculum should emphasise the international implications of librarianship;
(d) That basic qualifications should normally be generalist in nature;
(e) That courses in areas of 'post-basic' specialisations are required as a matter of urgency;
(f) That library schools are obligated to enter the field of continuing education with the community rather than for it.[172]

All the recommendations reflect increasing concern for library education to be made locally relevant. Dean,[173] in referring to the situation in the developing countries, argues that the trend towards 'relevance' is a major influence among other numerous factors governing curriculum development. The characteristics of hurdles to be cleared are, according to Dean:

(i)   Adequate back-up resources for teaching and a/v equipment;
(ii) Indigenous staff;
(iii) Accommodation
(iv) Type of student: qualities and suitability;
(v)   Language fluency for tertiary teaching and note making by students.

Dean is of course writing from valuable experience having served overseas (especially in Nigeria and Ghana) enough to know and be able to identify the peripheral problems affecting curriculum development activity in the library schools. His argument that the library pattern has in many cases been predetermined by colonial experiences and a system developed which is possibly not particularly appropriate for the environment, is quite valid and raises some questions. For example the author implied a re-definition of the future role of the professional in library and information services. The professional will be expected by his superiors, to carry out his duties effectively and in a manner appropriate to new forms of education and practice. Thus, in respect of what is expected of library educators, Dean submits, 'that curriculum rethinking in respect of objectives, content and teaching method is sadly lacking in most areas of the third world, and the habitual and familiar tend to be cherished.'[174]

However, in another study on curriculum development, Parr and Done[175] have jointly reported on the use of the Nominal Group Technique (N.G.T.) as a tool of curriculum renewal in their library school. The use of N.G.T. was decided upon with the aim of identifying curriculum areas of prime concern to library practitioners. The authors sampled 26 librarians (some of them former students of the library school) from senior and middle rank positions in academic, public, state, school and special libraries. Such technique as the N.G.T. was initiated and developed by Delbecq, *et. al.*[176] in 1968 as an alternative to the more conventional group formats such as open discussion or debate, and it was aimed at diffusing volatile or threatening group encounters as probable in such situations, thereby facilitating a more rational and comfortable decision making process.

Elsewhere in the literature, Delbecq and Van de Ven have in 1972 applied the N.G.T. concept to the field of exploratory health studies, but even more pertinent to this present work is that the NGT was for the first time applied to librarianship by Lonsdale[177] at the 1970 W.A.I.T. Colloquium. The procedure used was based on a nominal-group approach for small-group creative decision-making. All groups, drawn from Colloquium participants, had the same problem – to identify the most important attitudes, values, appreciations or feelings which should, in their view, be developed by a course in librarianship. In the analysis of results that followed, two areas of prime importance emerged:

(a)   Objectives relating to the relationship between the librarian and the library user: these are exemplified by such expressions as 'understanding the needs of users and a desire to serve them,' 'responsibility to clients,' 'desire to help,' 'attitude of service,' 'sensitive to people.'

b)   Objectives relating to the manner whereby the librarian approaches and solves problems.[178]

The list of objectives presented to the participants is not fully comprehensive nor do the results as outlined above truly represent the views of the participants. However, the study created a basis for discussion on the application of N.G.T. as demonstrated in Parr and Done's work. The advantages of N.G.T. have been outlined as consisting of four important elements necessary for obtaining relevant results from the participating practitioners:

(i)   N.G.T. encourages participation by each group member;
(ii)   It minimises threatening or stifling interaction between group members;
(iii) It focuses attention on ideas rather than on people;
(iv)   It produces an indication of the relative emphasis given by the group to the various issues raised during the discussion.

Clearly one disadvantage which may act as a hindrance to all the stated advantages above is the 'academic reality' that exists in higher institutions in the curriculum development process – curriculum innovation is hardly based on the opinions of practitioners where such expressed views cannot be quantified nor assessed objectively.

The views of practitioners may rightly be sought (as the authors have done) on curriculum content for library education because of the need to gain some measure of feedback as to the relative importance of the subject components to practice. The inclusion of former graduates of the W.A.I.T. library school amongst the 26 librarians who participated in the N.G.T. is reasonable to the extent that they would offer valuable comment from personal experiences on the effectiveness of the existing programme as a preparation for the field. In relating the N.G.T. items to the general results of the survey, it can be observed that **Philosophy and social context of libraries** (A) was considered by the participants to be the second most important element in the curriculum, occupying almost a quarter of the available time for study. **Administrative aspects** (C) was judged to be of 'great importance' as 'strong emphasis was placed upon the study of people **as individuals**' (my emphasis) within the organisation. '**Library skills**' (B) failed to make much impact as to rank alongside A and C, regardless of their tangible importance in the day-to-day running of the library.

In conclusion, Parr and Done argue that the view of the practitioners should be predominant in curriculum design; one may add that it is equally important that the library school is itself aware of expectations and changes in the field, and there are many avenues towards achieving this, for example, through active participation in continuing education schemes for professionals, research, consultancy and the like. On the whole, N.G.T. as a tool in curriculum development has its limitations as it has been discussed earlier, but the overriding factor is that it is an effective channel for obtaining current feedback from practitioners as regards library schools' courses, as well as a reliable medium for assessing practitioners' attitudes to curriculum innovation in the library schools.

India

Gupta[179] in a recent survey of library and information science curriculum, has related the nature of jobs performed by qualified library personnel with the content of library schools' courses in India. The results proved to be inconclusive and the report could only serve as basis for further discussion and debate. Similarly, Kanjilad[180] has attempted to trace modern trends in library education, only to devote considerable space and time to events happening overseas and leave very little room for the trends in India, presented as they were in breviate form.

However, by contrast, Kashyap[181] in a well-documented study on curriculum development considered the concept in its educational context, and following detailed examination of the curriculum development process, proposed that in its application to library and information education a 'systems' approach to curriculum development is preferable. Kashyap argues that because of the impact of systems philosophy, the curriculum is increasingly being regarded as a system of interrelated tasks designed to achieve certain ends. As a 'system,' the curriculum is defined in terms of its components such as, (a) objectives; (b) subject contents; (c) instructional materials; (d) teaching-learning strategies; (e) procedures for evaluation of students' progress; and (f) implementation programmes. The interaction of these elements provide the parameters for defining the curriculum as:

> A 'system' of planned action of instructions and evaluation methods of transmitting organized bodies of knowledge (subjects) to the learner, with the objective of increasing his knowledge and developing his intellectual ability, social behaviour and vocational aptitude.[182]

Within the 'system,' as proposed in Kashyap's definition of the curriculum, there exists an inter-active system of planning and development of a workable and effective curriculum design in an educational environment. Thus, the "systems" approach constitutes:

(a) *Determination and formulation of;*
    (i)   overall objectives of education
    (ii) level-wise objectives of curriculum
    (iii) subject-wise objectives of curriculum
(b) *Identification, selection and specification of core elements of the curriculum, namely;*
    (i)   subject contents to be learned by students
    (ii) teaching-learning strategies (methods)
    (iii) assessment procedure, i.e. how can the extent of learning of a student be measured
    (iv) instructional materials
(c) *Determination and formulation of objectives and functions of the core elements*
(d) *Establishing interrelation among the core elements*
(e) *Implementation and monitoring of the whole curriculum system*

It would seem from items (a) to (e) above that the 'system's' approach is heavily depenaent on implementation for successful course design. Even then, there will still be the need for evaluation of course materials. Kashyap refers to this last stage as 'a cycle of continuous revaluation and revision of curriculum,' thereby ensuring that what is taught is made relevant from time to time.

The author utilised relevant educational literature to good effect by working out a set of desired objectives for a new library and information science educational programme. The 'objectives' thus determined and specified will provide the guidelines for:

(a) Conceiving the whole structure of an educational programme and to measure the effectiveness of its final output.

(b) Rational selection and organisation of curriculum contents; identifying relevant teaching-learning processes; choice of suitable methods for evaluation and preparation as well as selection of instructional materials.

Educational literature is still largely used by library educators involved with selection and organisation of content. For example, Schwab suggests a 'structure of discipline' as a device for content selection. It covers three distinct but related sets of selection conditions as follows:

(a) The way in which accumulated knowledge is organised according to subjects or the way discrimination is made between areas of investigation.

(b) The set of basic methods and rules used within the framework of the discipline for providing evidence, in other words, the methods of enquiry unique for the discipline.

(c) The set of basic concepts used to describe a variety of phenomena within the boundaries of a discipline.[183]

Another educationist Dave refers to the selection and organisation of curriculum contents on the basis of:

(a) The curriculum area or subjects of study should be selected in such a manner that they provide a wide basis and choice for further education.

(b) While selecting subjects and organising their content, the nature of individual subjects must be taken into account. For example, subjects which undergo quick changes in respect of their content need frequent updating.

(c) In the process of selection and organisation of content, the emphasis should be shifted from specific bits of knowledge which quickly become obsolete, to those aspects which constitute the structure of the subject, key concepts of the curriculum area and tools and methods of inquiry specific to the subject....

(d) The curriculum content should have an appropriate mixture of work and study. Academic study should be interrelated with work situations wherever possible.

(e)   Each subject of study selected for inclusion in the curriculum should be examined in terms of the possibility of its acquisition and applicability.[184]

The important point to emerge from the above-mentioned citations (Schwab and Dave) is that library schools are suitably disposed to adopt the principles of selection as enunciated in the outlines such as, for example, in the area of restructuring the curriculum content. The developing countries too may use this as a leverage for indigenising their curricula so as to make them socially relevant. This is all the more important because in almost all cases of curriculum innovation in African library schools, the planner of the educational programme is not always presented with *tabula rasa*, from which to develop his course. Kashyap's contribution, apart from being of value to the developing countries in general, is a positive analysis on curriculum development as a process in professional education.

Review

The literature on curriculum development in library and information studies has been reviewed in this section to cover trends in the field from British, American, Nigerian and other countries' perspectives – such as Australia and India. Practically, all elements of curriculum design and change as surveyed in this present work indicate some form of pragmatic approach to the curriculum of librarianship. In some cases proposals for new curriculum have been made without due recourse to assessment of need, although this is more than compensated for in the renewed efforts by the library schools, especially in Nigeria, to localise the curriculum so as to make it socially relevant.

As can be observed from the review, curriculum development is a cyclic process with a continuity value in the field of education. In general, it is influenced by both 'inside' and 'outside' factors such as, social, economic, and political change in the society which library schools exist to serve. In view of the changes necessary to be made in response to these factors, efforts must now be directed further at developing new concepts such as the N.G.T. and applying them beneficially to the profession as a whole. As 'gatekeepers'[185] of the profession library schools are suitably placed to incur whatever changes are considered necessary in order to improve professional services through an active curriculum development process.

References

1. Hirst, P. H., 'The Logic of the Curriculum,' *Journal of Curriculum Studies*, 1(2), 1969: 142-158.

2. Hirst, P. H. and R. S. Peters, *The Logic of Education*, London: R. & K.P., 1970.

3. Phenix, P. H., *Realms of Meaning: A Philosophy of the Curriculum for General Education* New York: McGraw-Hill, 1964.

4. Ring, R., 'Curriculum Content: Principles of Selection' in: Lawton, D., *et al, Theory and Practice of Curriculum Studies,* London: Boutledge, 1978: 137-143.

5. Ring, *op. cit.*: 137.

6. Gleeson, D., 'Curriculum Development and Social change: Towards a Reappraisal of Teacher Action,' *Journal of Further and Higher Education*, 2(2), 1978: 41-51.

7. Lawton, D., Social Change, *Educational Theory and Curriculum Planning,* London: University of London Press/Hodder & Stoughton, 1968.

8. Ghuman, A. P., 'Problems and Approaches in Curriculum Development' in: *Workshop on Curriculum Development in Librarianship and Information Science,* College of Librarianship, Wales, 1977. London: BLRD, 1978: 2. Quotation from: Hirst, P. H. and H. S. Peters, the logic of education ... *op. cit.*

9. Bloom, B. S., ed., 'Taxonomy of Educational Objectives: The Classification of Educational Goals,' *Handbook I: Cognitive Domain,* Longmans, 1956.

10. Kratwohl, D. R., 'Stating Objectives Appropriately for Programme, for Curriculum, and for Instrumental Materials Development,' *Journal of Teacher Education,* 16, 1965: 83-92.

11. Musgrove, F., 'Curriculum Objectives', *Journal of Curriculum Studies,* 1(1), 1968: 1-18.

12. Stake, R. E., 'Objectives, Priorities and other Judgement Data', *Review of Educational Research,* 40(2), 1970: 181-212.

13. Gribble, J. H., 'Pandora's Box: The Effective Domain of Educational Objectives', *Journal of Curriculum Studies,* 2, 1970:11-24.

14. Kratwohl, D. R., *et al,* 'Taxonomy of Educational Objectives: The Classification of Educational Goals', *Handbook II: Affective Domain* London: Longmans, 1971.

15. Harlen, W., 'Formulating Objectives: Problems and Approaches', *British Journal of Educational Technology,* 3(3), 1972: 223-236.

16. Hogben, D., 'The Behavioural Objectives Approach: Some Problems and Some Dangers', *Journal of Curriculum Studies*, 4, 1972: 42-50.

17. Tyler, R. W., *Basic Principles of Curriculum and Instruction*, Chicago: University of Chicago Press, 1949.

18. Kratwohl, *et al ... op. cit.*, 1971: 6.

19. Pring, R., 'Bloom's Taxonomy: A Philosophical Critique' (2), *Cambridge Journal of Education*, 2, 1971: 83-91.

20. Bramley, G., *A History of Library Education*, London: Clive Bingley, 1969.

21. Bramley, G., *Apprentice to Graduate: a History of Library Education in the United Kingdom* London: Clive Bingley, 1981.

22. *Ibid.:* 7 : 176

23. Davinson, D., 'The Librarianship Board of the Council for National Academic Awards', *Journal of Librarianship*, 8(2), 1976: 84.

24. The Library Association Working party on the Future of Professional Qualifications: Recommendations and Implementation, *Supplement to Library Association Record*, 79(9), 1977.

25. Franz, E. G., 'Archives, Manpower Planning, Training Facilities and Preparation of Curricular for Regional Training Centres,' in: *Planning Information Manpower*, Paris: UNESCO, 1974: 31-68.

26. Havard-Williams, P., 'Librarianship and Documentation: Manpower Planning, Professional Structure, Education and Training, in: *Planning Information Manpower.* Paris: UNESCO, 1974: 1-29.

27. Schur, H., and W. L. Saunders (with the assistance of L. J. Pargeter), *Education and Training for Scientific and Technological Library and Information Work*, London: H.M.S.O., 1968.

28. Havard-Williams, P., 'Education for Library, Information and Archive Studies', *IFLA Journal*, 2(3), 1976: 137-145.

29. *Ibid:* 141.

30. Havard-Williams, P., 'The Role of Library Schools and Manpower Training,' in: the L.A. *Proceedings of the Study School and National Conference*, Brighton, 1978. London: L. A., 1978: 101-103 (p.101 *et seq.*)

31. *Ibid.:* 40

32. Grogan, D. J., 'Non-librarianship Elements in Library Education.' Paper given at the Library Association University, College and Research Section Meeting at College of Librarianship Wales, 8th April, 1978.

33. Wilson, T. D., 'Research: Its Influence on Curriculum Design and Development' in: *Workshop on Curriculum Development in Librarianship and Information Science*, Wales 1977, London: BLRD, 1978: 84-90.

34. *Ibid:* 84.

35. Holroyd, G., 'Assessment in Education for Librarianship: A Teacher's View', *Journal of Librarianship*, 2(2), 11970: 116-125.

36. Kaye, D. and A. J. Wood, 'Teaching and Testing in Library and Information Studies: The Rule of Assessed Course Work', *Journal of Librarianship*, 1975: 182-198.

37. Foskett, D. J., 'Information Science as an Emergent Discipline: Educational Implications', *Journal of Librarianship*, 5(3), 1973: 161-174.

38. Saunders, W. L., 'Professional Education, Research and Development,' in: Saunders, W. L., ed. *British Librarianship Today*, London: L. A., 1976:341-361.

39. Saunders, W. L., *Guidelines for Curriculum Development in Information Studies: Report*, PGI-78/WS/27. UNESCO/UNISIST, 1978.

40. Maguire, C., 'The Development of Educational Programs in Information Science': Opportunities and Problems,' *Information Bulletin of the Library Automated System Information Exchange* (LASIE), 8(4), 1978: 23-30.

41. Dudley, E. P., 'Curriculum Change in the Eighties: Time for Significant Developments', *Library Association Records*, 83(7), 1981: 332-334. (p. 333 *et seq.*)

42. Needham, C. D., 'The Design of Undergraduate Courses' in: *Workshop on Curriculum Development in Librarianship and Information Science*, Wales, 1977, London: BLRD, 1978:7-27.

43. *Ibid.:* 7-8

44. Wilson, T. D., 'Research: Its Influence on Curriculum Design and Development ...' *op.cit.:* 85

45. Davidson, D., 'Recent Developments in British Librarianship', *Herald of Library Science*, 16(4), 1977: 255-342.

46. Lawal, O. O., 'Elements of Degree Courses in Librarianship and Information Science,' (MA Thesis), Loughborough, L.U.T., 1979.

47. *Ibid.:* 183-4.

48. Burrell, T.W., 'Curriculum Development for Librarianship,' (PhD Thesis) Strathclyde: University of Strathclyde, 1982.

49. *Ibid.:* 302.

50. Burrell, *op. cit.:* 77-4-776.

51. Quotations in this section are all from the proposal and interim reports of the Curriculum Development Project as cited in the work of Burrell, T. W. Curriculum Development for Librarianship, *op. cit.* The full publication of the Report is presently being awaited.

52. Needham, C. D., 'The Design of Undergraduate Courses ...' *op. cit.*

53. Needham, C. D. 'The Common Core' Paper presented at the British Library R & D Department's curriculum development project meeting: curriculum change in the 80s: a seminar held at Cumberland Lodge. Windsor Great Parkm July 1980.

54. *Ibid.:* 15.

55. For example: Maltby, A., 'United Kingdom Catalogue use Survey: A Report', London: L.A., 1973.

56. Needham, C. D., 'The Common Core ...' *op. cit.:* 15

57. Dudley, E. P., 'Curriculum Change in the 80s: Time for Significant Developments', *Library Association Record,* 83(7), 1981:333.

58. *Ibid.:* 334

59. Eyre, J., *Teaching Students in Schools of Librarianship and Information Science about Computers and their Applications,* London: BLRD. 1979. (Report no. 5466).

60. Churchwell, C. D., 'Education for Librarianship in the U.S.: Some Factors which Influenced its Development Between 1919 and 1939,' University of Illinois, (PhD thesis), 1966. (Authorised facsimile printed by University Microfilms International, Ann Arbor: Michigan).

61. *Ibid.:* 8.

62. Reed, S. R., 'The Curriculum of Library Schools Today: A Historical Overview' in: Goldhor, H., ed. *Education for Librarianship: the Design of the Curriculum of Library Schools,* Urbana, Illinois: University of Illinois, Graduate School of Library Science, 1971:19-45.

63. Vann, S. K., 'Training for Librarianship Before 1923: Education for Librarianship Prior to the Publication of Williamson's Report on Training for Library Service,' Chicago: A. L. A., 1961: 33.

64. White, C. M., *The Origins of the American Library School,* New York: Scarecrow Press, 1961:94.

65. Carnegie Corporation of New York, 'Training for Library Service: A Report Prepared for the Carnegie Corporation of New York'. Prepared by C. C. Williamson, New York, 1923: 136-137: 143. 69, 1951, *Standards for Accreditation.*

66. Danton, J. P., 'Between MLS and PhD: A Study of Sixth-Year Specialist programmes in Accredited Library Schools,' Chicago: A. L. A., 1970.

67. Swank, R. C., 'The Graduate Library School Curriculum', in: *Institute on Problems of Library Schools Administration,* edited by S. R. Reed, Washington, D. C.,: US Office of Education, 1965: 20-27.

68. Fryden, F. N., 'Post-master's Degree Programmes in the Accredited US Library Schools,' *The Library Quarterly,* 39, 1969, 233-244.

69. Licklider, J. C. R., *Libraries of the Future,* Cambridge, Mass.: MIT Press, 1965.

70. Becker, J., 'Libraries, Society, and Technological Change,' *Library Trends,* 27(3), 1978: 409-416.

71. Goehlert, R. and G. Snowdon, 'Computer Programming in Library Education,' *Journal of Education for Librarianship,* 20(4), 1980: 251-260.

72. Rees, A. M. and D. Riccio, 'Information Science in Library School Curricula' in: *International Conference on Education for Scientific Information Work, Queen Elizabeth College, London, April 3-7, 1967,* The Hague, Netherlands, 1967: 29-37.

73. Rees, A. M. , 'The Impact of Computer Technology on Library Education,' *UNESCO Bulletin for Libraries,* 23, 1969: 25-29.

74. *Ibid.:* 26.

75. Rees and Riccio, *op. cit.* (listing of schools and course tiles).

76. Hayes, R. M., 'The Development of a Methodology for System Design and its Role in Library Education,' *Library Quarterly,* 34, 1964: 340.

77. Rees, R. M., The Impact of Computer Technology .... *op. cit:* 26.

78. Borko, H., 'Information Science: What is it?" *American Documentation,* 19, 1968: 3.

79. Hayes, R. M., 'The Development of a Methodology ...' *op. cit.:* p. 340.

80. Rees ... *op. cit.:* 29

81. Harlow, N., 'Changing the Curriculum,' *Journal of Education for Librarianship,* 10, 1969: 78-85.

82. *Ibid.:* 84.

83. Goldhor, H., ed., *Education for Librarianship: The Design of the Curriculum of Library Schools:* proceedings of papers presented at a Conference ... conducted by the University of Illinois Graduate School of Library Science, September 6-9, 1970.

84. Reed, S. R., ... *op. cit.*

85. Asheim, L. E., 'New Trends in the Curriculum of Library Schools", in: Goldhor, H. ed. *Education for Librarianship... op. cit.:* 59-79.

86. Shera, J. H., *The Foundations of Education for Librarianship,* Wiley-Becker and Hayes, 1972.

87. *Ibid.:* 362.

        : 362-3

88. Borko, H., ed., *Targets for Research in Library Education,* Chicago: A. L. A., 1973.

89. Jahoda, G., 'The Integration of Information Science and Library Automation into the Library School Educational Programme' in: Borko, H., ed., *Targets for Research ... op. cit.:* 49-64.

90. Hayes, R. M., 'The Development of a Methodology for System Design and its Role in Library Education,' *Library Quarterly,* 34, 1964: 330-351.

91. Hayes, R. M., 'Data Processing in the Library School Curriculum,' *ALA Bulletin,* 61, 1967: 662-669.

92. Hines, T. C., 'Salaries and Academic Training Programmes for Information Scientists,' *Journal of Chemical Documentation,* 7, 1967: 118-120

93. Taylor, R. S., 'The Interfaces between Librarianship and Information Science and Engineering,' *Special Libraries,* 58, 1967: 45-48.

94. Asheim, L. E., 'Education and Manpower for Librarianship,' *ALA Bulletin,* 62, 1968: 1-96-1106.

95. Wilson, M. L., ed., 'Papers Presented at a Workshop on the Integrated Core Curriculum, University of North Carolina,' March 6-8, 1977. in: *Journal of Education for Librarianship,* 19, 1978: 151-183.

96. *Ibid:* 152.

97. Asheim, L. E., 'The Core Curriculum,' in: Wilson, M. L., ed., *Papers Presented at a Workshop on the Integrated Core Curriculum ...* op. cit. 155.

98. Garrison, G., 'Needed, a Core Curriculum for a Diversifying Profession,' in: Wilson, M. L. ed., *Papers Presented at a Workshop on the Integrated Core Curriculum ... op. cit.:* 179.

99. *Ibid.:* 180

100. Quoted in: Downs, R.S., 'Education for Librarianship in U.S. and Canada,' in: Bone, L. E. ed., *Library Education: An International Survey,* Urbana: University of Illinois Graduate School of Library Science, 1968.

101 Williamson, C. C., 'Training for Library Service (1923),' in: *The Williamson Reports of 1921 and 1923,* Metuchen, New Jersey: Scarecrow Press, 1971:28.

102 Hansen, W. L. and R. H. Graham, *The Foreign Language Imbroglio in Graduate Education,* Medison: University of Wisconsin, 1968.

103. Alter, M. P., 'Thirty-six Reasons for Retaining Foreign Language Requirements,' *Bulletin of the Association of Departments of Foreign Languages,* 4, 1972: 10-12.

104. McGrath, E. J., *Liberal Education in the Professions,* New York Teachers College: Columbia University, 1959:16.

105. McGlothlin, W. J., *Patterns of Professional Education,* New York: Putnam, 1960.

106. *Ibid:*31.

107. Fisher, S. B. and W. J. Beck, 'Implications of the Foreign Language Requirement for the Library Schools,' *Journal of Education for Librarianship,* 19(1), 1978: 40-54.

108. Quoted by Fisher and Beck, in: 'Implications of the Foreign Language Requirement'.... *op. cit.* 45

109. Fisher, Suzanne, B. and William J. Beck, *op. cit.:* 45-46.

110. For example, Harris, C. D., 'Area Studies and Library Resources,' *Library Quarterly,* 35, 1965:214.

111. Hare, R., 'The Bibliographer in the Academic Library,' *Library Resources and Technical Services,* 13, 1969: 165-166.

112. Fisher and Beck, ... *op. cit.:* 53.

113. Usher, F. R., 'The Challenge for Library Schools an Employment View,' *Special Libraries,* 64, 1973: 439-444.

114. Lemke, A. B., 'Alternative Specialities in Library Education,' *Journal of Education for Librarianship,* 18, 1978: 285-294.

115. c.f. Brees, M. A., 'The Challenge for Library Schools: A Student's View,' *Special Libraries,* 64, 1973: 433-438.

116. Lemke, ... *op. cit.:* 291.

117. *Ibid.:* 286.

118. Dresang, E. T., 'An Application of Decision Making Theory to Curriculum Change in Library Education,' *Journal of Education for Librarianship,* 22 (1 and 2), 1981: 57-73.

119. Monroe ... *op. cit.:* 65.

120. Sexton, R. F. *and* R. A. Ungerer, *Rationale for Experiential Education,* Washington D. C., American Association for Higher Education, 1975. Quoted by Monroe ... *op. cit.:* 61.

121. Conant, R. W., 'The Conant Report: A Study of the Education of Librarians,' Massachusetts: MIT Press, 1980.

122. *Ibid.:* 24.

123. *Ibid.:* 25.

124. *Ibid.:* L 193-196 (Summarised).

125. Vitriolic comments have been made on the Conant Report by individual library educators and published in their Association Journal - *Journal of Education for Librarianship* (AALS) issue of 1981, e.g. Darling, R. L. A comment on the Final Conant Report, *Journal of Education for Librarianship,* 22 (1 and 2), 1981: 98-99.

126. Harreit, L., 'Promoting Knowledge through Publishing,' *West Africa,* 9 March, 1981, 500-502.

127. Zell, H., 'Publishing in West Africa: Producing Books against the Odds,' *West Africa,* 27 August, 1979: 1553-1556.

128. *Ibid,:* 1553

129. Akinyotu, A., 'Training and Education of Library Personnel in Nigeria — Comments and Proposals on its Objectives and Content,' *Nigeria Libraries,* 8(2), 1972: 103-116.
    c.f. Historical analysis of Nigerian library education by the same author.

130. Akinyotu, A., 'Training and Education of Library Personnel in Nigeria: A Historical Survey,' *West African Journal of Education,* 15(3), 1971: 195-200.

131. Bankole, E. B., ed., *Report* on 'Colloquium on Education and Training for Librarianship in Nigeria', *Nigerian Libraries,* 9(3), 1974: 169-171.

132. Department of Library Studies, University of Ibadan, *Report* on 'Colloquium on Education and Training for Librarianship in Nigeria,' *Nigerian Libraries,* 11 (1+2), 1975: 139-149.

133. Benge, R. C., 'Trends in the History of Library Education.' Paper Presented at the Colloquium on Education ..., University of Ibadan, 1974. (mimeo)

134. Chan, G. K. L., 'Third World Libraries and Cultural Imperialism,' *Assistant Librarian,* 72(10), 1979: 134-140 (Especially pp. 136, 138-9).

135. Dipeolu, J. O,. 'A Critical Examination of the Curricula of Library Schools

in Nigeria,' Paper presented at the Colloquium on Education and Training ..., University of Ibadan, 1974 (mimeo).

136. Ogunsheye, F. A., 'New Proposals for Structure of Personnel and Curricula for the Various Levels or Categories.' Paper presented at the Colloquium on Education and Training ... University of Ibadan, 1974. (mimeo).

137. Moid, A., 'New Proposals for Library Education in Nigeria: Co-operation between Library Schools, Exchange of Staff and Students, Standards and Equivalencies,' Paper presented at the Colloquium ..., University of Ibadan, 1974 (mimeo).

138. Obi, D. S., 'Education for Librarianship in Nigeria,' *Nigerian Libraries*, 11 (3), 1975: 221-251.

139. *Ibid,:* 245

140. Based on: Nzotta, B. C., 'The Teaching of Management in African Library Schools.' Unpublished M. A. Dissertation) Loughborough: L.U.T., 1975.

141. Nzotta, B. C., 'Education for Library Management in African Library Schools,' *Journal of Librarianship*, 9(2), 1977, 130-144.

142. Asheim, L. E., ed., 'The Core of Education for Librarianship'. Report of a workshop held under the auspices of the Graduate Library School, University of Chicago, August 10-15, 1953. A.L.A., 1954:1.

143. Mohammed, A. and J. Otim, 'The Problem of Relevance to Local Conditions in Professional Education Programmes in Africa: The Case of Librarianship.' Paper presented at the SCALS meeting, Ibadan, 3-10 May, 1978 (mimeo).

144. Benge, R. C., 'Library Studies and Indigenisation,' *The Library Scientist* (ABU, Zaria), 5, 1978: 65-70.

145. *Ibid:* 66-67

146. Ogunsheye, F. A., 'Formal Programme Development in Library Education in Nigeria', *Journal of Education for Librarianship*, Spring 1978: 140-150.

147. *Ibid.:* 146.

148. Fayose, O., 'Proposals for a One-Year Postgraduate Education for School Librarians in Nigeria,' *West African Journal of Education*. 11(2), 1980: 20-27.

149. Ene, N., 'The Place of Libraries in Educational Planning in Nigeria,' *Nigerian Libraries*, 10 (2 and 3), 1974: 169-174.

150. Allen, J., 'School Library: Some Problems and Possibilities'. Workshop on Rival Libraries held at Kano State College, 27-30 January 1975. Nigerian Library Association: Northern States Division, 1975. (mimeo)

151. Akinyotu, A., 'The State of Education and Library Services in West Africa: A Brief Review', *International Library Review*, 8, 1976: 217-229.

152. Ogunsheye, F. A., 'Formal Programme Development ...,' *op. cit.:* 142.

153. Aiyepeku, W. O., 'Teaching and Examining Methods for Library Education,' Paper Presented at the Colloquium on Education and Training ... University of Ibadan, 1974 (mimeo).

154. Edoka, B. E., 'Assessment Technique in Library Studies' *Nigerian Libraries*, 15 (1 and 2), 1979: 48-58.

155. Ogunsheye, F. A., 'Trends in Library Education: The Criteria for Evaluation, of Programmes.' Paper Presented at the SCALS, University of Ibadan, Ibadan 3-10 May, 1978: 18 (mimeo).

156. International Federation of Library Associations Standing Advisory Committee Section of Library Schools, *Standards for Library Schools*, 1978: xiii.

157. Wall, W. D., 'Examinations', *West African Journal of Education*, 8(2), 1964: 65.

158. Olden, E. A., 'The Development of the Department of Library Science, Ahmadu Bello University, and its Implications for the Planning of Library Education Programmes in English-Speaking Black African Countries,' (M.L.S. thesis) Zaria: Ahmadu Bello University, Department of Library Science, 1980.

159. *Ibid.:* 40

160. Aboyade, B. O., 'Education for Librarianship', *Nigerian Libraries,* 15(1 and 2), 1979: 27-34.

161. Mohammed, A. and M. Afolabi, 'Education for Librarianship in Nigeria', *Nigeria Libraries*, 15 (1 and 2), 1979: 35-47.

162. Aboyade, B. O., 'Education for Librarianship ...' *op. cit.*: 31.

163. Mohammed and Afolabi, 'Education for Librarianship' ... *op. cit.:* 40

164. Aboyade, B. O., ed., 'Education and Training for Library and Information Services in a Predominantly Non-literate Society,' Papers Presented at the FID/ET Technical Meeting, Ibadan, Nigeria 6-9 May, 1981, The Hague: FID, 1981.

165. Ogunsheye, F. A., 'Education and Training for Library and Information Services to Rural Communities,' in: Aboyade, B. O., ed., *Education and Training for Library and Information Services... op. cit.*: 87-103.

166. *Ibid.:* 91-102.

167. Ogunsheye, F. A., 'Formal Programme Development ...' *op. cit.*

168. Standing Conferences of African Library Schools. *Report* of meeting held at University of Dakar, Feb. 25-27, 1974.

169. Standing Conferences of African Library Schools. *Report* of meeting held at University of Ibadan, May 3-4, 1978.

170. Insdoc, *Training Course in Information Science: Prospectus and Syllabus,* Delhi: Indian National Documentation Centre, 1980.

171. Colloquium on Education for Librarianship. Western Australian Institute of Technology, Perth, August 28-30, 1973. *Curriculum Design in Librarianship: An International Approach.* Proceedings ... edited by E. A. Parr and E. J. Wainwright. Perth: WAIT Aid Ltd., 1974.

172. *Ibid.:* 3-4

173. Dean, J., 'Library Education and Curriculum Problems in the Development Countries" in: *Colloquium on Education for Librarianship,* WAIT. *op. cit.:* 98-98.

174. *Ibid.:* 95.

175. Parr, E. and M. Done, 'Curriculum Development and the Nominal Group Technique (N.G.T.), Gaining the Practitioners' View', *Journal of Education for Librarianship,* 19(3), 1979: 223-232.

176. Delbecq, A. L., A. H. Van de Ven, and D. H. Gustafson, *Group Techniques for Programme Planning: A Guide to NG and Delphi Processes,* Glenview, Illinois: Scott, Foresman & Co., 1975.

177. Lonsdale, A., 'Affective Objectives for Education for Librarianship' in: *Colloquium on Education for Librarianship,* WAIT ... *op. cit.:* 23-29.

178. *Ibid.:* 24 and 29.

179. Gupta, P. K., 'Library and Information Science Curriculum Development — A Survey', *Annals of Library Science and Documentation,* 25 (1-4), 1978: 3-21.

180. Kanjilad, S., 'Modern Trends in Library Education,' *Indian Journal of Library Science,* 4(1), 1978: 1-6.

181. Kashyap, M. M., 'Curriculum Development and Design Process: A Systems Approach,' *International Library Review,* 11(3), 1979: 353-365.

182. *Ibid.:* 356.

183. Schwab, J., 'The Structure of Natural Sciences, in: Ford, G. W. and L. Pugno, eds.' *The Structure of Knowledge and Curriculum,* Chicago: Rand McNally, 1964: 6-30.

184. Dave, R. H., *Life Long Education and School Curriculum,* Hamburg: UNESCO Institute of Education, 1973: 36-38.

185. Conant, R. W., *The Conant Report ... op. cit.:* 165-167.

3

Curriculum Objectives: Some Nigerian Library Schools

Definition and Scope

The present writer is an ample example of how 'objectives' in Nigerian library education (not to consider similar world trends on the subject) have been made to relate to the needs and 'functions' of personnel in library and information services, having first obtained the so-called 'para-professional' qualification after obtaining two G.C.E. Advanced Level subjects before proceeding to acquire degree after serving in junior and intermediate positions in the library since 1967. Likewise, the importance of 'objectives' are made inherently obvious to the present writer during and after serving in senior positions in libraries both in the U.K. and Nigeria after graduation. Thus, for the purposes of this present study, one may at this juncture ask, what constitutes the concept of 'objectives' from library education viewpoint?

'Objectives' are the planned ends of the classroom activities that make up the daily work of a known group of students in a particular institution, and the 'function' of the students when they upgrade to personnel status in libraries refers in terms of 'objective,' to the strictly factual statement of what the institution or a sub-unit within it, actually achieves, rather than what it may be designed to achieve, as a result of its activities . Therefore, it would seem from the present writer's experience that much has been written about the 'functions' of libraries, but very little has been written about the actual (achieved) function of the library schools. Admittedly, this unique way of looking at 'objectives' is open to different interpretations depending on the reader's own perspectives, but in the content of this present work, curriculum objectives can only be expressly derived in the light of the circumstances of a given institution and its personnel.

In its main essence, curriculum objectives are anticipatory and derive directly from the designer's apprehension of the kinds of generalists and specialist which will be necessary within the profession, not now, but in the years to come. It is possible to derive objectives from 'proximate' goal through ability to consider the students, teachers, and facilities of a given institution and tailoring a programme to precise and known needs. Hence, educational objectives are often cited as the most precise guide to curriculum development, since they represent the most specific statement of desired behavioural outcomes in the classrooms, this is true, but with the important proviso that it is necessary in the case of objectives, to **specify** which classroom is under consideration. Therefore educational objective can be derived from proximate goals only in the light of knowledge of the needs, progress and potential of the particular students identified as being at work in a particular classroom.

Perhaps an example will vindicate the foregoing statement: consider, for example, the study of computer technology upon which complete programmes have been based in North American library schools although for the most part 'objectives' are relatively limited, and so far imprecise, even by U.K standard (as a leading technological country). Experience in the North American continent elicits the following objectives:

(a)   To make students familiar enough to feel comfortable when talking to others in their field or to computer people;

(b)   To be familiar with terminology and have confidence when involved, and cope with discussion;

(c)   To be alert to the advantages and drawbacks of using a computer;

(d)   To manage information systems;

(e)   To be highly educated users themselves.[1]

However, no general consensus on the 'depth of penetration' in familiarisation with terminology has been reached, nor has familiarisation with the computer's actual 'technology' as reflected in the familiarisation expected to engender confidence in the average student been totally achieved. Indeed, item (d) above was regarded as being too advanced to be realistic by most practising library educators. Recent development however, dictate to the contrary with information librarians and scientists and an interchange and absorption of qualifications. Many schools in the U.K. are now advertising M.Sc in information management. Thus, 'objectives' are an important, if not all-significant aspect of library school curriculum, for it relates to the nature of the profession itself given the changing circumstances in the society as a whole. In this section, we shall be examining the objective of four existing library schools in Nigeria, i.e Ahmadu Bello University, Zaira; Bayero University, Kano; University of Ibadan; and University of Maiduguri respectively. As Dudley submits:

> A more effective assessment of the relevance to professional practice (of tomorrow not today) is more likely to be achieved through an examination of the objectives of courses and teaching syllabuses and the relationship between them.[2]

While this section is not entirely devoted to the teaching syllabuses *per se* it also examines the basis for objectives, the standards that should be conformed with and their planning in theory.

The Rationale for Objectives in Library Education

The study of objectives in any discipline raises fundamental questions as to the nature of practice in that discipline and consequently the structure of its professional education . The objective of library education in general, has been under scrutiny for some time. In a study based on the field of documentation Shera remarks that:

> ... the recruitment of technical information personnel is handicapped by our uncertainty as to the practice nature of the profession, the kind of people who should be brought into it, and the nature of the education the initiates should receive. Such uncertainties are not disastrous but their clarification would materially mitigate the problems of recruitment.[3]

The primary reason for the uncertainty as regards the precise nature of the profession is, as Shera concludes, 'because the profession is so young that it has never defined the parameters of its own discipline.'[4] That is, a kind of informed, disciplined and stringent analysis of what librarianship actually is.[5]

However, the importance of having clearly stated objectives has been persuasively put by Revill[6] in a study of the objectives of library education in the late sixties. Revill states that despite the semantic difficulties caused by a precise lack of definition of what librarianship is setting out to do, a statement of objectives is required if only to assist library educators in assessing their own objectives. The clarification sought for by Shera and others on the nature of objectives is not uncommon in educational literature. In Nigeria, it is fashionable for some library schools such as at Zaria and Kano to describe their courses as library science. Library science is a term which is defined, in the United Nations Bibliographic Information System (U.N.B.I.S.) Thesaurus, as 'the branch of learning concerned with collecting, storing and distributing written or printed records by means of libraries and of the management of libraries.'[7] From the understanding of the intellectual skills required of the librarian in 'collecting, storing and distributing written or printed record,' is the rationale on which basis a clarification of objectives in library education may be made. This can be considered in three ways:

(a)   The students;
(b)   The inter-relationship between the society; and
(c)   The knowledge component.

First, the students. A consideration of students in terms of their given abilities and proven professional outlook has so far been ignored in most librarianship curricula. While the technique and methodology of assessing students may vary from one library school to the other, it should be possible to identify objectives and make content of courses applicable to the different levels of ability range as in the three-tier structure of curriculum. The curriculum should therefore be student-centred in the sense of being related to areas of life and experience which they see as relevant to them, i.e. relevant in terms of specialisation or interest, and relevant in terms of the learning styles which equip them for the challenges of a changing profession and the society at large.

Secondly, in a society of considerable cultural tradition, technological complexity and general rapid change need for flexibility and adaptability becomes essential as both styles of work and leisure are affected.

Thirdly, the knowledge component should be determined in context of the level required for professional courses. For example, how far should library courses go in terms of academic subject study? How are the students' interest catered for in this respect? What about employment trends in the discipline, as well as the need of library employers? The foregoing recognition of objectives projects it as a basis for efficient learning and this in turn should lead to a more precise statement of objective appropriate to particular needs.

From this normative consideration of what should constitute a librarian's education, must be derived the objectives of the library school. These objectives, growing out of a soundly developed theory of librarianship, must provide a basis for the integration of dissident interests within the profession. The traditional definition of a library, as a collection of books organised for use, by implication defines the librarian as one who is little more than a keeper of the collection, and merely describes what is done in libraries with only the vaguest reference to specific social goals towards which the operations of the librarian are directed. The U.N.B.I.S. Thesaurus definition of 'Library Science,' however, shows the latest trend of implying that the librarian's duty extends beyond collecting, storing and disseminating records, but also of managing them.

Expressed in terms of education for librarianship, those professional activities relating to the collection, organisation and utilisation of written or printed record, requires to be emphasised in the curriculum. Stated in terms of their social objectives, these professional responsibilities are of two kinds:

(a)   Advancement of the general cultural level through the provision of library materials which enrich the experience of the individual.

(b)   Advancement of the 'scholarship' of the society, i.e. its scientific knowledge and managerial effectiveness, through provision of the specific information needed in the research, investigation, and decision-making processes.[8]

But as Shera warns, these two responsibilities stand almost in direct opposition. The first is focused upon the user – his tastes, education, interests, and experience, it implies an intimate and highly personal relationship between reader and book. The second, by contrast, is environment-oriented in that it relates to such variables in the situation as the subject field, the type of problem to be solved, the method or methods of investigation being used, or the kind of decision to be reached. Here the characteristics of the user, other than the librarian's capacity to understand what is set before him, are relatively unimportant.[9]

According to Shera, the lines of demarcation between the above-mentioned two responsibilities are not always clear and distinct, and though one may, in general, say that the first is the domain of the public, the school, and the academic library, and the second is the concern of special library or information centre, there is a constant recrossing of lines of responsibility. While this interrelationship may not be improper, it nevertheless causes some confusion in properly identifying the librarian's social and other roles, and consequently, confusion in respect of the kind of professional education the librarian will need.

Thus, in summarising the rationale for objectives by which the professional programme of library schools can be evaluated the following points emerge:

(i) Library schools' courses need to represent a well-developed theory of the social function of the library;

(ii) Library schools' courses need to extract from the totality of the librarian's knowledge and skills those which are professional;

(iii) Library schools' courses must present librarianship as a unified cluster of specialisations in preference to previous concept of educationally preparing a 'universal' librarian — the type John Dean refers to as the generalist of *Johannes factotum* at the basic professional level; and,

(iv) Librarianship courses need to be directed more toward the training of the intellect. Library schools in Nigeria are integral parts of the university community in which they exist. Only to the degree to which their programmes are intellectual can they be fully integrated with other academic departments.

In order to achieve and possibly maintain this rationale for objectives, some level of standards and planning need to be met. These are discussed in the following sections of this present work.

Standards and Library Schools' Objectives

In the area of curriculum objectives in library education, the need to conform to broad guidelines is essential especially in parts of the world where the formal establishment of library schools is a recent phenomenon. The usual channel for such conformity is through the provision of 'standards' in all spheres of professional practice of which library education is one. The merits and demerits of 'international' or 'national' 'standards' have been discussed in another chapter of this present work. However, it is pertinent here to unfold the importance of existing standards in library education as it affects the formulation, statement, and consequent evaluation of objectives for the programmes offered by the schools.

In the I.F.L.A. 1976 document titled *Standards for Library Schools,*[10] it is argued that the worldwide development of the library profession (including documentalist and information scientist) has brought into focus the necessity for high quality programmes in library education. Library education is regarded as very advanced in certain countries but functioning less satisfactorily in most areas of the world. The document further posits that there are basic differences to be found, from one region to another, in the level of the library education programmes, in their curricula, in their expectations of students, in the qualifications of their teaching staffs, and in their conditions of operation. Thus, in many instances these differences work to the disadvantage of library development in the regions which need it most.[11]

If the views expressed in the I.F.L.A. document is accepted, then it would seem that some form of criteria or 'standards' is essential for progress in education for librarianship. The next task is to determine the guiding principles for the stating of objectives as provided for in the I.F.L.A. standards. In the relevant section on 'objectives' it is expressly stated that:

> The school should have specific objectives, derived from its goals, which
> are clearly stated in a formal document.[12]

The goal statement is one of general purpose and long-range intentions of the school. The objectives statement is an expression of specific aims which are to be met (usually in a specified time span) and which can be evaluated in terms of their achievement or lack of it. Viewed as a totality, the curriculum, as the document suggests, should clearly offer a unified and coherent succession of studies and experiences which will support well-defined objectives. The objectives of the curriculum should be carefully expressed as specifically as possible, in a formal document which is periodically examined to assess its current validity, and revised as necessary.

As a corollary to curriculum objectives, institutional objectives are also viewed as of prime importance. For instance, the document advocates that considerations of future activity by the school should be prominent in the thinking of the staff and Head. Such considerations will be most effective if they are based upon prior formulations of goals and objectives.[13] This latter requirement from the library schools have varying implications for some schools, for example, from developing countries who cannot afford to meet the required minimum standard due to infrastructural exigencies.

As many library schools and library establishments are members of I.F.L.A., it is reasonable to expect favourable adoption of most, if not all of the recommendations as the obvious advantage is that it helps to maintain quality of the programmes offered as well as an international acceptability of the qualifications obtained. But the implications for planning policy of the library school needs to be assessed separately.

Planning: Library Schools' Policy on Objectives

If the criteria on 'objectives' as stated in the earlier section are neglected or even possibly ignored for one reason or another, then the absence of a clear statement of objectives will be 'a shortcoming which might lead to lack of direction and purpose.'[14] This lack of direction further manifests itself in confusion, inability to achieve, sudden changes in programmes, thereby, causing unnecessary nor desirable tinkering with the curriculum, and above all, futile efforts at launching unsuccessful programmes. The 'stating' of objectives requires planning so as to reflect the goals and objectives of the larger society, i.e whether it is an open democratic society where access to knowledge and information is considered the right of every individual or otherwise.

Besides, the statement of objectives (i.e. in its final written form) or any other form should also be clear on whether the institution plans to cover every cadre required in the profession or only particular levels such as middle or senior levels. As Ogunsheye observes:

> The ideal and the trend in Africa is to train for the various cadres within an institution. The older institutions in Africa at Ibadan, Accra, Kampala and Zaria run two or three levels of programmes:
> (a) Postgraduate programme for the specialist...
> (b) Undergraduate programme for the first professional
> (c) "sub-degree" programme for the para-professional.[15]

According to Professor Ogunsheye this seems to be the ideal in the present state of development in most African countries, because 'it has the advantages of utilizing fully the limited manpower for library education and of control of standard of training for all cadres in the profession.'[16] This assertion may very well be true in the light of existing circumstances of the burgeoning state of professional education especially at the postgraduate level in Africa, **but** the ultimate goals of the library schools also relate to people and ideas. For example, the library school assumes responsibility for the production of qualified personnel at every level **in response to local demand.**

Dean, in his seminal text on the subject of library education, suggest that when the demand for staff is not sufficient for the effective development of library systems, as is often the case in emergent areas, then the library school should make a determined attempt to change the employment pattern by indicating as persuasively as possible to employing authorities the extent to which their establishment fall short of their minimum requirements.[17] This assertion might have been true in the late sixties and early seventies but certainly if recent developments in Nigeria are any thing to go by, then the employment pattern seems to have been influenced by external forces such as social (e.g. educational expansion), economic (budget increases to institutions and establishment due to 'oil boom'), and the general rise in demand for information. In this situation, the library schools have been lucky not to be the agent of change and stimuli to the employment pattern as it affects librarianship.

However, the library schools still have obligations, in their planning, to undertake professional leadership. Indeed, this view is not new as Danton in 1949 has stressed the importance of undertaking such professional leadership:

> Unless library schools in some measure assume a role of leadership we can hardly expect more than the maintenance of the *status quo* and a static condition in librarianship; if progress and improvement are to be achieved they will come to a considerable degree from leadership exercised by the schools which must then be at least a step ahead of the libraries for which they prepare staff members.[18]

The library school should therefore be somewhere ahead of current professional thinking and constantly too. Dean has provided what amounts to 'specific objectives' which can be identified by the library school in the developing country:

(a) To ascertain curricular needs and the setting up of appropriate training courses at the levels required.

(b) To identify areas in which investigation is required and to establish research programmes, encompassing both group and individual projects.

(c) To publish monographs, textbooks, journals. As soon as a school is reasonably well-established, it should begin to think in terms of publication to invigorate local and indeed, national professional thinking.

(d) To undertake the creation of a resource centre in librarianship, i.e., the assembly of materials relevant to library studies generally upon selective basis and the assembly of local materials upon a comprehensive basis. The centre may well become the focus for the exchange of materials between institutions right around the world.

(e) To maintain continuous professional contact with alumni and to afford guidance after they have left the school.

(f) To contribute to continuing education in region served and to mobilise professional consciousness by seminars, short courses, and conferences.

(g) To hold exhibitions of current publications of new items of equipment, etc., in order to increase the school's impact upon its environment.

(h) To establish library pilot projects, where local services are deficient — the community must be brought into contact with effective library service by the creation of pilot projects as they may be required.

(i) To provide advisory and consultancy service when necessary. In developing countries with an overall lack of professional expertise, a number of library systems may appropriately take advantage of these facilities. At its most significant, this kind of activity is directed toward coherent library planning at the national level.

(j) To play an active role in the administrative, teaching and research functions

of the institution of higher education in which the school is situated.
(k)   To take some responsibility in creating appropriate international
relationships, i.e., to forge links between other library schools everywhere
and thus create a forum for the exchange of ideas.[19]

It is against this background of specific objectives (as listed above), which
can form the basis of a dynamic policy in respect of a library education
programme. that the case studies on Nigerian library schools will be conducted
and discussed.

Ahmadu Bello University Library School, Zaria

In the 1968/69 session at Ahmadu Bello University, Zaria, the Department of
Librarianship was founded 'to train librarians and assistants (B.L.S. degree and
diploma respectively) on all levels of librarianship with special emphasis on
librarianship in Africa.'[20] At the time this objective was stated, there seemed
little doubt as to the fact that the recruitment needs of Northern Nigeria were not
the same as the rest of the Federation, nor could anyone deny (as evidenced in
the pattern of admissions) that the first responsibility of the library school was
'to fulfil the staffing needs of the Northern States'[21] following the Sharr Report
which revealed enormous gaps with the South in this respect. However, by 1978
ten years after the inception of the school, the library school at Zaira (by now
formally established as Department of Library Science) expanded its objective to
include postgraduate programmes for the 'leadership' concept in the profession.[22]
However, by 1979, as Mohammed and Afolabi reported, the terminology
and scope of Ahmadu Bello University Library School's objectives changed
significantly. For instance, the statement of objective has been re-oriented 'to
train professional and para-professional library staff at all levels with well rounded
education up to **international standard** (my emphasis), for all states of the
federation, while placing emphasis on the problems facing libraries in Africa.'[23]
Certainly, this latter statement seems the most comprehensive when compared
with the earlier statement. Students are now viewed not as 'librarians' and
'assistants' but as 'professionals' and 'para-professionals.' This in itself reflects
current thinking in the library profession in Nigeria beset with determining a
specific pattern of recruitment into its professional cadres.
Similarly, the emphasis on 'international standard' is noteworthy in the
light of discussion in the earlier section on standards of library education in this
present work. It would seem that the library school at Zaria is keen to make its
programmes universally acceptable beyond the national frontiers. But the
determination of equivalencies would normally be based on evaluation report of
the programmes rather than through statement of objectives worthy though it
may seem.
Two other points emerge from this latest statement of objectives. One, the

desire to make the school national in outlook rather than existing mainly to serve the interests of northern states. After all, the graduates of the library school would stand to benefit in respect of employment opportunities in other parts of the country, but this cannot be achieved through a politics of isolation. On the credit side, the library school justifiably lays emphasis upon the problems facing libraries in performing their traditional functions in a society which cherishes its cultural values and traditional heritage. Somehow this progressive stance needs to be permeated with 'international standard' objective and all its implications.

Two, a further objective of the library school, which does not seem to be incorporated in the statement under discussion, but discovered by the present writer while on a visit to the library school is the orientation of the 'syllabus' to suit students' needs. Students' views on the design of the 'syllabus' have always been listened to and implemented. For example, at the students' request, the title of the Library and the Community course was changed to Sociology of Library Science. As Olden points out:

> Student representatives were members of the Curriculum Review Committee set up in 1978/79 and some of that committee's recommendations, as implemented in 1979/80, streamlined the B.L.S. syllabus and removed some over-lapping of courses.[24]

Naturally, one would expect that in normal circumstances the library school should involve its students in curriculum development, but as Dudley indicates, this is not always the case in the U.K., for example, in summarising the proceedings at the 1977 Workshop on curriculum development held in Wales, he observed that:

> ...the workshop rarely considered the problem of a curriculum as a whole... with whatever degree of internal cohesion and as experienced by students (intimately) and by Heads of Schools of Librarianship (distantly)...[25]

This view was also echoed by the students themselves two years after the workshop.[26] Thus, the involvement of students in curriculum objectives as practised in Zaria library school would seem to be a step in the right direction in any consideration of the professionalisation of education for librarianship in the country.

Bayero University Library School, Kano

The Department of Library Science at Bayero University, Kano has the following statement of objectives:

(i) To produce librarians with an adequate professional and academic background to work in the fast expanding school, public, academic and special libraries in Nigeria.

(ii) To help students develop an understanding of the role of the library in a rapidly changing society.

(iii)   To inculcate in students the value of continuing education and research.[27]

It is clear from the above statement that considerable attention is paid to students' needs within the overall planning of the curriculum. Preparing the student librarians for the varying challenges of library and information services entails developing their intellect and skill in the knowledge of the environment in which they are likely to work, as well as the subject background knowledge necessary to fulfil their professional responsibility in the collection, preservation, and disseminating written or printed record. For instance, in the B.A. (Library Science) programme, the purpose of the course is to provide a thorough grounding in professional subjects and sufficient background in some academic subjects[28] (two subjects from degree courses in other departments), in order to enable the student to shoulder responsibility in any type of library in which he is employed.

Ibadan University Library School, Ibadan

The first fully fledged library school to be established on a regional basis for West Africa was the Institute of Librarianship University of Ibadan, Nigeria. The library school is now the Department of Library, Archival & Information Studies with the pioneering objectives stated as follows:

> To help the development of libraries by training Librarians and investigating problems of librarianship and bibliography, with special reference to West Africa and with particular attention to the leadership level.[29]

There are three elements constituting this statement of objectives, i.e. the development of libraries, bibliography and postgraduate emphasis in professional education – styled as the 'leadership' level. The pursuance of the 'leadership' concept bears historical significance dating back to the decisions reached at the UNESCO seminar on the development of public libraries in Africa (1953), in which it was recommended that:

> A limited number of library schools of high calibre be established in Africa to provide full-scale professional training at the leadership level.[30]

And further that:

> Library schools located in Africa should require University graduation or its equivalent for admission to the programme of full-scale professional training at the leadership level.[31]

However, the decision of the Ibadan library school to give priority to training at the leadership level and therefore postgraduate level aroused some controversy in Nigeria. Despite the controversy, fifteen years after its inception, the objectives of the Ibadan school patently includes the leadership concept even though courses are now provided at sub-professional level. According to Ogunsheye, the original objective of Ibadan to educate the leaders of the profession has been expanded to include training of supportive 'para-professionals' and the research specialist at the apex of the professional ladder.[32] Thus, by the mid-seventies the statement of objectives were as follows:

(i)   To educate the leadership for the profession.
(ii)   To train supporting para-professional staff for libraries.
(iii)   To conduct research into the problems of libraries and library operations in Africa.
(iv)   To provide further educational opportunities for experienced members of the profession; and,
(v)   To provide a forum of discussion on problems of African librarianship.[33]

These objectives have been translated and applied in the development of courses at the different levels in the library school. Item (iii) above includes an element of continuing education, conferences, workshops and seminars, with the library school fulfilling its responsibility in this respect.

University of Maiduguri Library School, Maiduguri

At the University of Maiduguri, itself a young institution in comparison with the other main higher institutions of learning such as at Ibadan, Zaria, Lagos, Nsukka, and Ife, the Department of Library Studies was established in 1978 in the Faculty of Education offering a 'Bachelor of Library Science' degree programme. The objectives are as follows:

(i)   To produce graduates educated in the conceptual and technical skills of library and information work, i.e. library and information professionals well-grounded in relevant theoretical knowledge and equipped with the necessary skills and techniques.
(ii)   The products of the (B.L.S.) programme should be able to cope with the enormous rapidly growing flood of information and knowledge, modern management techniques, new media, new teaching methods at learning situations in educational institutions and in society at large.[34]

By April 1981, strict measures aimed at upholding the objective of enabling students to acquire knowledge in the processing of information based on the literature of modern and Arabic languages, were published.[35] This required that all students who did not meet the foreign language requirement must take and pass the two required courses in the chosen language before they can graduate. The approved languages are Arabic, French and German.

Needless to emphasise, from the present writer's point of view, the considerable academic strain this requirement on languages will bear on the student librarian, at a time when most schools in similar circumstances are relaxing such requirements to make them more flexible in terms of weighting and assessment in the final library science degree examination. In short, it is apparent that a forcible attempt is being made at upholding high 'standards' in the quality of the educational preparation of the librarian in Nigeria.

However, it needs to be pointed out too that the objective of producing graduates 'educated in the conceptual and technical skills of library and information work' seems to be a classic response to the protracted debate in the profession, as to the quality of the B.L.S. degree and the academic preparedness of its graduates to serve in demanding circumstances of library and information service most especially in the university and other academic libraries, and special libraries/information bureau. Thus, it would seem that the standard of education has been deliberately set high in view of current professional thinking aided by the powerful 'academic librarians' lobby in the profession as a whole special libraries/information bureau. Thus, it would seem that the standard of education has been deliberately set high in view of current professional thinking aided by the powerful 'academic librarians' lobby in the profession as a whole.

Summary

In summarising this section one can only relate the evidence that has emerged from the case studies of how the library schools in Nigeria state and pursue their curriculum objectives to why the objectives are themselves derived. Their derivation exists from growing professional pressure and 'needs' circumstances in the library and information field. An example of such pressure from the profession is the need for library schools to relate and reflect their courses on local problems of library and information practice, i.e. the need to make the courses socially relevant.

This in some cases places a strain on the library schools which have been established on traditional lines of librarianship as practised mainly in the 'advanced' countries of Europe and America. As a result, the schools find themselves chasing a chimera of high 'standards' on the one hand, and 'local relevance' on the other, and thereby struggle to maintain a balance between the two. This is a healthy situation to be in as it implies, as determined elsewhere in this present work, the professionalisation of education for librarianship in the country.

Missing from the available literature used in this section, is any clarification of the 'objectives' format, nor is there any appreciable guideline or proposal for a method of assessing if objectives are being met in the process of curriculum development. It is important to distinguish between 'institutional objectives' and 'course objectives.'

Institutional objectives are incorporated in the overall policy of the library school while 'course objectives' are fixed behavioural and educational capabilities expected of students. In the fulfilment of both functions, the library schools can be observed to have performed appreciably well, although, distinct demarcation lines need to be drawn if objectives are to be met and assessed satisfactorily to incorporate the needs of students, institutions and the whole society.

References

1. Adapted from British Library Research and Development Department: *Teaching Students in Schools of Librarianship and Information Science about Computers and their Applications: Report* 5466 by J. Eyre, London, BLRD, 1979.

2. Dudley, E. P., 'Curriculum Change in the Eighties: Time for Significant Development,' *Library Association Record*, 83(7), 1981:333.

3. Shera, J. H., *Libraries and the Organisation of Knowledge*, London: Crosby, Lockwood, 1965: 169.

4. *Ibid.:* 170

5. Foskett, D. J., 'The Intellectual and Social Challenge of the Library Service,' *Library Association Record*, 70(12), 1968: 302-304.

6. Revill, D. H., 'Education for Librarianship, Objectives and their Assessment,' *Library Association Record*, 71 (4), 1969: 106-109.

7. *UNBIS Thesaurus*, New York: United Nations, 1981: 109.

8. Egan, M. E., 'Education for Librarianship of the Future,' in: J. H. Shera *et al*, eds., *Documentation in Action*, New York: Reinhold, 1956: 206.

9. Shera, J. H., *The Foundation of Education for Librarianship*, New York: Wiley-Becker and Haynes, 1972: 359-360.

10. International Federation of Library Association Standing Advisory Committee Section of Library Schools, *Standards for Library Schools*. 1976 (mimeo).

11. *Ibid.:* (iii).

12. *Ibid.:* 2 (IIIC).

13. *Ibid.:* 24 (IIIR).

14. Ogunsheye, F. A., 'Trends in Library Education: The Criteria for Evaluation of Programmes.' Paper presented at the SCALS Conference University of Ibadan, 3-10 May, 1978. Ibadan, 1978: 8 (mimeo).

15. *Ibid.:* 8

16. *Ibid.*

17. Dean, J., *Planning Library Education Programme,*. London: Andre Deutsch, 1972: 33.

18. Danton, J. P., *Education for Librarianship*, Paris: UNESCO, 1949: 14 (Quoted by Dean, J ... *op. cit.:* 34).

19. Dean, J., *Planning Library Education ... op. cit.:* 34-35.

20. Ahmadu Bello University, Department of Librarianship, *Prospectus, 1970-71*. Zaria: Department of Librarianship, 1970: i (mimeo)

21. Benge, R., 'Return to West Africa: Some Notes on Library Education in Africa,' *Nigerian Libraries* 9(1 + 2), 1973: 97-100. (p.100, *et. seg.*)

22. Ogunsheye, F. A, 'Formal Programme Development in Library Education in Nigeria,' *Journal of Education for Librarianship*, Spring 1978: 43.

23. Mohammed, A. and M. Afolabi, 'Education for Librarianship in Nigeria,' *Nigerian Libraries* 15 (1 & 2), 1979: 35.

24. Olden, E. A., 'The Development of the Department of Library Science, A.B.U., Zaria, Nigeria, and its Implications for the Planning of Library Education Programmes in English-speaking Black African Countries (MIS thesis), Zaria, A.B.U.D.L.S., 1980:40.

25. Dudley, E. P., Summary, in: 'Workshop on Curriculum Development in Librarianship and Information Science, College of Librarianship,' Wales, London: BLRD, 1978: 134.

26. Campbell, C., 'Student View, Degrees of Librarianship: A Report on the AAL National Student Conference,' *Assistant Librarian*, 72(6), 1979: 88-89.

27. Bayero University, Kano, Faculty of Education, Department of Library Science, *B.A. (L.S.) Degree Programme*, May 1980:1.

28. *Ibid.*

29. Ibadan University, Institute of Librarianship, *Annual Report, Sessions 1959/60–1961/62*, Ibadan: Institute of Librarianship, 1962: i (mimeo).

30. Ibid. (c.f. UNESCO, *Development of Public Libraries in Africa, The Ibadan Seminar*, Paris: Unesco, 1954.

31. *Ibid.*

32. Ogunsheye, F. A., 'Formal Programme Development'... *op. cit.:* 143.

33. Ogunsheye, F. A., 'Library Education at Ibadan University, Nigeria', *UNESCO Bulletin for Libraries*, 28(5), 1974: 259-267.

34. As itemised by the present writer from written statements of objectives, in: 'University of Maiduguri, Faculty of Education, Department of Library Sciences, *Bachelor of Library Science (BLS) Degree Programme: 1980/81*, Maiduguri: Department of Library Studies, 1980 (mimeo).

35. University of Maiduguri, Faculty of Education, Department of Library Studies, *The Structure of the B.L.S Programme*, Maiduguri: Department of Library Studies, April 7, 1981.

4

The Professionalisation of Education for Librarianship

Introduction

Within the overall concept of professionalism, this chapter deals with an important criterion — its education system. By virtue of its nature, professional education contributes valuably to any occupation's claim to professional status. The system can thus be examined in its various facets, and with different objectives in indicating the trend on professionalism in Nigerian librarianship. Furthermore, it is important, perhaps illuminating, to consider the system of professional education for librarianship; the conceptual framework of its curriculum development; the factors of relevance, i.e., educational and developmental; evaluation (of curriculum and staff); philosophy of education for librarianship (covering the 'knowledge-base' theory, organisation of content in terms of academic versus professional elements of the curriculum); and finally, the role of the library school in research, and the nature and purpose of research degrees in librarianship. All these elements provide suitable basis from which to assess professional education within the overall concept of Nigerian library professionalism.

The immediate concern at present is to consider those forces and events which typify the process of 'professionalisation' in the educational preparation of the librarian. The approach adopted here is to demonstrate the facts as scrutinised through historical analysis of documents relating events and developments in the field of library education in the period 1950-1970. The first of the two decades (1950-1960) was a period of non-formal library education: but then, its significance is borne out by the fact that the foundation for a formal system of professional education was laid during this period. The second decade of 1960-1970 portrays the 'teething period' of uncertainty but also a time significant for the courage and tenacity of the pioneer library educators in Nigeria, who not only struggled to institutionalise the system of professional education through the traditional university system but also succeeded in handing over to their successors a sound and solid professional system of education, as integral parts of reputable graduate/undergraduate degree programmes in Nigerian universities.

The social events underlying the professionalisation process are discussed so as to illuminate the genesis of the problems encountered, and to enhance tacit understanding of how the ensuing difficulties were either tackled or surmounted. It is crucial to consider that such factors as; debates over the right kind of institution for library education and the consequences for qualification levels, e.g.: graduate or non-graduate entry into the profession; control of library education; library education statistics relating demand and supply situation of librarians in Nigeria and the like, are all factors that are recurrent and therefore proving inconclusive, *ad infinitum*.

Professionalisation

According to Carroll:

> ... professionalisation is defined as that dynamic social process whereby an occupation, or one or more aspects of an occupation, such as its educational system, can be observed to change certain of its crucial characteristics in the direction of a profession, thereby taking on more of the elements of an ideal type profession.[1]

The concept of an 'ideal type profession' and how this reflects on the overall concept of library professionalism has been thoroughly examined in the work of Combe in which the conclusion show that, 'there is a strong status-seeking ideology associated with the professionalisation process, and its connection with professional education movements... thus, librarianship has undergone and continues to undergo the professionalisation process.[2] It would seem that Combe's observation is consistent with Carroll's point that professionalisation of library education implies, 'the process whereby those concerned with training librarians seek to change the agencies involved to bring them into conformity with other professional schools.'[3] The status-seeking element is comparatively high in this latter observation.

Nevertheless, the origin of professionalisation is by itself status clad, Reader suggests that:

> One of the earliest developments in professionalisation was the passing of the Apothecaries Act of 1815. The Act did not forbid unqualified practice, though it did put obstacles in the path of it, and in this also it set a pattern for late legislation. If people wanted to go to quacks, it was felt, they should be free to do so.[4]

Not all occupational groups were controlled by statute, hence those occupations where statutory control existed were considered fortunate because they have experienced state-aided professionalisation. This did not imply that the government of the country (in England) was in any way supporting a highly lucrative monopolistic system for the professionally qualified. Hine and Jennifer[5] in an article considered the seeking of recognition by professions through Acts of Parliament or incorporation by Royal Charter. The same conclusion was reached as to the status-seeking symbol of professionalisation.

However, despite the odds that might have faced pioneer librarians in Britain, the nineteenth century marked a turning point in library history with the granting of a Royal Charter to the Library Association (L.A.) in 1898.[6] The Charter granted the L.A., a monopoly over professional qualifications and this was jealously guarded through the use of the professional register.[7] In general, the significance of the award of a Royal Charter in modern times has been stated by Millerson who wrote:

> A Charter has developed into an inter-association status symbol; a distinguishing mark, acknowledging supremacy in a particular field.[8]

On the part of the L.A., the Charter meant a regal acknowledgement that it was the supreme arbiter of all members concerned with professional library practice. According to Bramley, two of the clauses of the Charter laid a distinct responsibility upon it to assume complete responsibility for the education and training of librarians, notably:

(a) To promote whatever tends to the improvement of the position and qualifications of librarians;

(b) To hold examinations in librarianship and to issue certificates of efficiency.[9]

The resounding success of the professionalisation of British librarianship inevitably had salutary inferences in the English-speaking world where the only route to professional qualification was by passing the L.A. examinations. Thus, the characteristics of professionalisation as a process in the nineteenth and early twentieth centuries were, according to Reader status-based, because an occupation:

> ...needed a professional association to focus opinion, work up a body of knowledge, and insist upon a decent standard of conduct... should have a Royal Charter as a mark of recognition... to persuade parliament to pass an Act conferring something like monopoly powers on duly qualified practitioners, which meant practitioners who had followed a recognised course of training and passed recognised examinations. Right at the centre of the professional world therefore was this matter of training and examination.[10]

A change in emphasis of the curriculum and even more importantly, in the attitude of university administrators towards professional education has drastically altered the images of professionalisation as characterised by 19th Century charters. The pursuit of knowledge in professional education is now fully integrated with the realm of world of learning. No longer is the graduate of a professional course in librarianship compelled to register before he could practice. The attainment of degrees has relegated such requirements to the back-stage. Graduates now voluntarily join the L.A. on other basis such as, to further their professional interests through current trends in the field, associate with colleagues and peers, and exchange information for personal professional development.

The essential characteristics of the process of professionalisation now centre around; the planning and implementation of professional education programmes; structuring and restructuring diversifying elements of the qualification system; determining levels of educational attainments and organisational structure for different cadres of personnel; providing suitable programme of continuing education designed to disseminate new ideas and improvement of existing ones from professional schools to the practitioners and vice versa; co-ordinating library education statistics for the purpose of facilitating manpower planning; and finally, regulating the certification system through a retention of the in-house structure of licentiates, associates and fellowships.

Given the foregoing stated characteristics and the wind of educational change that has produced them, it is clear that professionalisation is self-generating in professional education systems. In the process, occupational groups place great emphasis on the education and qualification of practitioners for their business. Bennion refers to 'chartered status' as a symbol of possession of a hallmark of competence highly valued by the society:

> Few people will employ an architect, unless they have assurances of his quality, if he is not a member of the R.I.B.A. Similarly, those needing to employ an accountant or a surveyor will feel happier if he is 'chartered'.[11]

Thus, the statutory recognition of a qualification as represented by the designatory letters of the various institutions, is very much sought after by professional people, hence the reason for their preservation. Degree holders also seem to desire professional qualification (even though it does not affect the regulation of their practice) if only to achieve the high status of proven competence in their professional skills.

Early Library Education Provision in Nigeria, 1950-1970

The urgent need for library education in Nigeria, soon became apparent immediately after the establishment, in 1948, of the first university college located at Ibadan, Nigeria. Prior to this time, of course, some learned libraries in research institutes and advanced colleges of science and technology have been developed and equally expanding their services.[12,13] The decade 1950-1960 was, however, essentially one of foundations in preparing suitable grounds (in terms of finance, accommodation, and philosophy) for the formal establishment of library education in Nigeria. This important preparatory factor including social events and educational (training) activities in the period have, more often than not, been ignored in the professional literature. The pattern of the preparatory efforts to create a library school was first based on a regional basis, taking the whole of West Africa as a fegion for the purpose of library education, and Nigeria as the 'training centre' where the first school for English-speaking West African librarians was to be established at Ibadan. Unfortunately at the time, this was not to work out as smoothly as expected due to many constraints of finance, nationalism and regional distance (this will be expanded upon later).

The Period 1950-1960

Operational difficulties notwithstanding, some form of recognised 'training' did take place during the decade. 'Training' is deliberately used here as a synonym to describe the form of education which took place up to 1960. In this respect, the training factor consisted of organised courses which had the objective of privately preparing participants for the (British) L.A. examinations (from the First Professional Examination (F.P.E) stage to A.L.A. and the ultimate accolade of F.L.A.), and equipping them for better performance in their library assignments.

As mentioned earlier, the professionalisation process in Nigerian librarianship was already underway, boosted by the establishment of the University College of Ibadan library and the consequent growth in collection and staff. The library, which temporarily carried out national library functions with particular emphasis on bibliography was also responsible for the training of Nigeria's early librarians. Lawal[14] outlines the evidence of progress:

(a)   Two publications, the first of their kind — *'A Preliminary List of Serials in the Library'* (University College, Ibadan, 1949), and, *'A Guide to the Library'* (1950).[15]

(b)   The acquisition of a microcard reader in 1950, possibly the first such machine in any library in the British Commonwealth.

(c)   The celebration in December 1949 of the accessioning of the 10,000th volume. Nigeria at last had the basis for a scholarly research library, and for a national bibliography, as well as an effective staff to handle them.

(d)   In 1949, a group of experienced librarians met to discuss knowledge and skills and the subsequent booklet compiled afterwards, and published in Ibadan by the Western Province Education Department proved an occasion of the birth of the library profession in Nigeria.

The opportunity afforded for education and training was indeed enormous considering the above-mentioned developments. The group of librarians who met 'to discuss knowledge and skills' laid the foundation for professional education by publishing a tentative syllabus edited by Miss Joan Parkes.[16] The document preserved something of what was taught on that occasion, most being related to the development of skill. The admission requirements specified that participants 'should be literate in English and their general standard of education should not be below Middle II.'[17] The course was the forerunner of similar courses regularly organised in Northern Nigeria by Parkes as from 1952. Producing library workers in this way was both cheap and fast in view of the urgent need for library staff to keep up with the pace of development.

Public libraries were also used as centres for organising in-service training courses for junior library staff and success on the course is guaranteed by promotion up the career ladder. The Eastern Regional Library Board, perhaps the most effective library development Board at the time, also started a staff training scheme in 1956 with five assistants as the first intakes. The dual objective of preparing participants for the (British) L.A examinations and improving job performance was also the dominant factors at this stage. Similar in-service courses were run by the Western State Library until late 1968.

By 1959 beneficiaries of the in-service courses were recognised and being given the opportunity to supplement whatever assistance they could get with a full-time overseas course before qualifying finally as A.L.A.F.L.A. Most of those given in-service training leaves of absence to study abroad travelled to the U.K. where they completed the formal courses in librarianship; the others who stayed on at home studied privately through correspondence courses.

In addition to the educational activities as described above, the 'preparatory decade' 1950-1960 witnessed an era of concrete discussions as to how best library schools could be planned and established in the West African region. The UNESCO Seminar,[18] which was held at Ibadan in 1953 on the development of public libraries in Africa provided the added impetus for the planning of library development in Africa (c.f. seminar have since formed the philosophical basis of education for librarianship in Nigeria).

1960-1970

Unlike the present writer's tracing of library education history in Nigeria from 1950 onwards, writers such as Obi,[19] Akinyotu,[20] and others tend to observe 1960 as the commencement date for library education in Nigeria. But this approach is from institutional viewpoint, for the first library school was established as Institute of Librarianship at University of Ibadan in 1960. At the same time, the country attained political independence and consequently, the accelerated development in social and economic order created the basis for expansion in library services and, hence, demand for trained manpower in the field. An historical account of the development of the Institute of Librarianship, Ibadan, is contained in Obi's article[21] on library education in Nigeria.

Of particular significance in the historical analysis are the factors of students and the curriculum. The author pointed out that the first class consisted of four graduates and two non-graduates representing a compromise on admission requirements, in order to permit selection of candidates with at least two years full-time experience in a recognised library and who hold one part of the L.A registration examination. Non-graduates account for three out of ten students enrolled in 1961-72; four out of twelve in 1962-63; ten of twenty-three in 1963-64; and eleven of twenty-two in 1964-65. In 1965-66, the last year in which non-graduates were admitted to the programme, thirteen of the class were graduates and six non-graduates. By this time the Institute had produced sixty-nine professionally qualified librarians of whom fifty-three held the Institute's own diploma.[22] By implication, it is obvious that the library school was implementing the 'leadership', i.e. postgraduate philosophy as prescribed at the 1953 Ibadan Seminar.

With regards to the curriculum, the first curriculum was geared specifically to the L.A registration examination. Courses for the Diploma in Librarianship 1963/64 to 1965/66 comprised the following four papers; Administration, Book Course (i.e. Reference and Bibliography), Cataloguing and Classification, and Special subjects. 'The special subjects are included as options for public, university, special, school and children libraries.'[23]

With hindsight, perhaps the most significant document to emerge from the Institute in the mid-sixties was the one entitled *'Achievements and Future of the Institute,'* which was distributed within Nigeria and to other West African countries in order to give interested parties a brief survey of what the Institute had already accomplished and what it hoped to accomplish in the future. A resume of the publication is provided as a useful appendix in Dean's work on 'planning library education programmes.'[24] Some of the pertinent issues raised in the document, as indicated by Dean, are hereby reproduced to serve as a focus for appreciating the later shift in status for the library school (from Institute to full departmental status in the Faculty of Education):

Future of the Institute (Policy Statement, 1965)

Integration into the Constitutional Structure of the University

It is important that the Institute, which is now full fledged, be integrated into the constitutional structure of the University. The advantages are:

(a)   When the case of providing funds for the financing of the Institute in the next quinquennium, which begins in 1968/69 is presented, the work of the Institute will have been known and discussed in the Councils of the University for two years.

(b)   The Institute will be in a better position to call on other departments of the University for assistance in the teaching and research programme.

(c)   The present Board of Studies, which has done valuable work, is essentially a professional body. The association of other members of the academic staff in the affairs of the Institute will be of considerable advantage.

Research

It is vital for the Institute to develop research programmes. The need to stimulate research is paramount and the areas of enquiry are manifold.

Textbooks

The library field is generally conspicuous for the absence of acceptable textbooks. This fact is nowhere more obvious than in Africa. It is proposed that one of the projects of the Institute will be to produce a series of manuals for the use of students not only in Nigeria, but throughout Africa.

Co-operation in Africa

Chief Librarians in Africa will, in due course, be consulted with a view to discovering whether they would be interested in sending postgraduate students to the Institute for training... It should be emphasised that at the moment Nigeria is the only developing country in the anglophone or francophone territories of Africa offering a postgraduate course, and it is clear that Nigeria will be able to attract students from overseas....[25]

The text of the Institute's Policy Statement in 1965 provided the fulcrum for later developments in the library education scene.

However, it soon became clear that while Ibadan was steadily advancing the 'leadership' training philosophy and consolidating its own professionalisation, other equally significant efforts were being made in Northern Nigeria concerning the establishment of a library school to cater for the needs of the North. A survey was commissioned in 1963 to consider broadly the library needs of Northern Nigeria. The ensuing report by Sharr[26] received considerable attention both in and outside the profession. The commission was mandated:

(a)   To survey critically all existing libraries including public, university, school and special libraries, to study their development plans and to suggest improvement with a view to providing the best and most economic overall service to the Region;

(b)   To make recommendations on the division of responsibility between the government library services and the Native Authority services;

(c)   To survey the existing training schemes and to consider the establishment of a Central training school and in addition, to consider the possibility of local certification prior to fully recognised professional qualification;

(d)   To recommend the best means of producing a comprehensive regional bibliography.[27]

Given the above mandate, the Commission felt compelled to recognise the importance of professional education in relation to library needs and therefore Chapter II of the Report was devoted entirely to the necessity for having an organised form of professional education and training. One of the Commission's observation supports this view:

> Before there can be good libraries there must be qualified and trained librarians. There is no organised professional education and little training in the North: in ten years only one Northern librarian has qualified. There is a dual need: for in-service training... and for professional education which could best be given in a school of librarianship at Ahmadu bello University providing a combined course of general education and professional studies.[28]

Thus, the Sharr Report distinguished between 'education' and 'training' and in addition, precise mention was made as to the particular institution required for the education of librarians from the North and the nature of the course content. Understandably, one of the consequences of the Report was the formal establishment in 1968 of the Department of Librarianship at Ahmadu Bello University, Zaria. The Department was established 'to train librarians and assistants (B.L.S. Degree and Diploma respectively) at all levels of librarianship with special emphasis on librarianship in Africa.'[29] From 1971/72 session, the Library School at Zaria was renamed Department of Library Science. The historical detail of the development of the school is contained in the works of Obi[30] and Olden.[31]

Perhaps the whole essence of Sharr's Report revolves round the emphasis it placed on the idea of a profession which, the Report argues, 'rests on the possession of an intellectual technique acquired by special study and experience which is capable of application in some sphere of life.'[32] Professional education in Nigeria, it was further suggested, should be provided at 'international qualification standard on a sandwich course basis for Northern students and for those of other Regions, if they so desire.'[33] The successful commencement of Zaria's programmes, and the school's effective contribution to professional and non-professional library manpower suggests an attainment of professionalisation status in education for librarianship. The school's concern with professional development now transcends its original regional approach as its outlook is now national and international.

British, North American, and other International Influences

British Influences

Nigeria was in the early fifties one of the very few Commonwealth countries to benefit directly from international activity in the field of library development and education. The 1950s represented a period of determined efforts on the part of UNESCO to eradicate the universal disease of illiteracy in the Third World. Worthy as this cause seemed, it presented numerous planning difficulties. As a British colony, Nigeria received some form of British assistance in the education field on a variety of basis such as textbooks, expatriate manpower, British Council grants and other aid activities. Gunton[34] suggests that different aid agencies encouraged the development of reading materials suitable for Nigerian schools and also initiated publishing services. For instance, under the British Technical Assistance programme the British colonial administration expedited the growth of publishing in support of existing in-house printing that was being done locally. In addition, 'student edition' of expensive textbooks such as in medicine, engineering and the humanities were made available to Nigerian students under heavy subsidy.

The presence of expatriate professional personnel in many sectors of the Nigerian economy and social development has no less been effective. Dean states that:

> In the former colonial territories, many of the expatriates holding office immediately following independence were usually nationals of the former colonial power. This can be accounted for by the number of ties — economic, educational, linguistic and colonial power in spite of autonomy. However, after the first phase of independence, the structure of the expatriate group tended to become more cosmopolitan. The work of the United Nations, the specialist agencies and the American Foundations, in particular, has been responsible for the growing diversification of the expatriate community... (Thus,) Expatriates are active in all professional fields in the developing countries and not least in librarianship.[35]

British contribution in terms of professional service in Nigerian library education is immense. British experts have served as director of library schools — latterly as heads of department of library studies/science; as lecturers, external examiners and consultants on library education projects. By this effort, they have more than made up for the apparently divisive policy of regionalism which was initiated as part of the deal setting up the Ibadan library school. A case in point of the resultant divisiveness was the occurrence of nationalistic barriers and sentiments. Ghana felt strongly that the first library school, as intended for West Africa and deliberately set at university standard, should have been located not in Ibadan but Accra, 'which has superior public and special library services and a university library in no way inferior to that in Ibadan.'[36] But overall, the sequence of events which led to the cessation of the West African Library Association indicate that perhaps the right decision was taken at the time with regards to the location of the first library school in West Africa.

North American Influence

The timely assistance of the Americans enabled the planning of the first library school in West Africa to be formally implemented at Ibadan. In 1957, Harold Lancour was commissioned by the Carnegie Corporation of New York to undertake a survey of the libraries in (British) West Africa. In his report, Lancour[37] suggested that the area in which the Corporation could make its greatest contribution to library development in West Africa was that of recruitment and training of personnel. Thus, it was recommended that:

(a)   A grant of money be established for scholarship to send potential librarians to England and possibly to other countries;

(b)   To establish a library school in one of the West African countries, preferably at Ibadan; the location of such a school it was further suggested, should be in an institution of higher education.

As a direct result of these pungent recommendations, the Carnegie Corporation made a grant of $88,000 (dollars) available to University College, Ibadan for the purpose of establishing in 1959, a training scheme for librarians in the university libraries.[38] The library was used as training grounds for preparing students for the registration examination of the (British) L.A. examinations in one year. In addition to the A.L.A. examination, graduates were to be awarded a local diploma based on success in the A.L.A. plus additional work of special relevance to libraries in tropical Africa.

According to Burgess,[39] the choice of Ibadan as the first library school in West Africa was fortunate (since Ford Foundation's support for several other schools and departments was secured independently), therefore, placing the new library school in a rapidly developing university. However, additional grants insured the continued existence of the library school until 1968 at which point it was taken over by the university.[40]   Overall, the Ibadan library school was financed from 1960-1968 by the Carnegie Corporation of New York, with a total expenditure of $300,000 (dollars).[41]

It is pertinent to point out that in 1963, there was a complete reorganisation of the school following the Ford Foundation's renewal grant which ensured the appointment of an Advisory Director for the Institute of Librarianship at Ibadan for one year. The person given the job was Dr. Lieberman, Director of the University of Washington Library School, Seattle in the U.S.A. It is significant that one of the first changes to be instituted was the elimination of the (British) L.A syllabus, since in the view of the library school the institution was no longer prepared to teach an externally examined subject.

Even more significant, and perhaps an interesting phenomenon of the time, is the observation of the absence of American influence on the curriculum. Usually, institutions which are aided with American grants display some form of loyal affinity in the structure of the institution and its programmes. This was not the case at Ibadan except for original members of the teaching staff from the indigenous population whose traits reflect their American background in education and training but were not forceful enough to drastically influence a change in the *status quo*. Thus, in the crucial decade of formative library education provision (1960-1970), American influence was largely financial, but this was enough to give the profession a sure footing in its education system.

International Influences: UNESCO, UNISIST/NATIS (PGI), British Council, U.K. Ministry of Overseas Development, and Leverhulme Foundation

One of the first effective measures on the international scene was the sponsoring, by UNESCO in 1953, of the Ibadan Seminar on 'the development of public libraries in Africa.'[42] This seminar resulted in the establishment of the first regional library school in West Africa as stated earlier, though at this stage it was clear that the initiated discussion on library development was producing an emergence of a philosophical debate centred on two factors:

(a)   The desire and search for a theoretically-based education which would provide the initiate with the principles and philosophy of the library profession and leave the technical aspects of training to his employer, i.e. graduate education, to provide 'leaders' for the profession;

(b)   The insistence of some groups that urgent staffing needs be faced by providing vocational-type training which is rich in technical skills and would provide the profession with the urgently required level of staffing needs in libraries, i.e. non-graduate education to provide paraprofessionals.

What seemed to be forgotten by participants on the debate was that the country required the two staff cadres, whatever the urgency. On the 'leadership' issue, the undeviating zeal of John Harris brought to a conclusion a project he had long nurtured. Reference to this fact was reflected in the report of Group III of which Harris was a member at the Ibadan Seminar:

> ... the basic objective of full-scale library training in Africa should be to train leaders for the library profession.[43]

Carnell, in reviewing the report in *W.A.L.A. News*, however, was pronounced in her opposition to the 'leadership' philosophy:

> It is difficult to understand how anyone who has worked in Africa can support the statement that "the basic objective of full-scale library training should be to train **leaders** for the library profession." The basic need is **workers**. Leaders, in any case, are not produced by library schools ... the essentials are certain qualities of character... discipline... responsibility.[44]

Evans in her Presidential address to W.A.L.A. in 1957, concurred with Carnell:

> There is a suggestion from the Unesco Seminar that... Library schools located in Africa should require a University graduation for admission to the programme of full-scale professional training at leadership level. Does this give cognisance to the fact that the Fellowship of the Library Association approximates in standard to a university degree? Is it necessary for a librarian to have two degrees... ?[45]

However, Carnegie's enthusiasm for high education was expressed in the desire for a postgraduate school of librarianship despite the objections to the 'leadership' philosophy.

In the area of education of teachers of librarianship in the developing countries, UNESCO, the British Council, and the Ministry of Overseas Aid and Development have contributed significantly in offering technical assistance for the education of library educators from the developing countries. Such practical assistance was tailored to suit the education of the educators from the viewpoint of their own environments. The assistance was crystallised at the N.A.T.I.S. Intergovernmental Conference (1974):

> The training of the teachers especially for new schools in developing countries was also a problem. Unesco was urged to give more assistance to such training schemes for the teachers as had been organised and sponsored by the Royal School of Librarianship, Denmark, and Loughborough University, U.K.[46]

The N.A.T.I.S. Conference preceded the commencement of the Loughborough University course by ten days. Prior to the conference, UNESCO and the Department of Library and Information Studies of Loughborough University have conferred with the latter, agreeing to investigate the response from library educationalists in the developing countries as to the establishment of a course that would assist in satisfying their demands and which grant successful participants a Master of Arts degree in Archives, Library and Information Studies and Education (M.A./A.L.I.S.E.).[47]

Loughborough University agreed to the establishment of such a degree course and UNESCO, through the Department of Documentation, Libraries and Archives drew up a contract defining its support for such a course.

UNESCO agreed to three awards: three library educators from Africa to receive priority in the first year and three from Asia in the second year in part fulfilment of objective 13(iii) of the N.A.T.I.S. Conference which concerned itself with the programme for professional education.[48] The British Council and the U.K. Ministry of Overseas Development offered practical support with scholarships and technical assistance training awards respectively. The Leverhulme Foundation agreed to meet the salary and related expenses of the course tutor for the experimental period.[49]

Thus, was established a unique M.A. programme which is the first and only course of its kind in the world. Lawal observes:

> The M.A. (A.L.I.S.E.) is an international qualification and the course draws students, with their own distinctive cultural mix, from various countries; for example, from October 1974 to September 1979, 43. Students have completed the course, represented by: Nigeria, 10; Brazil, 7; Ghana, 4; U.K.,4; Denmark, 1; Iraw, 1; Ivory Coast, 1, Kenya, 1; Malaysia, 1;

Mauritius, 1: Norway, 1; Pakistan, 1; Sierra-Leone, 1; South Africa, 1; Tanzania, 1: Thailand, 1; Uganda, 1... So far on the programme since 1974/ 78 not less than 21 countries have been represented (on the M.A. (A.L.I.S.E.) course).[50]

As can be observed from the list of beneficiaries of the M.A. (A.L.I.S.E.) course, Nigeria has done well by topping the list although the library needs of each country differ. The training of library educators is thus an enormous boost for Nigeria's manpower requirements in this area. This could not have been possible, nor the achievement sustainable, without the tacit support of the international agencies involved in setting up the course primarily for the benefit of teachers of library education in the developing countries.

In addition to the varying curricula demands made within the country, on the library schools, Nigerian library educators have had to reckon also with international demands in library and information studies. Aboyade identifies the factors of international influence thus:

> The international developments in the profession that have been having repercussions on education for librarianship in recent times are principally the concepts of UNISIST, NATIS (PGI), UBC (Universal Bibliographic control) and the newest arrival on the horizon — UAP (Universal Availability of Publications). These phenomena have since gone beyond the conceptual stage to the development of concrete proposals and programmes of action to make them a reality in our time.[51]

By implication, the planning objectives of the international agencies, which include fostering closer co-operation between documentalists, librarians and archivist, require the harmonisation of training in librarianship, information science, and archival administration. From the viewpoint of economy, this arrangement has proved valuable for Nigerian library schools as courses that could not be offered separately, e.g. 'information science', have been integrated as viable units of the curriculum. In essence, the 1974 UNESCO Paris consultation with a group of experts on the 'harmonisation of methodology and curriculum in the training of documentalists, librarians and archivists', engendered the foundation of broad common interest among library educators teaching in at least two of the three fields of information, with the sole purpose of harmonising programmes for each of the services and identifying items to be included in a common core curriculum for each one separately. In general, therefore, the major international efforts directed at enhancing the professional process of education for librarianship have proved rewarding in Nigeria much as in other parts of the library world.

Summary

With the evidence produced and examined in this section concerning the events leading up to and including, formal establishment of library education in Nigeria, it would conclusively seem that the attainment of professionalisation is assured. The status-seeking criterion has proved instrumental as one of the factors which have helped to shape the trend in professionalisation. Chronologically, the two decades 1950–1960, and 1960-1970 have their distinctive significance in contributing to professionalism in Nigerian librarianship. The underlying elements of the events contributing to the 'professional' status of librarianship in Nigeria, are of historical significance. But their current development when put into perspective, shows a capacity for absorbing new trends, such as in the areas of the curriculum, professional relevance, evaluation and perhaps analytical view of current needs for philosophy. With these elements, the fundamental achievement of having local schools of librarianship has promoted kindred overseas interests not in the country's professional education system but its absorption of international trends in library development.

References

1. Carroll, C. E., *The Professionalisation of Education for Librarianship with Special Reference to the Years 1940 – 1960*, Metuchen, N. J.: The Scarecrow Press Inc., 1970: 248.

2. Combe, N. R., 'The Professionalisation of Librarianship' (M.Sc. Dissertation), University of Sheffield, 1973: 68.

3. Carroll, C. E., *The Professionalisation of Education for Librarianship...* *op. cit.:* 10.

4. Reader, W. J., *Professional Men: The Rise of the Professional Classes in Nineteenth Century England*, London: Weidenfeld & Nicholson, 1966: 52.

5. Hine, S. and S. Jennifer, 'Professional Bodies in the United Kingdom," *Public Administration*, 37 (Summer), 1959: 165-178.

6. Bramley, G., *Apprentice to Graduate*, London: Clive Bingley, 1981: 28-29.

7. Harrison, K. C., 'One Hundred Years of Professionalism: The L.A. 1877-1977,' *Herald of Library Science*, 16(4), 1979: 370-376.

8. Millerson, G., *The Qualifying Associations*, London: Routhledge & Kegan Paul, 1964:91.

9. Ramley, G., *Apprentice to Graduate ... op. cit.*: 29.

10. Reader, W. J., *Professional Men ... op. cit.:* 71

11. Bennion, F. A. R., *Professional Ethics: The Consultant Professions and their Code*, London: Charles Knight, 1969: 36.

12. Harris, J., 'Libraries of Learning and Research in Nigeria,' *Library World* 64 (745), 1962: 68-80.

13. Harris, J., ' Libraries and Librarianship in Nigeria of Mid-century,' *Nigerian Libraries*, 6 (1 and 2), 1970: 26-40.

14. Lawal, O. O., *Library in Nigeria*, Birmingham School of Librarianship, (Spring) 1978:5-6.

15. Ibid, (Quoting: *Nigerian Publications, 1950-52*, Ibadan: University College Library, 1953: iii.)

16. Parkes, J. ed., *Notes on Method for Training Native Authority Librarians*, Ibadan: Western Provinces Education Department, 1952.

17. *Ibid.:* 1.

C.O./*Development of Public Libraries in Africa: The Ibadan*
Paris: UNESCO, 1954.

., 'Education for Librarianship in Nigeria,' *Nigerian Libraries,*
5: 221.

, A. "Training and Education of Library Personnel in Nigeria,"
Libraries, 8(2), 1972:103.

Education for Librarianship... op. cit.: 222-229.

, *Planning Library Education Programmes,* London: Andre
1972: 115-117.

26. Sharr, F. A., *The Library Needs of Northern Nigeria: A Report Prepared
under the Special Commonwealth, African Assistance Plan,* Kaduna:
Ministry of Information, Government Printer, 1963.

27. *Ibid. (Letter of Committal,* by F. A. Sharr): 1-2.

28. *Ibid.:* 4-5

29. Ahmadu Bello University, Department of Librarianship, *Prospectus, 1970/
71,* Zaria, Department of Librarianship, 1970: 1(mimeo)

30. Obi, D., *Education for Librarianship ... op. cit:* 235-242.

31. Olden, E. A., 'The Development of the Department of Library Science,
Ahmadu Bello University, and its Implications for the Planning of Library
Education Programmes in English -speaking black African Countries" (MLS
thesis), Zaria: Department of Library Science, 1980.

32. Sharr, F. A., *The Library Needs ... op. cit.*: 34.

33. *Ibid.:* 42

34. Gunton, D., 'Books, Libraries, and aid, in Particular British Aid in Nigeria
during the Development Decade,' *1960-1969.* (MA thesis) University of
Sheffield, 1974, 43-84.

35. Dean, J., *Planning Library Education Programmes ... op. cit.:* 118-9.

36. Ofori, A. G. T., 'The Organisation of the Library Profession in West Africa',
in: Chaplin, A. H., ed., *The Organisation of the Library Profession: a
Symposium based on Contributions to the 37th Session of the IFLA
General Council, Liverpool, 1971,* Pullach. Munchen: Verlag
Dokumentation, 1973: 80.

37.   Lancour, H., 'Libraries in British West Africa: A Report of a Survey for the Carnegie Corporation of New York, October-November 1957, Urbana: University of Illinois, Graduate School of Library Science, 1958. (Occasional paper no. 53.)

38.   Ogunsheye, F. A. 'Formal Programme Development in Library Education in Nigeria, *Journal of Education for Librarianship*, 19(2), 1978: 140.

39.   Burgess, R. S., 'Education for Librarianship: U.S. Assistance,' *Library Trends*, 20(3), 1972: 519.

40.   Ogunsheye, F. A., *Formal Programme Development ... op. cit.:* 140

41.   Burgess, R. S., *Education for Librarianship ... op. cit.:* 519.

42.   UNESCO, *Development of Public Libraries in Africa: The Ibadan Seminar,* Paris: UNESCO, 1954.

43.   *Ibid.:* 100

44.   Carnell, J., Review 'Development of Public Libraries in Africa: The Ibadan Seminar', *West African Library Association (WALA) News,* 2(2), 1955: 46-47. (Journal discontinued).

45.   Evans, E., 'Training for Librarianship,' *WALA News,* 2(3), 1956: 67-72 (p.68 *et seq*).

46.   UNESCO, *Intergovernmental Conference on the Planning of National Documentation, Library and Archives in Infrastructures, Paris, 23-27 September, 1974. Final Report.* Paris: UNESCO, 1975:13.

47.   'M. A. in Library Education', *UNESCO Bulletin for Libraries,* 27(5), 1973: item 378 (Quoted) in: Bowden, R., Improving Library Education in the Developing Countries: a UNESCO and Loughborough University Experiment,' *UNESCO Bulletin for Libraries,* 30(5), 1976: 256.

48.   UNESCO *Intergovernmental Conference ... op. cit.:* 32

49.   Bowden, R., *Improving Library Education... op. cit.:* 256.

50.   Lawal, O. O., 'Elements of Degree Courses in Librarianship and Information Science', (MA thesis) Loughborough University of Technology, 1979: 86-87.

51.   Aboyade, B. O., 'Education for Librarianship,' *Nigerian Libraries,* 15(1 + 2), 1979: 29.

5

The Search for Relevance

'To those who cannot read, libraries hold little attraction'
— *Lester Asheim (1966)*[1]

Introduction

The concept of 'relevance' consists of many aspects from which it may be viewed and applied. In relation to learning, the use of the term implied the appropriateness of educational provision to the society in which such learning process takes place. It is possible to look broadly at 'whole' systems such as institutions: universities; teachers and other academic personnel; Librarians; language (medium of instruction); culture (the effect of literacy on local traditions) and the process of national development. The library is inextricably linked to these social institutions.

However, it is also beneficial to examine specific aspects of relevance within the given systems. For instance, one may select the area of curriculum development in any national or local needs. Thus, the application of concept of relevance to particular situation will need to take account of its varying nature. It is important to specify: **Relevance to what**?

Similarly, the circumstance for obtaining specific interpretation may prove all – inclusive if, as it is possible, the analysis cuts across a wide spectrum of factors which describe the '**what**' element. As a case in point, the university is expected to be conventionally dominated by a sense of reality and have relevance to the society which supports it. That the university should promote change is not in question, but there are widely differing view on the ills of society and on the means of correction. Education which would promote change must be *per se* still take cognisance of, and relate to, the current scene. A division from this view point often results in problems of relevance. Thus, an assumption can be derived that the university not only gets its support and its authority from society but also takes direction from it and is accountable to it. This implies that the educational programmes of the university are required to be responsive to society's needs and concerns.

However, in the commitment to learning, the university cannot be held entirely responsible for digressing from local needs even at critical periods of change in the society. Other factors influence the incapacity to cope with change especially when such changes have to be related to tradition. It may be argued further that societal needs may usually be determined through appropriate research, but while research is essential to learning, the university is not primarily a research institution but a medium for motivating students to learn and focusing on the nature of what is to be learned. Accordingly, the **search for relevance** is influenced in the main by both educational and developmental factors which tend to define the problems of relevance in perspectives.

The analysis that follows in the work as set in this section, relate principally to the educational and development factors of relevance. The objective is to provide an in-depth analysis of the genesis of the problem and to show how the search for a solution is affecting education for librarianship in Nigeria.

The professionalisation of education for librarianship in Nigeria incur scrutinisation of programmes offered from the viewpoint of relevance to national or local needs.

The Criteria of Relevance

One of the persistent problems to emerge from all kinds of discussion on relevance is a lack of standard for judging the parameters of the subject and consequently its effects on social systems. In the case of librarianship, the criteria of relevance derive from the activities of libraries in promoting social change.

(a) *The Education System:* Its appropriateness and validity in traditional social systems. Unlike in metropolitan countries of Europe and North America with a sure assumption of full literacy, homogeneous culture and language, oral traditional societies offer alternative systems of acculturisation. In this way, the values and norms of the society are not only preserved but enhanced in the educational process.

(b) *Social-Political Effects of Colonialism:* The evolution of foreign ideas of administration and political organisation for the purposes of government. These ideas form the basis of undue influence and therefore, unrelated societal values in the generation, organisation and dissemination of written records on which information is usually based on all aspects of societal life. Librarians inherited the accumulative records showing Arabic influence of Islamic education and European type education as introduced by the Christian missionaries. These Islamic records have sometimes been perceived by writers[2,3] as indigenous literature, yet they are the products of another form of imperialism.

(c) *Curriculum Renewal and Oral-aural Culture:* Librarianship in its own curriculum renewal has taken account of society's oral-aural culture but to what extent? Cynics claim that indigenisation has been 'carried out only to a superficial degree.' Perhaps it is understandable that such criticisms are made in view of the radical nature of curriculum renewal detracting from the principles of librarianship which have a political content rooted in various interpretations of democracy.

Thus, it is clear from the above criteria that the search for relevance derives from the needs and concerns of the society either as a group or as a nation. Professional education should take cognisance of this fact, especially as socio-economic forces influencing the curriculum are deeply rooted in objectives of national development. For instance in political terms, one of the most explicitly nationalist criteria of relevance is the 'Africanisation' of the curriculum in African institutions. There is a deep routed feeling that first, the staff should be Africanised and second, that the curriculum should also be Africanised. This follows the rationale that there are times when it is generally assumed that the curriculum and entire syllabus cannot effectively be localised unless the staff itself is local. But rejection of aliens and their ideas or ideologies is surely not a positive approach to indigenisation of curriculum and staff as Benge[4, 5] and Mazrui[6] have observed. The quest for a reduction of foreigners or their ideologies does not lie in restricting the curriculum to the study of African phenomena only. The greater challenge is to study a variety of other intellectual riches but from an African perspective.

'Localisation,' 'Nigerianisation,' and 'Indigenisation': Postulate of Relevance

In the field of education in general, and library education in particular, the overall concept of relevance has drawn the fervent attention of sociologists who view the minutiae of events in the discipline with some concern.

The concerns relate to the disparities and diversities of social behaviour in many African countries in which the consequence of behavioural differences shows in ethnic and religious customs and urban-rural life styles. Such diversities make the curriculum planners' task most arduous and complex. The complexity is compounded when there is greater demand for promoting indigenous culture through the curriculum at all levels of education.

However, education whether modern or ancient, aims at perpetuating the culture of society wherever this may be. In the African context, traditional education attaches considerable importance to this aspect of training the individual. In most cases, traditional education is thus imparted without elaborate equipment or complicated teaching methods. In Nigeria, for instance, the child grows into and within the cultural heritage of his people: he imbibes it. Culture in traditional society is not taught: it is caught, through what sociologists describe as the 'socialisation process.'

The child observes, imitates and mimics the actions of his elders and siblings. He watches the naming ceremonies, religious services, marriage rituals, funeral obsequies. He witnesses the coronation of a king or chief, the annual yam festival, the annual dance and acrobatic displays of guilds and age-sets, and 'often participates with his own age-group or his relations in the activities.' The core of European or American criticism of this system of traditional education is that it tends to be conservative and conforming, in that it does not train the child to challenge or **change** those aspects that are considered unprogressive within the system. The gradual build-up and consequent strengthening of this position among African elites has led to the recurring dilemma of local relevance in the system of education.

In Nigeria, the elites form the core of administrators and educators; these two groups in particular share a common belief that there is considerable weakness in traditional education since any form of change in the system is considered as taboo by elders of the various cultural organisations in the country. But can this be a disadvantage? Recent attempts to neutralise the cultural debate have always pointed at some sort of compromise. According to Taylor:

> In the past few years there has been a new determination in Nigeria's search
> for a curriculum which seeks to develop a national 'supra-tribal' identity as
> a precursor to modernity in a multilingual and multicultural country.[7]

The theory of ethnocentrism does not, however, presuppose 'supra-tribal' sentiments. Educational sociologists use supra-ethnic entity to refer to the phenomenon of national identity: that which surpasses the beliefs and tradition of any one group in the country. Therefore in the search for curriculum relevance, the Western European model of education system is constantly being re-examined in areas of obvious local content. The dismay of educationalists is reflected in Fafunwa's observation:

> If education is the aggregate of all the processes by which a person develops
> abilities, attitudes and other forms of behaviour of positive and meaningful
> value in the society in which he lives, if it is a system based on certain
> philosophical or theoretical assumptions and seeks to justify its usefulness
> in terms of its practices and results, then most of the educational systems
> in Africa South of the Sahara and north of the Limpopo today can hardly
> stand the test.[8]

Thus, it is clear that the imported 'modern' system of education, instead of developing positive cultural values in the society in which the African child lives, tends to alienate him from his own cultural environment. The 'modern' system educates the child out of his environment regardless of the positive or negative aspects of this situation. As a prominent educator has observed, there is a strong feeling among all educationalists today that traditional western education has contributed in no small measure to the failure of social and economic progress in Africa: it has disorganised and disoriented African societies, thereby divorcing the educational needs of Africa from the economic imperatives.

However, the feature of concern here is to consider the various terminologies that have emerged as a direct result of the search for relevance. The terminologies as outlined below, derive from their general, sometimes confused, application in the humanities literature. These are now considered as follows:

Localisation

The term 'localisation' in African education system refers to the decolonising of the process of modernisation without ending it. Although an interpretation of the definition seems close to neo-colonialism, in fact it is different from any such connotation. It implies merely, the creation of an indigenous system in every sphere of social activity within the universal concept of modernisation. Thus, localisation is analogous to Africanisation in the way the term is usually applied in African literature. Sometimes, it reflects the replacement of expatriate staff in institutions of higher learning and other related establishments, and at other times, the removal of foreign ideals from the curriculum in response to local needs.

Furthermore, it is desirable to grasp an understanding of both terms in the light of current events in the search for relevance. While localisation is specific in its application to particular environments in the society, 'Africanisation' is much more of a wider term putting in perspective many interrelated elements such as: not only in terms of implementation of educational reforms to suit African needs, but also inculcating replacement of expatriate staff or a drastic reduction in their quota, in favour of indigenous manpower. Usually this is more noticeable in top administrative or teaching positions.

Localisation varies intently in perspective. For instance, if education whether African, Western or Eastern European, is viewed as the totality of experience in response to nature and the environment, it follows that it may differ in style, approach, and emphasis mainly because of local needs and conditions. One may offer the hypothesis that both traditional and modern systems have positive and negative aspects. Hence, localisation implies the essence of utilising what is positive when formulating a new system which will be **relevant** to the needs and conditions of the locality in a society. A rejection of negative aspects of modern education system in African societies should not represent a criticism or an indictment of its philosophy. Rather, it could be viewed as a meaningful departure from unreality — a classic disposal of Utopian ideal of ultimately attaining full developmental status in the nation's socio-economic adventure.

Equally, it is clear that Africanisation derives from the principle that all modern education systems are commercially based and not in the interests of Africans because, according to radical elites in African universities, modern education lacks the necessary foundations that should have been built on African traditions and values, for example:

(a)   African respect for humanity and human dignity;

(b)   African sense of community;

(c)   African respect for **legitimate** and **human** authority;

(d)   African respect for authentic and positive African moral and religious values and cultures;

(e)   African respect for the dignity of labour;

(f)   Motivation and stimulation of creativity.[9]

Against this background, modern education system in Africa at present views technology and scientific achievements as ultimate educational aims which are not necessarily ideal for existing situation. Localisation, as a tool of relevance, ensures pertinent readjustment of the *status quo* in educational provision to suit local needs.

Nigerianisation

Presently, curriculum development is still dominated by the desire to shape a 'Nigerianess' and the majority of professional educators accept this goal. Two specific strategies are often adopted:

(a)   An extension of opportunities for more children to attend school via the introduction of the Universal Primary Education Scheme, begun in 1976;

(b)   A language policy to provide a national *lingua franca* which will equip individuals with a working knowledge of a Nigerian language other than the local vernacular.[10]

Both strategies are commonly acceptable in the education circle since they provide the necessary itinerary for Nigerianisation of the modern education system. It was the declared policy of the government to Nigerianise both the civil service and administrative sectors of institutions of higher learning in the country immediately after political independence in 1960. However, it should be noted that the implementation of the policy to Nigerianise was inevitably linked with the sensitive ethnic political rivalries existing in the country,[11] perhaps more predominant at the time.

'Nigerianisation' can therefore be defined as follows:

> The appointment of qualified Nigerians to higher and responsible posts both in government and educational sectors.

The commitment here is deeper than the Africanisation issue because the implementation of the Nigerianisation policy depends to a very large extent on the urgent need to provide institutions in Nigeria for the supply of needed manpower for national development.

Furthermore, growth of institutions is simultaneously accompanied by

Nigerianisation of the faculties mostly in terms of staff. The ultimate aim of Nigerianisation is therefore to promote concerns of relevance to national purpose and national identity. Nigerian universities have particularly witnessed the effects of the Nigerianisation policy in their faculties and departments. But the policy has drawn the attention of educationalists from Western Europe. Taylor, for instance, observes that:

> While the Nigerian people collectively may have discovered nationalism, many as individuals feel that local geography, local anthropology, local studies are hindrances to their personal educational developments.[12]

Taylor's observation sums up the typical neo-colonialist attitude of regarding local education materials as 'inferior' and foreign ideals such as the study of 'Shakespeare's works' or the 'geography of the British Isles' as 'superior.' The essential point in the search for relevance is to sever links with 'colonial mentality' and wake up to the realism of local relevance in the education system, be it through staffing or the curriculum. Benge aptly suggests that:

> A consequence of cultural dependence is that perceptions are blocked or distorted so that people are prevented **from seeing their own world:** They are using borrowed coloured spectacles. With regard to education for librarians, this causes the unfortunate students to concentrate on non-problems and provide answers to questions which should not have been asked. It is of course true that the textbooks are inappropriate, but that is partially true of all textbooks: **The teacher's task is one of interpretation and eventually to provide his own text.** (My emphasis).[13]

The essence of Nigerianisation should be to enable teachers to use their own indigenous upbringing in relating courses to the local environment. The malign influences of a metropolitan education system cannot be allowed to detract from this project. According to Taylor:

> If the Nigerian pupils accept that the curriculum is designed to socialise and Nigerianise as well as to prepare for higher education and future occupations, the experiment may succeed. But at present the problem has psychological, sociological and pedagogical ramifications about which the government's think-tank has not yet commented.... There has been no assessment of parental or pupil interests and needs... (nor) child-centred needs determining either teaching content or method.[14]

In a development situation, the characteristics of democratic thinking inherently displayed in Taylor's quotation above is nothing but a luxury in many developing countries. Many departmental research conducted by Nigerian educationalists, though not publicised nor published in conventional form, have found their way to the necessary government quarters to facilitate the decision-making process. Besides, evaluation of any kind has many constraints such as, political, financial, and reliability. Given these constraints and the consequent ethnic feeling likely to be engendered, it seems reasonable to pursue a policy of restraint in making public comments on the issues of relevance arising from Nigerianisation of the education system. National objectives have priority in such matters.

However, there are other significant problems of Nigerianisation. Consider, for example, the *lingua franca* factor. According to John:

> When an education system forces children to express themselves in a language which is not their own, it not only becomes difficult for them to articulate their ideas but they also tend to lack the confidence which they would show when using their native tongue.[15]

In the Nigerian context, the problem is made more complex as there are many languages to choose from for a national *lingua franca*. Politically, it is emotive; sociologically, it seems impractical; educationally, it may prove costly and retrogressive; but realistically, it is an essential corollary of relevance in the education system. Consider for instance, the effect on writers of indigenous textbooks, novels, and other works.

Hypothetically, in an already literate society a change of official language does not alter the status quo of writers, regardless of the literacy rate in such a society. The problem, however, is not the inability of writers to detach themselves from the subjects they wish to write about, but the difficulty of having to use another language. The likely effect is that writers would become frustrated by their inadequate command of the new language. But if the introduction of a new language is made at lower levels of education (such as primary and secondary), it can be realistically expected that at a future date, say in two decades, the necessary foundation for a *lingua franca* would have been laid. Thus, it would be possible to obtain locally-produced documents to support pedagogical work.

The *FESTAC Colloquium[16] produced resolutions which called for total 'reorganisation or revolution' of most of the current school systems in Africa from the primary school level to the university level. The starting point of the 'revolution' is seen as the introduction of an indigenous language or mother tongue as the medium of instruction. This is already taking place in most schools although much more at lower levels of education. Language, it was further hypothesised, is a vehicle which transmits knowledge to the child; such vehicle must of a necessity be that which the child is most familiar with and which relates to his everyday life and understood by his parents and society. The attainment of an 'ideal' language for medium of instruction will definitely take some time. Current efforts, however, show that this objective can be met. In Nigeria, for example, Yoruba is presently being used as a medium of instruction predominantly at lower levels of education but gradually being introduced in some courses at the university level. In this connection, mention was made at the FESTAC

Colloquium of efforts being made 'to create technical vocabulary either by selecting indigenous words or Africanisation of foreign words through borrowing'[17] — further evidence of creating and showing a desire to shape a 'Nigerianness' in the education system.

Indigenisation

This can be defined as a common term used in the developing countries to denote emancipation from economic domination by foreigners (Lawal, 1993). The aliens are backed by the dominant power of rich nations who, in theory, determine to a large extent the pattern of international trade, terms of technology transfer, foreign aid, and direct investment in Africa, Asia, and the Caribbean. Since the end of World War II, Nigerians have tried to analyse the reasons for the low levels of indigenous participation in the modern sector of African economies.[18,19] It has been a classic Legacy of 'Africans have the land, Asians have the money, Europeans control the government' syndrome.[20] In order to overcome this legacy, Nigerians distributed 'a wide range of extant and proposed programmes to assist indigenous investors.'[21] Thus, with the attainment of political independence in 1960, the first order of business was the Africanisation of the civil service to pave the way for indigenisation of the economy. But the country's industry and trade remained an almost exclusive preserve of the expatriates, and Nigerians did not like this.[22] The Nigerian Indigenisation decrees of 1972 and 1977 therefore came as no surprise, given the unexpected transformation of the economy by the oil boom of the 1970s.

Thus, 'indigenisation' is an elusive term in the social sciences. The term means different things, in different places, and at different periods in a nation's history. In social and political context, for instance, prior to Nigerian independence, in the 1950s indigenisation at the university level meant Nigerianisation of staff. Furthermore, indigenisation is used to describe curriculum renewal and innovations which relate to local and national conditions.[23]

This latter development of the concept of indigenisation is of central concern in the search for relevance. Despite intense preoccupation with the concept in the 1970s, Nigeria has today not achieved much by way of economic self-reliance or economic independence. According to Balabkins:

> Indigenisation can be conceived of as an integral part of the economic evolution of or a vital component of the socio-economic development strategy of Nigeria. One of the most important elements in this strategy is the way in which the Nigerian masses perceive and interpret the prevailing economic opportunities in their country.[24]

The importance of self-reliance cuts across frontiers in social and economic development. As part of the development strategy, indigenisation of the curriculum is seen to promote social change, but as Balabkins warns, there are limits to be reached:

> The roots of modernization go back to the 18th century, to the philosophers of the Enlightenment. This **Weltanschanung** has three basic ideas: reason, nature, progress. In the philosophy of Enlightenment, the environmental conditions, be they the existing legislation, customs, or traditions, can corrupt and prevent the normal physiological application of reason.[25]

To improve matters, the subscribers to the philosophy of enlightenment held that certain environmental changes are indispensable for the building of a better world for the masses. They believed in and advocated what was known as 'social engineering.' The indigenisation process is perceived as a mechanical way, say for example, by which libraries could respond to the growing needs of the community in sustaining society's self-reliance in knowledge and information.

Educational Factor of Relevance

The underlying elements that created the irrelevance in the modern education system, can be traced to Nigeria's colonial past. Details of the link with colonialism cannot be justifiably treated here, but these are adequately covered in studies by Koehl,[26, 27] Kay and Nystrom,[28] and Mazrui.[29] In the cited works, European motives for the cultural penetration of Africa were analysed to the effect that the penetration was found to result in the emergence of the university as the most sophisticated instrument of 'cultural dependency.' For instance, Mazrui argues that university graduates in Africa are the most culturally dependent because they are the most deeply westernised Africans.[30] Integration with metropolitan systems have always formed the basis of the priorities of African scholars. In West Africa, Greek, Latin, and European history formed the core of the humanities. For many years, no African language, not even Arabic, could be studied at the university level.[31]

Having been educated, African elites, like their colleagues of the same social stratum in other parts of the 'Third World,' pride themselves more on the basis of the prestige and status of the higher institutions they attended rather than what they could achieve for the benefit of the society who trained them. High profile institutions such as Harvard, Yale, Oxford, Cambridge, University College, London, and the former University College, Ibadan (now University of Ibadan), are recognised publicly as status symbols for appointments into the public service. Thus, as evidence of cultural dependency, the personal educational achievements of elites in the African society tend to rank higher than their capacity for social responsibility and service. The question of value therefore arises. This can be approached from two dimensions:

(a) Practical relevance — which focuses on issues of skills; and,
(b) Cultural relevance — which relates to issues of values.

Practical relevance in African universities should be concerned with whether or not universities are producing the right kind of personnel for the processes of economic and social development. The emphasis must be on skill. For example, in areas such as political science, management studies, sociology, and librarianship, the curricula changes so far seem to reflect **what** is studied rather than **how** it is studied. More and more courses on Africa and on the economics of development have been introduced, but few methodological innovations (such as being applied in 'oral tradition in history'). Relevance may in this way gradually vanish into oblivion or at best become a utopian ideal.

Cultural relevance, on the other hand, ensures relatively of theory with past and existing tradition in the society. The traditional values of the society are not lost but incorporated in the learning process, regardless of other forces that may influence the curriculum. The ultimate aim is to enhance greater understanding of the indigenous social system and thereby improve the level of services and the general quality of life in the society.

Nigerian Education System

The objective in this section of the study is to provide an insight into the nature of the education system in Nigeria (excluding the higher education sector). The education structure that evolves is then related to the perspectives of relevance under discussion. A consideration of factors in the education system thus provides an opportunity of a suitable background from which to assess professional education.

Traditional Education

In Northern Nigeria, which is predominantly Muslim (except for areas such as Plateau, Kaduna, and Bauchi States which are not predominantly Muslim), an Islamic educational system has been in operation since the 15th century,[32] long before Europeans intervened. Until the 19th century, it was mainly a peripatetic system but some educational institutions did exist. In Kano alone in the late 15th century there were an estimated 3000 mallams.[33] Teaching and learning were by *lectio* and *memoriter* (i.e. reading aloud and rote memorisation). With time the peripatetic system gave way, never completely, to a formalised, institutionalised system of Quranic education.

Thus, over many centuries an educational system and an ideology which suited the Muslim population of Northern Nigeria was in existence. The introduction of westernised education did not go unchallenged. In this context, various appreciation and analysis as regards the role of Islam in the process of development and modernisation have emerged in sociological and historical literature. Weber,[34] for instance, considers Islam as a relatively non-progressive, conservative force. But according to Ajayi and Oloruntimehin:

...for the vast majority of West Africans in the first three-quarters of the 19th century Islam, not the Christian abolitionist movement, was the revolutionary factor creating larger political systems with new economic opportunities and establishing new religious obligations and social values.[35]

The social values, still existing today, are difficult to eradicate even by modern standards. Apart from Islamic education, other aspects of traditional education exists with the following common goals:

(a)   Developing the child's latent physical skills;
(b)   Developing character;
(c)   Inculcating respect for elders and those in position of authority;
(d)   Developing intellectual skills;
(e)   Acquiring specific vocational training and developing a healthy attitude towards honest labour;
(f)   Developing a sense of belonging and participating actively in family and community affairs;
(g)   Understanding, appreciating, and promoting the cultural heritage of the community at large.

These common goals, in Fafunwa's view,[36] enhance greater understanding of traditional values in Nigerian education. In addition, there are 'hidden' values in the traditional system of education:

> For the select or the elect (apprentice/practitioner) secret cults served as institutions of higher or further education. It was at this level that the secret of power (real or imaginary), profound native philosophy, science and religion were mastered. Irrespective of the level of education and training given during the pre-colonial days in Africa, it was functional because the curriculum was relevant to the needs of society.[37]

The issues raised in the above quotation are still pertinent today, but with an increased awareness for public recognition of traditional institutions. As Taiwo submits, 'at present, in addition to the formal education offered in schools, Nigerian children are subject (in varying degrees) to some traditional education.'[38]

In respect of the **content**, Taiwo states that traditional education consists of:

(i)   Education for living in conformity with the traditions of the community;
(ii)   Education for occupations and economic self-reliance;
(iii) Education for special occupations such as family crafts, secret organisations, religious priesthood, divination, medicine and surgery.

Given the content as stated in (i) to (iii) above, it was obligatory to expose every child to the first type of education, which was basic. Fadipe, a Nigerian sociologist, suggests that:

> ... the child's teachers directly or indirectly were his parents, as well as the various members of his family and household, his extended family (usually

located in the same compound), his kindred and his neighbourhood to call a person "uneducated" in this sense was a great insult to the person and his family.[39]

The social environment reinforced these accepted values, but as Taiwo suggests, the traditional methods of education that are observable today are no longer in their former setting: The factors which influence the methods of education have changed. The aims of education have been broadened out to keep step with the age of science and technology. Reading and writing which were unknown are the basic tools of education, which every child should acquire as the first essentials. Education has become complex, far beyond the grip of any one father, mother or older child in the family or any adult in the compound to impart. The content of education has also increased and deepened many times over. The environment has also changed.[40]

The change in environment has resulted in the child being less acquainted with farm life, its animals, birds and plants more in contact with artificial surroundings with social provision such as air, sea and road transportation, shops, theatres and libraries. The rural area being transformed into more complex environment and now societies are emerging. These change have affected traditional values and methods of education.[41]

With regards to problems encountered in the organisation of the content of traditional education, some elements are discernible:

(i) The problem of language defies solution at present because African languages, when placed in context of mathematics, science, technology or political science, seem clearly to be inadequate in the universal pursuit of knowledge;

(ii) The curriculum of traditional education is often presented in a way that it emphasises living in society other than creativity;

(iii) Teachers and their education rarely take full account of intellectual requirement of traditional values and norms.

Teachers should know the qualities which have sustained the community and the methods of imparting them, otherwise, their contribution to education would remain superficial.

Against this background of change and the resultant problems of traditional education system. For instance, does the philosophy of education in the formal system adequately cover the final state in the traditional system. i.e., in terms of definite structure and its relation to national development objective?

Philosophy

In general, the foundation of the Nigerian government policy are the five main national objectives[42] which it is widely believed that education can promote. The philosophy is that education is recognised as the greatest force that can be used to foster in the much needed unity of Nigeria and to correct the quick development of the greatest investment that can make for the quick development of the economic, political, sociological and human resource of the country.

The government therefore aims at providing equal educational opportunities for all the citizens of the nation at the primary, secondary and tertiary levels, both inside and outside the formal school system with a view to integrate the individual fully into a sound and effective citizen, useful to himself and his society, and the nation. It is fervently considered that education will bring about self-realisation, better human relationships, individual and national efficiency, effective citizenship, national consciousness, national unity, as well as social, cultural, economic, political, scientific and technological progress. The government considers it to be in the interest of national unity that each child should be encouraged to learn one of the three major languages (Hausa, Igbo, and Yoruba) as well as his mother tongue. [43]

Primary Education (age 6 to 11+)

Free Universal Primary Education (UPE) was available to all Nigerian children (effective, September 1976) and was later made compulsory. The curriculum is aimed at permanent literacy and numeracy and effective communication. The medium of instruction is the mother tongue or the language of the immediate community, and at a later stage, English. Islamic 'protests of corrective censure,' made against the U.P.E. scheme are in line with the emphasis that the cultural heritage of the people of Nigeria must be preserved, that a foreign model of these must be developed, and that in some instances, these emphases have already had their effect.[44] The move to make Hausa the medium of instruction in the Northern state in 1976 has assisted in the development of a Nigerian educational system which takes cognisance of the modern and useful aspect of the traditional.

Secondary Education (age 11+ to 17+)

Secondary education is aimed at preparing individuals for useful living in the society and for those willing and able to further their studies at higher education level. It is a six-year course (effective 1982) and it is in two stages of three years each, known as the junior and the senior stages of schools respectively. It is both academic and pre-vocational, and sufficient as preparing for trade and vocational training. The senior secondary school is comprehensive. Admission to the university will be directly from the six-year secondary school.

Technical Education

This is broadly defined as 'that aspect of education which leads to the acquisition of practical and applied skills as well as basic scientific knowledge'[45] outside the university, there are five types of technical education institutions, comprising pre-vocational and vocational schools at both post-primary and post-secondary levels. At the technical education level in librarianship, for instance, the new professional course — Nigerian National Diploma in Library Studies (4 years) (now re-styled HND Library Studies) — has been introduced. Although Owerri College of Science and Technology (Nekade Polytechnic) is already implementing the course, the final draft of the curriculum took some time to be approved by the government sponsors and the profession.[46]

Adult and Non-formal Education

The National Policy document on education provides for nationwide mass literacy campaign which was planned for a limited duration of ten years during which all available resources were to be mobilised towards the achievement of total eradication of illiteracy. The realisation of this aim is proving rather difficult.

In improving the education of those adults who, for various reasons, are unable to go to normal universities for further studies, there is provision for an Open University (O.U) system to enable the adult workers to study for and gain degrees initially in subjects related to national development objectives. Obasi[47] and Lawal[48] have in separate articles examined the bases and importance of the O.U. system and the implications for library services.

Overall, the pattern of Nigerian education system is represented in the structure and levels of learning. It appears the issue of relevance is illuminative, not in the structure itself, but in the organisation and selection of content for the curriculum. The universality of knowledge as sometimes assumed in the literature, makes the present educational structure seem inevitable, but knowledge is also a social construct which draws its intellectual wealth from local circumstances in an environment. Thus, it is possible to make courses relevant to local needs without necessarily dismantling the structure of the education system due to its 'foreignness.'

The Higher Education System

A practical point from which to start the analysis is to assume that educational culture is a dynamic system of behaviour implementing a dominant group's values and expectations concerning the preparation of children, young people, and adults for living on after the older generation pass away. The higher education system is an avenue, not only for expanding knowledge frontiers, but for conserving and propagating aspects of societal values. If not handled rationally, the higher education system may be used by some groups as breeding ground for social revolution and consequently leading to confrontation in the society which the institutions exist to serve. African societies have assimilated many aspects of European educational tradition by establishing formal institutions for education and certification, and 'acting in a mediating role for transforming the society along indigenous lines.[49]

In 1972, the Association of African Universities held an important education seminar at Accra, Ghana. The theme of the seminar was 'Creating the African University: Emerging Issues of the 1970s.'

An envisaged African university was defined as:

> A community essentially of African scholars, men and women, old and young, lettered and unlettered, dedicated to serve its community and committed to the total development of African society with the objective of the total liberation of the common man from all that hampered his well being physically, materially and intellectually. [50]

The African concept of university system as indicated in the above quotation implies not only a commitment to knowledge but one of social responsibility as well. Clearly, this is a challenge to all Africans because it calls for a re-evaluation of the present European and African models in favour of a nationalist pattern. The political undertones, such as 'total liberation of the common man,' derive from the existing marriage of convenience between politics and the system of higher education in African countries. But university education is international phenomenon often in defiance of political rhetorics. According to Bereday:

> Not only do the substance and procedure of university study partake of universality, but they are from the beginning of the modern age, and still at present, derived from the accomplishment of academics and amateurs of the western, central and northern European culture area including the North America, the very areas of the world against which the twentieth-century nationalism of Asia, Africa and Latin America is asserting itself.[51]

Agbowuro adds that:

> What, to my mind, the Africans call the Africanized system of higher education, is a system whose task, in part, is to propagate a universal culture and to contribute to its growth, while simultaneously cultivating and developing the indigenous actual and potential national culture and enhancing national life.[52]

In the pursuit of the dual objective as suggested by Agbowuro, the existing model of the university needs to be retained even though it is a foreign transplant. However, what is taught in the institutions is a different issue altogether. The curriculum will need to relate to the local environment. As Fafunwa argues:

> (The curriculum) should be designed to interpret the nation's culture, history, geography, religion, philosophy and to control the physical forces of the students' environment for the benefit of the whole nation.[53]

Having stated the determining factors of establishments in the higher education system, and the primary function of advancing knowledge plus the enhancement of traditional values and skills in curricula provision, attention may now be paid to the specific issues of relevance in the higher education system of which professional education is a significant part.

Mazrui writes:

> Debates about practical relevance in African universities have been concerned with whether universities are producing appropriate personnel for the processes of economic and social development. Is there enough emphasis on training people skilled in modern agriculture? Are universities sensitive to the need for veterinarians in pastoral regions? Do they emphasise Shakespeare more than rural development?[54]

Though writing from a political viewpoint, the focus of Mazrui's observation seems to cut across the broad spectrum of social issues.

In the field of education, many African universities started as liberal-arts colleges, not as training centres for skilled manpower. Part of the prejudice against technical courses was inherited from the metropolitan powers. Thus, the higher education system was producing more leaders than the required level of technicians. Nigeria's premier university (Ibadan) offered courses in Latin, Greek, Christian Doctrine and Medieval European History long before it recognised the need for courses in engineering, economics, public administration, or librarianship.[55]

However, there were strenuous efforts on the part of politicians and educators alike to make the courses offered in the universities locally relevant. Despite the ardent wish to forge an adaptable system of education, the problems of conservatism, scholasticism, romanticism, and a colonial outlook joined forces to frustrate curriculum reform of higher education from the time Ibadan opened its door in 1948 until the early 1960s when the four universities entered the scene.[56] The root of the problem lies in the attitude of Nigerian scholars trained in Britain, who believed, perhaps curiously, that any programme that diverged at all from what they themselves have gone through in the U.K. would not be good enough. A change, in their view, would be tantamount to lowering of standards. Ashby observes that:

> ...some African intellectuals, especially those educated in Britain, resist changes in curriculum or in pattern of courses because they confuse such changes with a lowering of standards. They are accordingly suspicious of any divergence from the British pattern. Some of them are particularly the British pattern. Some of them are particularly allergic to proposals for incorporating African studies into the curriculum in this, they say, the first step toward disarming us intellectually; to substitute Arabic and African languages for the classics; to teach English to Africans as Chinese is taught to Englishmen, not as Englishmen learn English at Cambridge; to neglect

Tudor history in favour of the history of Africa; to regard oral tradition as legitimate material for scholarship.[57]

Nigerian intellectuals display open maternal allegiance to their *alma mater* until recently, these institutions are mostly overseas-based. In view of this trend, the restructuring of the curriculum in terms of social relevance has been rather slow in the universities. The education of professionals in the universities now thrives on a curriculum aimed at producing knowledgeable but practical men while at the same time structuring the professional programmes to reflect national needs.

Development Factor of Relevance

The idea of 'development' derives from a generalisation that presupposes: (a) cultural awareness, and (b) social commitment to change. On grounds of economic principles, the generalisation is further widened to contain the element of growth. The cultural and social aspects of development create a process usually described in the literature as 'nation-building.' This is a process of reducing ethnic cleavages while at the same time promoting a common national heritage. Thus, in the context of development, the search for relevance involves relating socio-cultural activities to national purpose and identity.

Socio-economic and Educational Interpretation of Development

Modernisation and dependency theory provide the basis for three characterisations of the relationship between education and development. The developmentalist perspective is based on the notion that education can provide the skills, motivations, and personality traits required for an industrialising society. From the nationalist's viewpoint, LaBelle and Verhine[58] argue that education based on Western or neo-colonial models has not furthered national development, but has simply enabled those who control the schools to control the work place as well.

The dependency perspective is that the failure of peripheral nations to develop is not the result of their educational systems, whether Western, or nationalistic types, but of the specific role they play in the division of world labour. Existing educational systems are both a consequence of and a means of reinforcing this dependent position.

According to some developmentalists[59, 60, 61] education has two key functions: it should respond to national needs for trained manpower, and it should socialise a nation's population into modern values, attitudes, and personalities. This viewpoint assumes that the major reason for the Third World's failure to develop is that most of its people do not have 'sufficient education' to support a modern occupational structure, and are too traditional in outlook to participate in a modern world. Within this assumption, however, the mechanism of change has not been taken into account thereby weakening the strength of the proposition. To the developmentalists, since educational modernisation is expected to upgrade labour, it is considered an investment in human capital which will yield a substantial return in the form of increased national prosperity. The problem is perceived in terms of individuals, or an aggregate of individuals, rather than the social structure at the national and international level.

Another dimension of development and its relationship with education and occupation is that high levels of education are associated with high-status and high-paying jobs. This relationship points to the possibility that a higher general level of education will lead to the formation of a more modern occupational structure. Walters suggests that evidence from Africa indicates that educational expansion 'simply increases the number of credentials required for a particular job, and has little effect on the occupational structure; throughout the periphery, education has expanded tremendously, but national economic growth has not.'[62]

Furthermore, any interpretation of development needs to encompass social, psychological, and educational elements of change. Modernisation is the process of social change in which development is the economic component.[63] Investment in education, or more broadly in human resources, may be perceived as a major and critical basis of societal change.

Thus, in its socio-economic interpretation, development is 'concerned with the human capital and how to mobilise the latter for the enhancement of the quality of life of the majority of the citizens in a society.'[64] Elsewhere in the literature, Sanda[65] states that development has been erroneously equated with industrialisation or modernisation, even with Westernisation. The recent experience of many industrialising but developing countries points to the fact that premature industrialisation may constitute a stumbling block to the process of development in certain situations whereby workers are withdrawn from, say, the agricultural sector (without the location of an adequate substitute of source of food production), and into an industrial sector with limited capacity for the absorption of unskilled workers. This situation has created numerous problems of underdevelopment for some Third World societies.

Similarly, it is significant to draw a parallel with education activities where curriculum planners and planners of educational expansion perceive 'development' as synonymous to 'modernisation.' In many developing countries, there is a new concentration on the building of schools and colleges, expansion of enrolment at all levels of education and in adult education, extension of the coverage of mass media particularly through radio and television, growth in the number of health centres and medical establishments to create healthy learning situations, provision of better housing, libraries, and other social facilities complementing the role of education in enhancing quality of life.

In terms of the generation and dissemination of information, this is why in the development context, it has become important to deliberately create and institutionalise one or many agencies to provide the channel for a two-way information flow. In Nigeria, as in other African or Asian countries, these agencies include, for example, the agricultural extension worker, the co-operative officer, the community development officers, or even 'Extension/Information Counsellor Librarian'[66] as recently proposed by Ogunsheye. It is important to reflect this information need in the education process.

For instance, the extension worker is at present often regarded by many as the most important of information agencies. His role is to ensure a sufficient flow of information to the rural populace concerning the need for and the advantages of change; to teach people the skills needed for this change through demonstrations, explanation and persuasion; and to encourage them to participate fully in all the relevant processes of decision-making. In this way, a curriculum that reflects social development needs, may be said to attain relevance to national purpose and identity. This in turn reflects on the scale of professionalism in the various occupational activities.

Librarianship and the Concept of Local Relevance

The Problem

In the preceding sections, the education system in general, and higher education was examined specifically. It is clear that higher education has been slow to absorb the teaching of practical subject-matter usually associated with the professions. Even more important, is the trend that emerges from the current demand being made upon the educated for skills they do not have, and perhaps more likely, that they are unwilling to exercise. In order to meet this demand, the professions have effectively broken through the barriers of academic tradition in the universities by establishing and expanding their own knowledge frontiers. But the problem of professional relevance remains. In most cases, this is often generated in the field and spills over to the professional schools and vice-versa. So, how is librarianship faring?

Libraries, as social agencies, represent the traditions of society. Librarianship as a social institution is a foreign ideal which the developing countries of the world perceive largely as an essential agency to expedite social development and to facilitate exchange of information on the required knowledge for agricultural, scientific and technological advances. Basically, the philosophy and principles of librarianship are universal, but there is an increasing trend towards differentiating the emphasis on practice. Most developing countries have begun to question the rationale of providing libraries stocked with up-to-date reading materials in a largely non-literate society and rural environments occupied by local farmers, petty traders, and market men and women enjoying life to the full. To these groups of people, education is still restrictive no matter what significant development is taking place on the economic front. The restrictiveness implies unmotivated need for access to information, knowledge, and ideas which could substantially improve their economic performance as well as their personal development in the society. Thus, the circumstances surrounding the evolution of libraries in Nigeria and the attendant role of the services in education more than the social sector, is the root cause of the problem of professional relevance. Many regard library institutions as existing at present, as a *fait accompli* of neo-colonialist influence on Africa. The appeal of the opening quotation[1] to this work rests on a radical departure from what is considered 'traditional' in conventional library practice especially where this relates to a predominant non-literate society.

The challenge of 'relevance' is therefore a stimulating phenomenon in almost all kinds of professional activity. Europeans questioned the value of their professional education in the sixties and seventies – a period of economic boom and general educational expansion. But in the context of American and European experience, Havard-Williams suggests that relevance, a keyword in the sixties and seventies, is still alive, but perhaps not so relevant as it once was.[67] It is not a question of cultural stalemate but one of values in a changing society.

Criticisms of library schools as regard to what is taught and learned, and the nature of professional services in times of change, have reached endemic proportions in the literature concerning developing countries. The root cause of the problem, which is being analysed in this present work, has scarcely been explored by contributors to the debate. Perhaps an outstanding view in respect of the library school's curriculum is that put forward by Dean who states that:

> The library pattern (in developing countries) has in many cases been predetermined by **colonial experiences** (my emphasis) and a system developed which is possibly not particularly appropriate for the environment... This kind of situation calls for a good deal of insight on the part of the planner in determining precisely the programmes (that) are called for to satisfy the needs of the library systems of the country.[68]

Assuming that 'colonial experiences' is the root cause of the problem on professional relevance, how valid is this hypothesis, and how can the visible effects of colonialism be neutralised through cultural reawakening? The validity of 'colonial experiences' as a rhetoric for under-development was critically examined by the world renown American economist, Professor Galbraith, who states that:

> The ideas that interpreted capitalism, at least its early stages, were reasonably candid. The ideas that justified colonialism have never been candid. There

is nothing remarkable about this. On many matters men sense that the underlying reasons for action are best concealed. Conscience is better served by a myth. And to persuade others, one needs first of all, to persuade oneself. Myth has always been especially important where war was concerned. Men must have a fairly elevated motive for getting themselves killed. To die to protect or enhance the wealth, power or privilege of someone else, the most common reason for conflict over the centuries, lacks beauty. The case of colonialism is the same.[69]

History has run its course in the shaping of the affairs of men. The insatiable desire for world power in terms of political and economic gains led to adventures of colonialism, thereby creating in its trail a cultural subjugation of the weaker nations. However, with political independence, the search for relevance in the developing countries has no less been radical as the foreign ideals through which they have been subjugated. Critics of 'colonial experiences' do not recognise that there are limits to be reached in making such claims.

According to Galbraith:

> No memory is so deep and enduring as that of colonial humiliation and injustice. But it must also be added, nothing serves so well as an alibi. In the newly independent countries, the colonial experience remains the prime excuse whenever something goes wrong. In these countries much does go wrong. So, in this respect too, colonialism remains a lively source of myth. Once the myth was made by those who colonized. Now by those who were colonized.[70]

When narrowed down to the field of librarianship, unlike other sensitive areas of political organisation, administration, and economic services, 'colonial experience' becomes a burden rather than any form of alibi in places where things go wrong, hence the need for relevance. As one considers the need to relate library functions to local needs, political insinuations must be detracted from the inappropriateness of the system handed over to the new generation of Nigerians by the colonialists. Holdsworth, for example, emphasised that the need for relevance arises from the notable effects of colonialism:

> Library development was used by the colonial administration to perpetuate the 'proper exercise' of the function of a State (i.e. the Colonial power) and for the work of industry, trade and professional classes, through libraries of institutions of higher learning to finally public libraries, which in a way reflects colonial interests and priorities.[71]

The curriculum of Nigerian library schools until the late sixties reflected the colonialist's urge, which could not have been easily dispensed with in the first decade of independence. The urge was to propagate British culture and thus, seek its assimilation from their "subjects": Latin, English and Mathematics became the core of the curriculum, the study of Shakespearean works is still emphasised even today in the Literature curriculum. The immediate effects on the curriculum of library and information studies have been highlighted in this study.

Ekpe[72] argues that the impact of colonialism was so deep-rooted in the socio-economic and political life of Nigeria that librarianship had no ultimate philosophy of its own for the indigenous population. Calls similar to Ekpe's, have therefore been made for professional services to relate both to traditional Nigerian values and development needs.[73,74,75] Aina[76] and Ogunsheye[77] have also examined and discussed the conventional problems of attaining metropolitan status and how librarianship can best cope with achieving national identity. For instance, Ogunsheye found that:

.... Africa consists of communities and cultures with oral traditions, and communities whose information and recreation needs cannot be met by the conventional media – the book. The records of our culture are not in book form, but are alive in our oral poetry, drama, praise sayings, religious chants, festivals and art works. They carry records of our philosophy, religion and literature; of our crafts and technology; our cultural norms therefore our laws, politics, sociology and history.[78]

Libraries can in this way attract those members of the community who have not had the privileges of formal education, by relating the social aspects of the service to the norms of society.

International Dimensions

In the field of librarianship, the concept of professional relevance has wide international connotations. The challenge to traditional values usually is based on the claim that they do not today have relevance. The attacks on education in general, and library education in particular, often feel obliged to make no more specific indictment than that.[79] But 'relevance to what' is seldom defined, although the context sometimes suggests the nature of the complaints. On an international basis, postulatory views have been expressed as to the ideal role of the librarian in the society.[80,81,82]

Given the change in emphasis with regards to the library's role in all categories of information transmission (such as, in the area of information technology and its accompanying innovations), the claims for relevance often turn out to be simply utilitarian in ideals by prescribing specific learning situations to tackle specific tasks confronting the modern librarian. Asheim observes that when a procedure, considered by its originators as being of standard is abandoned, the justification is that it is no longer relevant to current professional needs.[83] At present, there is no evidence in the literature to prove otherwise.

Boaz comments on the problem by stating:

> The issues of core curriculum and electives of a liberal education and specialization, of graduate and undergraduate programmes are questions which continue to be of concern. The themes are old, the problems are ever present, the solutions (if found) will be new. [84]

One way of seeking relevance in the curriculum is through the optional and other specialised courses which usually address themselves to topical issues. The library school in the setting of a developing country will find it difficult to vigorously pursue wide ranging electives or specialisation in its curriculum mainly because of problems of staffing, finance, and inconsistent demand from the profession (which, in order to make the courses viable, must be on a continuous basis).

Glazer,[85] writing on the United States of America, observed that:

> ... the 'better' schools of librarianship tend to place their emphasis on that content which prepares higher administrators, research workers and potential teachers in library school to the alleged neglect of training for the central role of the practitioner.[86]

Another factor to emerge from concentrating courses designed for top management positions in libraries other than for levels at the lower end of the scale, is the relationship of librarianship qualifications to professional performance output. Mayhew cites a number of studies which seem to indicate that there is a minimal positive or even slightly negative relationship between job performance and length and level of education. The author suggests further that:

> If such studies are further validated, professional schools, if they are to continue to warrant the support and regard they have achieved in the past, will be forced into radical revision of the entire process of education, beginning with techniques of admission and extending to organisation of courses and requirements for graduation.[87]

Such radical reorganisation of the 'entire process of education' will derive from changing practices in the field and, at times, the irrelevance of the librarian's own qualifications to the job in hand.

As regards those members of the profession who are advocating radical improvements due to the factor of relevance in education, Jencks and Riesman observed that:

> The reformers in any given profession are disproportionately concentrated in its training institutions ... at any given moment the quality of practice taught at a professional school is likely to be higher than that actually carried on by the alumni of that school. Indeed the exalted image of a

profession provided by its better schools may first help it attract better recruits than it deserves and then help sustain these men in the face of its often sordid and tedious reality.[88]

As for the recruitment pattern into the profession of librarianship, a lot will depend on the individual who aspires to become a professional. This element can hardly be predicted aforehand in the library school's curriculum, thus, the claims of irrelevance in this respect would seem unjustified.

On the sociological issues of library and information service, in terms of relevance, the American experience seems to be of practical value. The demand for relevance by the Social Responsibilities Round Table and related movements in the American Library Association, can be traced back to the 19th century faith in the public library as a social force that would, 'through the promotion of reading, save mankind from poverty, crime, vice, alcoholism, and almost every other evil to which flesh is heir.'[89] From the 1930s through 1970s, the sociological roots of American librarianship derived from pleas for social action, that the librarian should have a vigorous and vocal social consciousness. According to Shera[90] and Ashei,[91] this conviction was especially strong among a relatively small group of young librarians who were demanding an end to conservatism and complacency, with development in their stead; the group also advocated for a dynamic social role for the library.

Earlier advocates for an investment into the impact of social change on the utilisation of human resources, staked their claims on the grounds that 'the librarian should concern himself with society and must teach himself to develop 'attitudes of foresight.'[92] In writing a *credo* for the youth of his generation, Martin argues tenuously that the core of the library's being 'is the transmission of group culture and knowledge as recorded in printed materials.'[93] The author thereby derived the social functions of the public library as an agency of social control which conserves and transmits the social heritage, and inculcates the experiences and values of the past to its contemporary society in order to promote social solidarity and unity. The heavy emphasis on 'printed material' tragically ignored other important, perhaps, more significant forms, of information transmission in society.[94]

The viewpoints of the 1930s spread through three decades of professional uncertainty, hence the persistent calls for relevance in a society prone to change. Perhaps, as Wheeler observes, the library profession has suffered from 'a well-meant overdose of social viewpoint.'[95]

Indigenisation and Library Studies in Nigeria

One aspect of relevance that draws the undivided attention of librarians and educators alike in Nigeria concerns the indigenous elements of the curriculum in library schools. The demands for local relevance in the curriculum seem to have triggered off efforts in that direction. The work in this section attempts to analyse current trends in the indigenisation of library and information studies, based upon derived needs for local relevance.

Nature and Purpose of Local Relevance

Nigerian library educators, in considering the relevance of their programmes to the community, readily admit that this is an area constituting 'a major academic problem for the library schools.'[96] It is generally felt that while mindful of the development in the profession on the international plane, education for librarianship should also reflect local needs. There seems to be an inclination towards the social functions of libraries. Aboyade's observation in this respect is pertinent:

> For us in Nigeria, as indeed for Africa in general, the question of relevance has to do mainly with service to a predominantly orally literate and non-literate people when the institution itself is heavily print oriented.[97]

The emphasis on oral tradition is a direct result of the UNESCO-sponsored Standing Conference of African Library Schools meeting held in Dakar in 1974, where the need to indigenise the curriculum was formally recognised and recommendations put forward to the effect that the curriculum in African library schools should include courses on African history, sociology and literature, oral tradition and audio-visual materials and technology. Library schools in Nigeria have since taken up this challenge. However, in view of the slow progress so far made, the process of indigenisation of the curriculum seem to be stagnating. But the saturation point is far from reached because there is still plenty of scope for making the library school curriculum socially relevant.

Ogunsheye provided some clues:

> Research is an instrument for discovering new knowledge and this is very necessary in the African situation where we are still rather uniformed about the behaviour and information of our local clientele, where we need to record and document our cultural, literary, and information material resources. The tendency is for academic personnel to be guided solely by interest, in their selection of topic for research. The factor of relevance must strongly be considered in the African situation where funds generally are in short supply.[98]

One valuable approach to indigenisation of the curriculum is through pure and applied research, but this method may prove expensive and time consuming in a dynamic situation requiring urgent solutions.

Mohammed and Otim[99] have shown another approach to indigenisation by relating professional education in librarianship to the realities of the library school's environment and to the goals of societal aspiration in general. The

authors perceived a relevant curriculum as geared towards defining and meeting developmental needs and requirements through the teaching of 'appropriate' courses. To illustrate the appropriateness, Zaria teaches two main course types:
(i)   Bibliographic study of source materials on Africa (area study); and
(ii)   A sociological course.

The content of the courses reflects a wide connotation of the concept of local relevance in that, it digs deeply into societal concerns such as librarians' need to recognise cultural liberation and be aware of change in respect of education for national development.

Other approaches to indigenisation, which are far less ingenious and outwardly superficial are represented by the commonly used cue in examinations – 'with special reference to ...' (Nigerian situation), 'with particular emphasis on...' and the like. If, as stated earlier, it is accepted that knowledge is a social construct, then it follows that the problems of professional practice under consideration in written examinations, essays, thesis or whatever, should be perceived as unique to the local environment. If the teaching has adequately reflected on this element during the course, then evaluation through examination will achieve original results without recourse to superficial cue such as, 'with special reference to.' Students need to be encouraged to develop aesthetic perception of trends in the field and to apply this in their practical work situations.

According to Benge,

> A consequence of cultural dependence is that perceptions are blocked or distorted, so that people are **prevented from seeing their own world:** they are using borrowed coloured spectacles.[100]

The root cause of the search for relevance derives from colonial experiences which in turn affect traditional pursuits in education.

Furthermore, a common explanation for failure to indigenise aspects of the librarianship curriculum is through using a measure of **excellence**, which in the sociological literature is tied up as a mythical international standard that must be achieved. African educators run the risk of conceding that anything indigenous is 'inferior' while foreign traditions and specifications in the same field are considered as 'superior' and of **standard.** The tendency is for developing countries to be dismayed by the constraints, as Ogunsheye has found out:

> Standards are ... related to the ability of the country or nation to afford the specifications. It is also significant to note that these standards which are specifications for the ideal have a dynamic relationship with sociology. They therefore change according to the financial and other economic and social conditions of the country.[100]

A strong motivation in the factor of relevance should be the developmental factor of relevance to national needs and identity rather than consideration of 'ability to pay the minimum standard of excellence required.'

The inability of some educators to detach their reasoning from cultural dependency has led observers on the trend of indigenisation to make overt comments on the inability of the library schools to indigenise. For example Benge with good intentions, considers that:

> ... a major reason for this relative failure arises from an inability to appreciate what is required .... In the modern world, ideals and concepts are necessarily international and these include the principles of librarianship which have a political content rooted in various interpretations of democracy. What is rightly condemned is the attempt to transfer technology or ideals to African countries without reference to local needs and circumstances. Basic theory is international; its interpretation is not.[102]

The political content of librarianship which Benge considers as rooted in various interpretations of democracy,' is seldom realised nor admitted by contributors to the analysis of relevance. Theoretical suppositions derived from foreign ideals are but offshoots of cultural dependency; they may or may not be international.

Similarly, Tjoumas and Hauptman[103] citing Nigerian studies on 'non-traditional' (i.e. European) approach to public library service, discover that the ultimate aid of the persistent efforts towards indigenisation is to transform the librarian from a member of an advantaged group serving the elite into a servant of the people. According to the authors, the key to this transformation is trifurcate:

(a)   The potential librarian must be educated so that he will be capable of performing his tasks: further, he must be stimulated to desire to do so;

(b)   The attitude of the educators must indicate that library work with the disadvantaged is both honourable and professionally rewarding; and,

(c)   The monetary compensation that librarians receive for this difficult job must be commensurate with the salaries of academic and special librarians.[104]

Interpretations differ as to who is 'disadvantaged' in the community. Unfortunately, the authors did not address themselves properly to defining the specific group of clientele they have in mind. No one wishes to be 'disadvantaged' in any society either as a minority group or a pressure group. The work of Obi,[105] which the authors relied heavily upon, refers to the rural community who cannot be called 'disadvantaged' due to the nature of their location and activities in the society. Surely, there are other potent factors that could beneficially be examined in the context of local relevance.

Some examples

Having analysed the issues and approaches to indigenisation in library and information studies, it is perhaps important now to concentrate on few examples where training is designed to suit local needs.

The IDUPÓM[106] research project is a case in point, based on heuristic information and professional relevance (with particular emphasis on Selective Dissemination of Information – S.D.I. – services) in Nigerian civil service. The characteristics of development information was used to determine the content of the project. These characteristics are derived from the assumption that most 'Third World' countries having found themselves in a 'world development order' have no alternative but to make the most of their available resources for better improvement of their social systems. For instance, in determining the characteristics of civil servants' information needs, Aiyepeku states:

> ... it would obviously be more helpful to know in detail the information needs of Nigerian civil servants than some universal knowledge of the information needs of a civil servant stereotype.[107]

Thus, among Nigerian civil servants, it has been possible to identify the following categories of potential information seekers/users according to the orientation of their functions:

(a) Policy-makers with respect to socio-economic development at governmental and non-governmental levels, nationally and internationally;

(b) Planners of socio-economic development project and programmes, including those responsible for the formulation of social and economic indicators; forecasting and pre-investment studies; technological-economic and social surveys, including the scanning of the socio-economic and socio-political environment; and assessment and performance evaluation of projects and programmes;

(c) Managers of development projects and programmes in the field and in central authorities;

(d) Researchers and teachers of socio-economic development subjects and those involved in management of research projects and programmes;

(e) Financiers who provide resources and technical cooperation for development projects and programmes. Likewise those who provide consultancy and advisory services;

(f) Communicators who attempt to convey information about development policies, plans, programmes and projects in easily assimilated language to the population at large or to particular segments of it;

(g) Personnel concerned with information analysis and products thereof (i.e. monographs, data compilations, trend reports, forecasts, etc.) as support service to those involved in the types of work mentioned in (a) to (f).[108]

The spectrum of potential users, the project refers to as 'development community.' Local needs on development information are self-generating; the community has itself produced or caused to be produced various kinds of information under the generic title of 'Government.' The IDUPOM Project is an attempt to create an information system, which can maximize information input in policy decision-making process of development planning. Apart from introducing the use of SDI service to retrieve information from development literature, the Project failed to suggest ways of organising the local materials for effective dissemination to users.

Another example of attempts at relevance in librarianship is as contained in Aboyade's paper presented at the FID/Education and Training Technical Meeting held at Ibadan in 1981.[109] The paper dealt with the state of documentation in rural development and how information transfer could be facilitated. The author argues that within the worldwide information system network for agriculture, such as: AGRIS, it is possible for information materials which is locally generated either through research or other activities, to be stored and then transferred to users, nationally and internationally. In national terms, the rural people whose main occupation is farming, producing agricultural products would benefit substantially from such effective communication system. At present, Aboyade points out quite rightly the missing communication link which is due to the fact that, 'appropriate information borne out of an intimate understanding and knowledge of the prevailing conditions in specific rural communities may be lacking.' [110] Nigeria, as one of the first countries to join AGRIS system, has not effectively exploited the resources of the body such as Tunisia and Egypt. One could have expected Professor Aboyade's paper to go a step further by suggesting measures that should be taken in order to facilitate access to information by non-literate rural farmers.

Perhaps other examples of actual and potential indigenisation areas of the librarianship curriculum are best illustrated under specific subject categories. Benge, in a recent study, [111] specified some topics, which the present writer will now consider under the appropriate headings:

Library History

Indigenisation does not imply automatic discard of comparative study of overseas institutions such as the history of librarians in Babylonia, ancient Rome, Greece, in the European Middle Ages, or present-day USA or USSR. As a library educator in Nigeria observes:

> ... (students) conclude that we can achieve local relevance by increasing the number of details about time to be spent on the rest; that is not what we mean by indigenisation.[112]

The study of history in relation to overseas institutions is relevant, not so much as to learn what should be done, but to learn from the country's own mistakes. Thus, the study of history is not in the first instance a guide to action but a key to understanding both the universal past and present, i.e., including the indigenous present. It will augur well for the new zest of librarians, who have begun the process of collecting, organising, and disseminating the intellectual contents of Nigeria's oral tradition and history, to study in greater detail elements of local and national history so as to provide a more relevant service to the community. The cultural function of libraries in the society cannot be performed satisfactorily without detailed reference to, and proper understanding of the place of history. The study of overseas institutions should act as a supplementary focus from which to measure national links with international community. Thus, any move to straighten the content of the curriculum with regard to library history in terms of its evolution in Nigeria and inter-connecting international events which have helped to shape that history, to be a welcome innovation. One cannot look into the future without understanding the past and present. The main philosophy is guided not by nationalistic feelings, but by pertinent desire to create conditions suitable for professionals relevant in the community of which the library is an important part.

Library Management

In this subject, most of the materials used for teaching are from overseas as Nzotta's [113] detailed analysis shows. Even though it is questionable whether the orthodox theories of management are appropriate to Nigerian circumstances, it seems at present that little can be done to radicalise the predominance of foreign ideals. This is due to a strenuous problem of lack of documentation of indigenous experiences in the field on the part of practitioners and educators alike. The fact remains that in Nigeria, the principle of management proceeds from invalid assumption which are not part of management theory but derive from social conditions in other countries.

Thus, the principles of management when transformed to a different environment are not wrong but irrelevant, and education which ignores these differences in social reality cannot be said to be indigenous. This view is consistent with the observation of Benge, a former librarian school professor in Nigeria, who in a recent article [114] argued the problem of finding suitable materials for teaching 'scientific library management,' from local experiences such as social and psychological factors. The problem may be there, but the possibilities of indigenising the library management curriculum offers great scope for optimism as projects work for students, consultancy projects and other research, and increasing documentation in a field tend to illustrate.

Book Selection

The emphasis on evaluation of books in areas such as: children literature, recreation reading and development literature, vary significantly from those of other countries. The objective is to enable the librarian to promote imaginative experience in children through indigenous literature, which reflect the course of events, folklore and culture in the children's environment. Furthermore, the librarian could help to develop recreational reading habits in individuals through a knowledge of indigenous novel literature. Thus, popular readership would depart from a different cultural setting and concentrate on locally generated events in the people's culture and life-styles.

The basic universal principles of 'selection' and general collection development procedures are, however, important features that need to be retained, constantly reviewed and applied in library situations, which present a less radical front for indigenous participation. For instance, in book selection, the training of librarians for university, college, or special library services will tend to emphasise the theoretical precepts than would be the case for public, national or state librarianship where local needs tend to influence the selection process in the promotion of socio-cultural values.

Summary

The concept of 'relevance' has been examined in the context of socio-economic phenomena, in particular, Nigeria's education system, and specifically, in relation to curricula provision in professional library and information studies. The educational and developmental factors of relevance, which have been examined, show an unrelenting trend towards indigenisation in the cases cited. The search for relevance thus implies re-orientation of national values within the overall concept of 'professionalism' not to detract from the quality and standards of professional service but to add, for its enrichment, local tradition and culture. In addition to being a process of individuation, modern education is a process of universalisation and professionalism, as it applies to all fields of activity, and should take account of knowledge from existing local tradition and values.

References

1. Asheim, L. E., *Librarianship in the Developing Countries,* Urbana, Chicago: University of Illinois Press, 1966: 49.

2. Whitting, C. E., ' The unpublished indigenous Arabic literature of Northern Nigeria', *Journal of the Royal Asitic Society of Great Britain and Ireland,* Parts I and II, April 1943: 20-26.

3. Wilks, I., 'The Transmission of Islamic Learning in the Western Sudan' in: Goody, J., *Literacy in Traditional Societies,* London: Cambridge University Press, 1968: 162-97.

4. Benge, R. C., 'Library Studies and Indigenisation', *Library Scientist,* Zaria, Nigeria, 5 March 1978: 66.

5. *Ibid.*

6. Mazrui, A. A., *Political Values and the Educated Class in Africa,* London: Heinemann, 1978: 187-231.

7. Taylor, W. H., 'Nigeria's Search for Curriculum Relevance,' *Compare,* 11(1), 1981: 99.

8. Fafunwa, A. B., *History of Education in Nigeria,* London: George, Allen & Unwin, 1974: 48.

9. Fafunwa, A. B., 'History of Education' ... *op. cit.:* 194.

10. *Ibid.:* 194.

11. Amoda, M., ed., 'FESTAC Colloquium and Black World Development: Working Group I, Report" (Part 3), *Nigeria Magazine,* Lagos: 1978: 193.

    a) Facts used here are gathered in fragmented form from two major publications of the Federal Government of Nigeria (12b and 13):

    b) Nigeria Federal Government. The 1977 White Paper: *National Policy on Education,* Lagos: Federal Ministry of Education, 1977.

12. The Implementation Committee's *Blueprint,* Lagos: Federal Ministry of Information, 1979.

13. Benge, R.C., *Cultural Crisis and Libraries in the Third World,* London: Clivee Bingley, 1979:213.

14. Taylor, W. H., *Nigeria's Search... op. cit.:* 102.

15. John, M., 'Libraries in Oral-traditional Societies,' *International Library Review,* 11(3), 1979: 329.

16. FESTAC - Festival of Arts and Culture (of Black and African World), For Colloquium, c.f. Amoda, M. ed. ... *op. cit.*

17. Amoda, M. ed., FESTAC Colloquium ... *op. cit.*: 194.

18. Nafzinger, E.W., *African Capitalism: A Case Study in Nigerian Entrepreneurship*, Stanford, California: Hoover Institution Press, 1977: 3-6.

19. Akeredolu-Ale, E.O., 'Private Foreign Investment and the Underdevelopment of Indigenous Entrepreneurship in Nigeria', in: Williams, G. ed. *Nigeria: Economy and Society*, London: Rex Collings, 1976: 106-112.

20. Shepherd, G. W. (Jnr.), *The Politics of African Nationalism: Challenge to American Policy*, New York: F. A. Praegar, 1962: 54.

21. Schatz, S. P., *Nigerian Capitalism*, Berkeley, California: University of California Press, 1977: 56.

22. See, for example: Ogunsheye, A., 'The Experience of the Universities in Indigenisation' in: Udo-Aka, U., Alile, H., and Kayode, M. eds., *Management Development in Nigeria: The Challenge of Indigenisation*, Ibadan: O.U.P., 1977: 91.

23. Balabkins, N., *Indigenisation and Economic Development: The Nigerian Experience*, Greenwich, Connecticut/London: Jai Press Inc. 1982: 242.

24. *Ibid.*: 247

25. Koehl, R., 'The Uses of the University: Past and Present in Nigerian Educational Culture, Part I,' *Comparative Educational Review*, 15(2), 1971: 114-131.

26. Koehl, R., 'The Uses of the University: Past and Present in Nigerian Educational Culture, Part II,' *Comparative Education Review*, 15(3), 1971: 367-377.

27. Kay, S. and B. Nystrom, 'Education and Colonialism in Africa,' *Comparative Education Review*, 15(2), 1971: 240-260.

28. Mazrul, A. A., 'The African University as a Multinational Corporation: Problems of Penetration and Dependency,' in: Altbach, P. G. and G. P. Kelly, *Education and Colonialism*, New York: Longman, 1978, 331-363.

29. *Ibid.*: 334.

30. *Ibid.*: 336

    See the work of:

31. Hiskett, M., 'Material relating to the state of learning among the Fulani before their Jihad' School of Oriental and African Studies, *Bulletin*, London, XIX, 1957: 550-578.

See also:

32. Hiskett, M., 'The song of Bagada, a Hausa Kinglist and homily in verse', School of Oriental and African Studies, *Bulletin,* London, 27(30, 1964: 540-567; *Bulletin,* 28(1, 1965: 122-136.

33. Quoted in: Roth, G. and C. Wittich, eds., *Economy and Society, Vol. 3.* New York: 1968: 1095.

34. Ajayi, J. F. A. and B. O. Oloruntimehin, Quoted in: Flint, J. E., ed., *Cambridge History of Africa, Vol. 5.* London: Cambridge University press, 1976: 2-00-221; (chapter 6).

35. Fafunwa, A. B., *History of Education in Nigeria ... op. cit.:* 20-49.

36. *Ibid.:* 16

37. Taiwo, C. O., *The Nigerian Education System: Past, Present, and Future,* Ikeja: Thomas Nelson, 1980: 179.

38. Fadipe, N. A., *The Sociology of the Yoruba,* Ibadan: Ibadan University Press, 1970: 311.

39. Taiwo, C. O., *The Nigerian Education System ... op. cit.:* 179

40. *Ibid.:* 181.

41. Nigeria, Federal Government, *National Policy on Education,* Lagos: Government Printer, 1977: 165.

The importance of the mother tongue is analysed in detail in a very useful work in this respect:

42. Taiwo, C. O., *The Mother Tongue as a Means of Promoting Equal Access to Education in Nigeria,* Paris: UNESCO, 1972: 423. (Ed/WA/307).

43. Clarke, P. B. 'Islam, Education and the Developmental Process in Nigeria,' *Comparative Education,* 1292), 1978: 133-141 (p.140 *et seq.*)

44. Nigeria. Federal Government, *National Policy on Education, ... op. cit.;* 19

45. Nndlis Programme Letter: from A. Olu. Olafioye to O. O. Lawal, National Library of Nigeria (Lagos), 3rd August, 1981: NL 990/T1/2, The position remains the same at present.

46. Obasi, J., 'Open University,' *West Africa,* March 1, 1982: 587-590.

47. Lawal, O. O., 'Open to Whom?' *West Africa,* (3372), March 22, 1982: 780-790

48. Koehl, R., 'The Uses of University ... Part I,' *op. cit.;* 115.

49. Yesufu, T. M., ed., *Creating the African University: Emerging Issues in the 1970s,* Ibadan: O.U.P., 76.

50. Quoted in; Agbowuro, J., *Nigerianisation and the Nigerian Universities, ... op. cit.:* 250.

51. *Ibid.:* 250.

52. Fafunwa, A.B., *A History of Nigerian Higher Education,* Lagos; Macmillan, 1971; 271.

53. Mazrui, A. A., 'The African University as a Multinational Corporation: Problems of Penetration and Dependency,' in: Altbach, P. G. ... *op. cit.*: 342.

54. Historical details of course development contained in: Ajayi, J. F. A. and T. N. Tamuno, eds, *The University of Ibadan, 1948-1973: A History of the First Twenty-five Years,* Ibadan: Ibadan University Press, 1973.

55. Fafunwa, A. B., *A History of Nigerian Higher Education... op. cit.:* 271

56. Ashby, E., *Universities: British, Indian and African,* Cambridge, Massachusetts: Harvard University press, 1966: 246-247.

57. LaBelle, T. J. and R. E. Verhine, 'Non-formal Education and Occupational Stratification: Implications for Latin America,' *Harvard Educational Review,* 56, 1975: 191-210.

58. Inkeles, A. and D. B. Holsinger, eds., *Education and Individual Modernity in Developing Countries,* Leiden, The Netherlands: Brill, 1974.

59. Klineberg, S. L., 'Parents, Schools and Modernity' in: Inkeles, A. and D. B. Holsinger, eds., *Education and Individual, ... op. cit.:* 69.

60. Sack, R., 'The Impact of Education on Individual Modernity in Tunisia,' in: Inkeles, A. and D. B. Holsinger, eds. ... *op.cit.*: 88.

61. Walters, P. B., 'Educational Change and National Economic Development,' *Harvard Educational Review,* 51(1), 1981: 97.

62. Lerner, D., 'Social Aspects of Modernisation,' in: Sills, D.L., ed. *International Encyclopaedia of the Social Sciences, v.10,* New York: 1968: 387.

63. Sanda, A. O., 'Social and Economic Development in Nigeria: Problems and Solutions,' Lecture Delivered at the National Youth Service Corps (NYSC) Orientation Courses, Ibadan, Nigeria, August 1980: 3(mimeo).

64. Sanda, A. O., 'Ethnocentrism and Theories of Modernisation,' *Nigerian Journal of Sociology and Anthropology*, 2(1), 1975: 65-74.

65. Ogunsheye, F. A., "Education and Training for Library and Information Services to Rural Communities,' in: Aboyade, B. O. ed. *Problems of Identifying Training Needs for Library and Information Services in a Predominantly Non-Literate Society — with Particular References to Agricultural, and Rural Development.* The Hague: FID, 1981: 93.

66. Havard-Williams, P., 'Oration in Honour of Lord Weinstock, on the conferment of al honorary degree', in: Loughborough University of Technology Gazette (65), September 1981: 7.

67. Dean, J., 'Library Education and Curriculum Problems in the Developing Countries', in: PARR, E. A. and E. J. Wainwright, eds., *Curriculum Design in Librarianship: An International Approach*, Perth, W.A.I.T. Aid inc., 1974: 91.

68. Galbraith, J. K., *The Age of Uncertainty*, London: BBC/Andre Deutsch, 1977: 111.

69. *Ibid.:* 112.

70. Holsworth, H., 'University and Special Libraries and Higher Education in Africa,' *UNESCO Bulletin for Libraries*, 15, 1961: 254.

71. Ekpe, F. C., 'The Colonial Situation and Library Development Nigeria,' *International Library Review*, 11(1), 1979: 5-18 (p.7 *et. seq.*)

72. Aradeon, S. E., 'Towards More Relevant Libraries,' *Nigerian Libraries*, 10(1), 1974: 51-56.

73. Anyim, J. C., 'Public Libraries as Cultural Centres,' *Nigerian Libraries*, 8(1), 1972: 15-19.

74. Wynter, J. H., 'Some Problems in Nigerian Library Development Since 1960,' *International Library Review*, 11(1), 1979: 19-44.

75. Aina, L. O., 'Factors Affecting Development of Librarianship in Nigeria,' *International Library Review*, 11(1), 1979: 57-67.

76. Ogunsheye, F. A., 'The Future of Library Education in Africa,' *Libri*, 26(4), 1976: 268-280.

77. *Ibid.:* 270.

78. A full discussion on the subject is contained in: Asheim, L., 'New Trends in the Curriculum of Library Schools,' in: Goldhor, H., ed., *Education for Librarianship: The Design of the Curriculum of Library Schools*, Urbana, Illinois: University of Illinois, Graduate School of Library Science, 1971:75.

79. Boaz, M., 'Library Education: Relevance to the Future,' *American Libraries,* 1(10), 1970: 937-938.

80. Marco, G. A., 'A Rationale for International Library Education,' *International Library Review,* 9, 1977: 355-362.

81. Ogunsheye, F. A., *The Future of Library Education... op. cit.*

82. Asheim, L., *New Trends in the Curriculum of Library Schools ... op. cit.:* 76

83. Boaz, M., *Library Education... op. cit.:* 937

84. Glazer, N., 'The Schools of the Minor Professions,' *Minerva,* New York: 12, 1974: 346-364.

85. *Ibid,* 357.

86. Mayhew, L. B., *Changing Practices in Education for the Professions,* Atlanta: Southern Regional Educational Board, 1971: 10.

87. Jencks, C. and D. Riesman, *The Academic Revolution,* Garden City, New York: Doubleday, 1968: 251.

88. Shera, J. H., *The Foundations of Education for Librarianship,* New York: Wiley-Becker and Hayes, 1972: 295.

89. Shera, J. H., 'Plus ca change,' *Library Journal,* 95, 1970: 979-986.

90. Asheim, L., 'Librarians as Professionals,' *Library Trends,* 27(3), 1979: 225-257.

91. Ogburn, W. F., 'Recent Social Trends: Their Implications for Libraries,' *Library Trends* (University of Chicago Press), 1937: 1 and 12.

92. Martin, L. A., 'The American Public Library as a Social Institutions,' *Library Quarterly,* 7, 1937: 549.

93. *c.f.* Hoyle, N., 'Oral History,' *Library Trends,* 21(1), 1972: 60-82.

94. Wheeler, J. L., *Process and Problems in Education for Librarianship,* New York: Carnegie Corporation of New York, 1946: 9.

95. Mohammed, A. and M. Afolabi, 'Education for Librarianship in Nigeria', *Nigerian Libraries,* 15 (1 and 2), 1979: 40.

96. Aboyade, B. O., 'Education for Librarianship,' *Nigerian Libraries.* 15 (1 and 2), 1979:30.

97. Ogunsheye, F. A., *Trends in Library Education: The Criteria for Evaluation of Programmes,* Ibadan: Department of Library Studies, University of Ibadan, 1978: 20-21 (Mimeo).

98. Mohammed, A. and J. Otim, 'The Problem of Relevance to Local Conditions

in Professional Education Programmes in Africa: The Case of Librarianship,' Zaria: Ahmadu Bello University, 1978: 2 (mimeo).

99. Benge, R. C., *'Cultural Crisis and Libraries in the Third World,'* London: Clive Bingley, 1979: 213.

100. Ogunsheye, F. A., *Trends in Library Education... op. cit.:* 2

101. Benge, R. G., 'Library Studies and Indigenisation,' *Library Scientist*, 5, 1978: 66.

102. Tjoumas, R. and R. Hauptman, 'Education for Librarianship in the Developing Countries: A Radical Departure,' *Libri*, 32(2), 1982: 91-108.

103. *Ibid.:* 99.

104. Obi, D. S., 'The Curriculum Needs of the Sub-Saharan African Library School' (PhD Dissertation), Graduate School of Library and Information Science, University of Pittsburgh, 1974: 211.

105. Idupom — 'Information Dissemination to, and its Utilization' by, Policy Makers in Nigeria. (Project leader) Consultant: Dr. W. O. Aiyepeku, Department of Library Studies, University of Ibadan, 1980.

106. *Ibid.:* 3-4

107. *Ibid.:* 5

108. Aboyade, B. O., 'Communication and Transfer of Information in Non-literate Societies,' in: *Problems of Identifying Training Needs for Library and Information Services in a Predominantly Non-literate Society... op. cit.:* 13-29.

109. *Ibid.:* 19

110. Benge, R. C., *Cultural Crisis and Libraries... op. cit.:* 213-214.

111. *Ibid.*

112. Nzotta, B. C., 'Education for Library Management in African Schools,' *Journal of Librarianship*, 9, 1777: 130-143.

113. Benge, R. C., 'Teaching the Theories of Management in an African Library School,' *Information and Library Manager*, 1(2), 1981: 47-49.

6

Philosophy of Education for Librarianship

Of all professions, that of the Librarian is probably the most derivative and synthetic, is the most dependent upon the more formal disciplines for the derivation of its own theoretical structure and its corpus of practice. In the past, Librarians have been disposed to view this characteristic as a fundamental weakness, and it has therefore generated a considerable feeling of professional inferiority. Yet this very quality has given Librarianship a uniquely strategic position of leadership in the integration of human knowledge, and it could make of Librarianship a uniquely strategic position of leadership in the integration of human knowledge, and it could make of librarianship a great unifying force, not only in the world of scholarship, but also throughout all human life.

— Jesse H. Shera (1972)[1]

Introduction

In William Maidment's *The Professions: Librarianship,* the philosophy of librarianship was viewed and presented wholly from public libraries' perspective thereby indicating assumed aims and attitudes of librarians to the work they do.[2] This basis for presenting librarians' work and their attitudes to the outside observer seems to be common in the literature, with other professions such as teaching, law, medicine, and the clergy being used by writers to draw comparison with librarianship. For example, Broadfield,[3] Butler,[4] Emery,[5] and Grimshaw,[6] among others, have distinctly professed the cultural function of the library mainly from the public service viewpoint perhaps to the obvious neglect of the educational function of the library and its probity for important access to information.

Butler, for instance, formulated statements like: the cultural motivation of librarianship is the promotion of wisdom in the individual and the community.[7]

Though the use of 'wisdom' is lacking in clarity it can only imply, based on the cultural factor, an understanding of the society in which an individual lives. The library is therefore presented clearly as a public warehouse of knowledge, which is not strictly subject-based, i.e. in terms of actual contribution to knowledge, but merely as a general-purpose facility for the seeking of leisure. This is perhaps understandable in mid 20th century librarianship [but attitudes of this kind have persisted). Emery, in his contribution adds that:

> ... a philosophy of librarianship could critically examine beliefs.... The basis upon which libraries exist, that is conceptions of their nature in relation to society in general; and the relationship of librarianship to other branches of knowledge (my emphasis).[8]

The latter part of the quotation as emphasised above implies specialisation. The bases of modern librarianship is inextricably linked with changes in society's need for information and the means of making such information available for the enhancement of knowledge.[9-11] Thus it is possible to derive an assumption that **libraries have a generic relationship with the world of learning.** As man acquires more and more knowledge about the world around him, he inevitably preserves it in documents, which have to be organised, stored, and retrieved in order to generate learning. This element of the overall philosophy of librarianship paves the way for a proper insight into the philosophy of education for librarianship.

However, the 'public service' image of the library profession is not being totally dispensed with here as its central issue can be used to show the fundamental difference in the present writer's approach to the subject. Writers like Grimshaw submit that:

> Librarianship is cleaning up after toddlers and/or dogs, the latter who have wandered in to inspect the library without the benefit of an owner ...

> Librarianship is improving one's vocabulary ... not from the less refined readers or the children from 'poor' homes but from literature-thirsting populace of the area ...

> Librarianship is being interrupted at least a dozen times whilst trying to 'do' the monthly statistics.[12]

Grimshaw's observation is applicable only to small or branch libraries but the parallel effect is the same because in most cases at present, the library staff are more to the intellectual content of librarianship than it is portrayed in the above quotations. The question arises as to how this is reflected in the planning and implementation of library education programmes, i.e., the central issue of the field's classification in the academic cadre; the function of education in the library profession; the knowledge-base of the discipline; its resource support unit; and its universality (home or abroad). These elements need to be linked from a philosophical viewpoint in order to demonstrate that the rationale for library education need not be measured tacitly by functions performed in the field **but** by the educational preparedness of the librarian and the ability to relate this to his task variables. To this end, a consideration of the philosophy of education for librarianship is a vital adjunct to the study of library professionalism.

Some Definitions

In this work wherever the term 'librarianship' is used, it is meant to be read in its broadest sense, i.e. as including the relevant concepts of information 'science' and documentation in general; wherever the term 'libraries' is used, the current models of media centres, learning or educational resource centres, information, documentation, and referral centres are also assumed. The specification of both terms as emphasised here is necessary in order to avoid the cumbersome process of repeating the entire gamut of variations and expansions often incurred in the professional literature.

Equally it is important to establish a working definition of 'philosophy' as it will relate to education for librarianship. The present writer submits that no philosophical issue solitarily exists in a vacuum. Usually such issue is connected to the primary source of the general concept of philosophy and within the purview of the appropriate subject field being considered.

Thus, when viewed on the basis of all known disciplines 'philosophy' is the pursuit of wisdom and knowledge, i.e. 'the knowledge of the causes and laws of all things' (OED). It is an art, which purposefully sets out the principles underlying any department of knowledge; philosophy therefore provides the basis for theoretical derivation from principles and practice of the discipline.

The central question of whether libraries (and librarianship) has ultimate philosophy of its own is a subject debate in the professional literature but this is not the main concern here. It is possible and in fact enriching for a philosophy of librarianship to be diversified in its perspectives, and these can be made manifest through the formulation of hypotheses such as: 'libraries help promote individual attainment though through adult education,' libraries profess the aims of civilisation,' libraries promote culture,' and that 'libraries as learning forum, are quite essential to higher education and research' — the list of such hypotheses may be unlimited. For instance, other conceptions evolve from formulating library's relationship with business, politics, and society as a whole, other than purely in terms of educational function.

Against this background, one may assume the existence of varying philosophy in librarianship and a model (for example, of library education) or models (for example, of the custodian, humanitarian, promoter, documentalist roles of the library) may be predicted to describe the appropriate philosophy in a distinct manner. In the context of library education, therefore, philosophy implies a system of theories on the nature of the principles and practice of education for librarianship as experienced both by staff and students of library schools.

The definition as provided here portrays the socialisation that takes place in the community of staff and students in schools of librarianship in terms of available choice of course and place of study; the indispensable tradition that the schools and the professors pass on values; the norms and objectives which lead student librarians to identify with the profession; and the library schools' approach to curriculum development as demonstrated by the content — 'academic' (i.e. general education) and 'professional' (i.e. core and specialized options' study of librarianship). These elements are indicative of the broad perspective of philosophy of library education.

Objective and Scope of Study

The work in this section is designed not to emphasise normative analysis of philosophy of librarianship, but to identify the prevailing philosophy in the education system of the library profession, with emphasis on Nigeria wherever practicable.

The scope is confined to critical examination of the factors customarily dismissed as problems but nevertheless requiring urgent clarification. Such factors include:

(a) Clarification on the faculty status, hence classification, of librarianship in the university system, i.e. in the system of the sciences, art, or humanities;

(b) A clarification of 'knowledge-base' theory and how librarianship features as in other disciplines;

(c) The 'universality' of library education and its dysfunction in terms of location of study, i.e 'home' or 'abroad';

(d) The importance and functioning of resource support units or centres in the library schools visited.

The nature of librarianship practice and the intellectual contents of its formal courses confer on the library schools unlimited monopoly in the educational preparation and certification of competence both of the generalist and specialist staff with subject qualification to enable them to work in libraries. In this respect, a framework is provided in this section to take account of the processes of socialisation which directly or indirectly influence the professionalisation of education for librarianship within the overall concept of library professionalism.

The 'Classification' Factor

In general, library schools are of the same kind everywhere but due to different emphasis in philosophy the schools' programmes are in most cases variously presented in form and content. Even where the title of courses are similarly styled, the content always seems to differ in emphasis. This can hardly be surprising as the problem of attaching the library school to a specific faculty in the system of the sciences, arts, or humanities is rather fragmented worldwide. For instance, existing library schools are Departments in their own rights both within the university system and other higher education establishments such as colleges and polytechnics. But the crucial point is that they are all linked differently with Faculty or School: Social Sciences; Education; Education and Humanities; Arts; and there are varying degree of nomenclatures in the field of librarianship such as, 'Bachelor of Library Science' (or studies); 'Bachelor of Arts in Librarianship'; 'Bachelor of Arts in Library Science'; 'Bachelor of Science' (Library Studies); and complex array of similar structure in master and doctoral programmes. The structure of courses indicates that through studies of a mainly vocational degree, students receive a liberal education, which prepares them not only for librarianship but other careers as well. Thus the Batesonian [13] view that librarianship is not a degree-worthy discipline is both curious and inaccurate.

'Inaccurate' though it may seem, but elements of Batesonian conservatism still persists today. For instance, according to Benge:

> At a deeper level and without reference to particular countries it has to be recognised that there is something inherent in library and information work which renders it less urgent or vital than the activities of doctors or lawyers, or even priests. ... Like teachers, librarians are embedded in the foundations of the cultural process; their tragedy is that they ought to be most noticeable when they are not there, but in many countries this does not happen.[14]

This kind of situation, as described in Benge's claims calls for a good deal of insight into the precise nature of the educational programmes designed for librarians, and in addition, the task performance of librarians need to be related also to their intellectual level of preparedness to handle complex information materials. It is only in this way that the professional rating of the librarian can at present be determined, bearing in mind the multifarious nature of his clients.

Meanwhile, in referring to library education in Nigeria in terms of curriculum development, Benge suggests further that the type of programme to be introduced in Nigerian new library schools — apart from Ibadan and Zaria — 'will be largely determined by factors which are not strictly academic and this is how it should be.'[15] Again, Benge's prescription remains unclear and the conclusions that can be drawn from the evaluation conducted in this present work, based on the programmes of the new school as well as the old ones certainly suggest to the contrary of Benge's expectation. This begs the vexed question of the intellectual content of librarianship and its 'right' kind of knowledge 'classification' in the academic context.

Writing historically on the concept of 'modern librarianship', White seems to be in no doubt as to what kind of education is required:

> Limits were being reached beyond which the mind could not keep up with or fully utilize the learning that was accumulating without relying upon the speciality which the library profession was to rise to handle .... It was up to somebody to assemble, organise, and make available this expanding record of the mind. It could no longer be done by private individuals who

took on the responsibility as a side job while doing other things. To develop this emerging speciality in scale with the times, library service would have to be organised and supported along the lines of other public responsibilities like police protection, formal schooling, and public health. High standard of service would be required for all classes of people, of all ages, and steady financing in terms of programme needs would be called for.[16]

From the above quotation, one can deduce that librarianship is perceived as a public utility for which no great educational preparation is required for the professional staff. However, in 1964, when White's statement was made, librarianship was experiencing accelerated changes in its education system. Many institutions began to offer degree courses in librarianship; the demand on the profession was also changing significantly with technological innovations and rapid expansion in the higher education system as a whole. There were also considerable advances in major fields of activity, such as in business industry. This resulted in a more sophisticated and information-conscious society eager to take advantage of library services. Furthermore, there has been an unprecedented increase in publishing all over the world, coupled with development in the field of information technology, increase in literacy, and the resultant growth in the complexity of documentation and information needs. Therefore, the tradition of librarianship no longer seems to reside in 'public utility' sense but can also be observed to encompass other vital elements of communication at all stages and levels of activity.

The organisation of the library profession itself has made significant progress in the past two decades. It has grown in influence and stature and successfully negotiated public policy and maintained standardisation in such areas as training and continuing education. As learning advance and became increasingly specialised, this was reflected in the professional associations and in their journal output. Though this specialised journal were designed to meet the need of their immediate clientele, the wider dissemination of such publication brought the innovation and discoveries of the fields to the scholars of another, and thus made possible the development of social cohesion among groups, the members of which, might otherwise have found communication difficult.

In the light of professional developments described above, the classification of librarianship requires to be clarified in the academic system. This will enhance better understanding of the function of professional education and in addition illuminate the knowledge-base criterion of library professionalism.

Science , Art or Technique

The problem of classifying librarianship in a particular branch of learning can be rather complicated due to the interdisciplinary nature of the profession. Regardless of this fact, public recognition and hence the status of the profession seem to reflect the uncertainty as to whether librarianship is an art (skills), science, or technique (craft).

As the opening quotation at the beginning of this work shows, the knowledge required of the librarian is derivative and synthetic, based upon the more formal disciplines drawn from academic subjects such as: history, psychology, logic, mathematics, sociology and education. The requirements for such knowledge in library and information work are fundamental to the process of selection of content in librarianship curriculum. The curriculum therefore contains both the academic and professional elements integrated for the purpose of preparing the student for a career, having attained a liberal education background in librarianship.

As an Art

As an **art**, librarianship, like any other profession, is a composite of theory and practice, i.e. knowledge and skills, and the one without the other is barren and sterile. Shera [17] argues that if librarians have anything of importance to contribute to the culture of their society it must be transmitted by those special skills that they have developed through centuries of practice. Such interaction of 'special skills' often result when transmitted to other disciplines via scholastics exchange. In the province of art all skill relates to a system of some kind, for example, to a coherent set of quantities, properties, and relationships, which have been, or may be abstracted from the totality of the environment.

The successful exercise of any skill depends upon the ability to create an abstract system from the complexities that comprise the real world in which the practitioner is operating. By implication, the skill of the librarian will depend upon his ability to abstract a system from the intellectual, emotional, social, and physical world around him, i.e. the world he 'serves', be it that of the housebound or other outreach services, the college student, the business man or industry experts, of the general public, or of the scholar in all kinds of institutions and research centres.

Communication of information thus becomes essential to the librarian's system where 'information' is to be understood as written or unwritten records of human minds which are made manifest through a maze of intellectual activity. An example of skill that can be acquired by the librarian is in recording transcripts, storing and dissemination of the intellectual content of oral history. This form of intricate pattern of communications reflects the abstraction of librarianship and the librarian can be sought.

As a Science

As a **science**, the general understanding of librarianship by those who profess the science terminology seems baffling. One is tempted to enquire what the science is in library science. The usage of the term is shrouded in a quagmire of mystery. Librarianship is no exception to the mysteries of terminology. Line[18] estimates that the mystique of librarianship is possibly stronger than its mystery. He submits that:

> All professions gather around themselves a mystique. One way of persuading the world that one's job is a profession is to require an initiation ceremony, often of considerable length and difficulty. And to surround the job with an impenetrable air of mystery. Manifestations of mystique are not hard to find. Examination papers in librarianship would quickly frighten off any non-librarian, if only by the terminology used. Professional conferences where acronyms are commonly bandied about at a fearful rate, are another manifestation. One of the most pervasive mystifications is the misuse of 'information science', a perfectly good term for the theory and study of information, in the sense of 'practical information work in industry...[19]

Probable clue to the mystery of science in library studies are there in the above quotation but these are inconclusive. Khan however addresses the problem differently by stating:

> In the last quarter of the nineteenth century there was a trend to call any human activity where some literature had accumulated a 'science' particularly in non-English speaking countries like Germany, France, and USSR. This was hardly relevant in the English-speaking world where science was considered (as) comprising observations made by performing experiments, formulating hypotheses and theories and employing the tools of mathematics and formal logic. The term 'science' however enjoyed some prestige. 'Library Economy' was therefore changed to 'library science' without much of opposition from the academicians. This change did not, however, mean that scientific methods had been applied to the study of libraries. It merely enhanced the prestige of the profession to bring it at par with medical and engineering professions.[20]

It would seem practical to suggest from the foregoing considerations, that the term science has been introduced into librarianship mainly to enhance the status of the qualifications, which the term describes.

Librarianship within the system of the sciences has attracted the attention of many experts in the field in various countries. Butler suggests that the intellectual content of librarianship consists of the following:
(a) It deals with things (materials) and principles that must be scientifically handled;
(b) With processes and apparatus that require special understanding and skills for their operation;

(c)   With cultural motivations that can be apprehended only humanistically.[21]

Of particular relevance to this analysis is the 'scientific' handling of library matters. If by implication this includes the processing of information and its retrieval using modern technology, then there is a *de facto* case for that element of 'science' in librarianship. One may augment this factor with the tasks of compiling bibliography, indexing and abstracting of science materials. Cubarian,[22] in representing the views of Soviet experts in a report, suggests that librarianship is inter-related with other sciences. He contends that the strengthening and broadening of the inter-relationship of librarianship with other sciences, and their possible integration, has three aims[23] (these are discussed in *seriatim*):

(i)   The definition of the problems of library research against the broad background of the achievements, conclusions, and theoretical propositions of other sciences.

This view as presented in (i) above is supported mainly by Soviet experience where it was found that the successes of sociology (for example) have enabled librarians to study readers from a special point of view, and to conduct library research in conjunction with problems such as the socio-demographic composition of society, the use of leisure, and the people's use of mass communication media. It was further suggested that the influence of science reflected on the problem of library and bibliographical information retrieval systems, which depends upon modern technology. This trend was set as a result of developments in electric computer science. Further involvement of the sciences with library processes emerged from the scientific elaboration of the distribution of library networks, which have become possible mainly as a result of its integration with the achievements of various social structure of the population and urbanisation.

(ii)   The use of research methods of various sciences to raise the level of library theory.

The wide use of the research methods of other sciences has generally raised theoretical standards in librarianship and this factor had decidedly influenced library research by overcoming the speculative character of some of its conclusions and propositions. Methods identified include the use of questionnaires, interviewing, 'social experiment', and expert evaluation.

(iii)   The use of factual material, conclusions, and propositions obtained from librarianship for the enrichment of other sciences.

Sociological applications of reading habits, readers' interests, and the spiritual life of the community – all derived from conclusions of library research.

An overview of Cubarian's paper seems to place librarianship firmly in the system of the social sciences, although there are elements from the nurture of librarianship, which suggest that an inter-relationship exists with the science of communication, i.e. information technology. This is pertinent at a time when the tradition of library practice are being urgently re-examined in the light of growth in modern technology and its impact on library and information work. The librarian, archivist, and information officer, will need to be educationally equipped to accept this challenge and responsibility. They need also to be prepared to exploit the materials and resources of a modern library and resource centre both in terms of scientific and social utility.

As a Technique

As a Technique (Craft); the portrayal of librarianship as a craft fits Grimshaw's description as quoted earlier.

Librarians working in rural or suburban libraries are likely to be less challenged with urgent tasks and usually under the circumstances there is a fusion of professional and non-professional duties as the 'professional' may very well be an administrator, cleaner, technician, and readers' adviser, in conjunction with doing his professional tasks. In most cases where this situation arises, collection development is usually centralised in the system i.e. from the parent library, and all that the branch librarian and his assistants do is to fulfil the clerical and other routines according to their own schedule. The activities carried out in this kind of libraries can be learned effectively on the job without the undue necessity of a formal education and training.

Nevertheless, the library clientele revere their 'librarian' and they are only too grateful to him for any assistance he may render in the course of their enquiries.

In advanced countries of Europe and North America for instance, it is not unusual to find graduate employees in libraries of the type described above. The present writer's recent experience on a visit to France and West Germany has influenced the viewpoint expressed here. In Britain too, some graduates for various reasons such as unemployment, matrimonial and material factors, and regional mobility, choose to work in the quiet of the suburban library. However, as West African experience shows, many library workers, especially in the French-speaking regions, are termed as 'librarians' regardless of the level or quality of qualification status of the staff.[24] This is still a dilemma for the library profession, which is struggling at present to define the parameters of professional and non-professional duties in libraries.

The professional literature is indicative of the mistrust felt by some writers[25,26,27] as to whether librarianship is not indeed a 'technique'. According to Butler:

> ... the librarian's self-identification has been retarded by another error. Persuaded of his own professional status, he has always been inclined to imitate the outward forms of the other professions before attaining the corresponding internal development.[28]

The problem, as Butler has stated, arose from a consideration of the inception of education for librarianship in North America. The main purpose of the 'founding fathers' was to provide vocational training. However, they were also influenced by the idea that librarianship should have its professional schools because the other professions have theirs. Library education was therefore conceived of as primarily a training in the 'niceties' of cataloguing and classification with the attendant result that a core curriculum became crystallised which even by 1950s standard, resists dissolution and makes educational reforms more difficult than they should be. In this context, librarians have developed a simplistic view of the demands of their job and therefore the kind of training required. Some writers such as Messenger[29] and Jesson[30] criticised the library schools for being too theoretical and less inclined to teach the rudiments of practice, factors which they claim are in the best interests of the student who is more than likely to face such problems in his job.

Jesson for instance, observes that:

> For far too long, we have taught and examined in 'education' and allowed 'training' to be picked up on the job.... Education is thought of as 'professional', training as mechanical; the two as mutually exclusive.[31]

Clearly an assessment of this nature is in disregard of the primary function of the library schools, i.e., to educate students who are aspiring to become full-fledged professionals. The library schools are also aware of their responsibility concerning training and this is reflected in the curriculum as indicated in the section on evaluation.

Having considered the problem of classification a positive determination of 'librarianship' and 'library science' in the realm of academics remains pertinent.

Dean, in his seminal work 'Planning Library Education Programmes,' examined the nature and objectives of librarianship and derived a working definition of the discipline as:

> The **professional** discipline concerned with the accumulation, storage and transfer of recorded knowledge.[32]

From this definition Dean views the goal of library education as being, to produce a person of general competence in theories and techniques associated with library studies as good educational background, a willingness to serve his community and the courage to defend his professional convictions with tenacity.

In pursuance of this goal the positive contribution of the library schools to professional development in terms of manpower and innovation of services, cannot be underestimated. However, a comprehensive definition of the processes of librarianship is as stated in IFLA's 1976 *Standards for Library Schools* in which 'librarianship' is defined as:

> The profession that is concerned with the systematic organisation of

knowledge in all its various formats and its dissemination for the purpose of preserving the society's cultural heritage, promoting scholarship and the generation of new knowledge. The practitioners employ the skills and processes of library science, documentation and information science to make graphic records available to meet the specific needs.[34]

The term 'library science' evolves from this definition as a separate entity of its own. When probed further in the Standards, 'library science' is described as,

The study of the principles and skills of processes and operations for systematic organisation of societies' intellectual heritage in the form of graphic and non-graphic records in libraries. It is also concerned with creating ready access to these records and the maximization of their use by matching clientele and appropriately.[35]

Thus, from these two definitions cited above, librarianship is portrayed as **the profession** and library science as **the study** of the principles and processes of the profession. This is consistent with the latest description of library science as entered in the United Nations Bibliographic Information System (UNBIS) Thesaurus, 1981:

The branch of learning concerned with collecting, storing and distributing written or printed records by means of libraries and of the management of libraries.[36]

The description provides suitable explanation for the 'science' that is in 'library science.' It can also be inferred that whatever title is adopted in course descriptions e.g. B.Lib., B.L. Science, B.L. Studies or whatever, the concept is broadly the same. Traditional librarianship is in transition and its new elements avail the professional, complex skills and specialised knowledge that could only be systematically implanted in the library schools. The horizon of library practice has widened by events to enhance the status of the librarian to that of information professional or manager, while the information scientist will be the core of specialists in practice.

The Function of Professional Education

Professional education has been described variously by different writers in the literature but at least on one cardinal point, there seems to be unanimous agreement — that professional education has three basic functions within the concept of professionalism. These include:

(a) It systematically determines who enters the profession and what qualifications and educational standards they must meet to qualify for professional practice;

(b) It provides formal teaching and learning situation of which the most important purpose is to provide students who seek to qualify with an understanding of the mission and practice of the profession.

(c)   It supplies the profession with qualified people, provides continuing education, defines the objectives of the profession and anticipates its future needs through a comprehensive feedback system of its own activity.

In general, professional education prognosticates trends in professional development through its research channel, although this is by no means the only basis for stimulating developments in the profession.

Churchwell suggests that:

> Professional education for an occupation has always been a subsequent development of the occupation itself. As the knowledge of an occupation accumulate and its techniques became more complex, the methods of education evolved from that of apprenticeship programs, the earliest and simplest form of professional education, to the highly organised professional school. Professional education has become, therefore the most widely used method of transmitting knowledge and techniques of an occupation from the skilled practitioner and theoretician to the unskilled beginner.[37]

Library practice was in existence even before the establishment of the first library school in North America, U.K., and Nigeria. In fact, in the case of Nigeria the profession was already consolidated in function by the time the Ibadan library school opened its doors for the first time in 1960. In this context, it is certainly appropriate to state, as Churchwell has done, that professional education is a subsequent development of an occupation.

It is significant to mention that professional education has, since the beginning of the twentieth century, invariably become associated with higher education. In an attempt to determine its nature within the higher education system McGlothlin considers that:

> Professional education is the most complex and difficult of all forms of higher education. Professional schools cannot be content merely with transmitting knowledge, although knowledge is important to them; they must make sure that the graduates are both knowledgeable and competent to practice.[38]

The practical orientation of most professional courses is attributable to some form of hindrance to its early acceptability into the university system.[39] However, it is characteristic of professional education not to begin at a lower level institution other than that afforded in the higher education system. Therefore ensuring that professional education prepares students 'competently' for practice is an obligation on the part of the institution, though more pressing issues of developing knowledge seem primarily to be the urgent task-in-hand for the schools.

To the independent observer, professional education represents, calling or employment.[40] This implies an all-inclusive interpretation of the phenomenon in that professional education may be differentiated, on the one hand, from vocational education, which relates to those employment not generally recognised as professions, and on the other hand, from general (liberal) education which has no specific practical application in view.

However, the latest trend for professional schools working within university establishments is to orientate their education system (especially at the undergraduate level) towards preparing students to receive a liberal education, through the study of a mainly vocational degree.[41] While most students enter the information field, for example, a degree in archive, library or information studies can serve as a preparation for other careers.[42]

The responsibility of professional education is therefore not only to function, in Conant's phrase, as 'the natural gatekeepers of the profession'[43] but also to prepare students liberally so that they are able to comprehend the world within the terms of their professional education and training.

Progress is visibly being made in many library schools in respect of harmonisation of the curriculum which incorporates teaching of the elements of archive, library, and documentation studies in an integrated fashion. This process of education is not new but it serves to mesh the much-desired theory with practical developments in the field. Saunder's observation in this respect is pertinent:

> The firmer the theoretical framework, the easier it will be to teach library and information science at the level of principles rather than through a detailed description of practice.[44]

But practice in any profession is the *raison d'etre* of its education system. The present trend is for most library schools to offer full-time programme of courses, but the important 'fieldwork' element as a corollary to education, still requires wider definition in relation to theoretical derivations of the principles and practice of the discipline. For instance, it could be necessary to provide training facilities, which will enhance deeper and more specialised knowledge of skills as librarians' need for them becomes apparent. However, the constraint on the library schools especially in the developing countries is as always that of cost.

It is also the function of professional education to provide intellectual leadership in the profession. If this hypothesis sounds like preaching to the converted,' it maybe illuminating to find out why in universal terms the professionals always seem to be at loggerheads with the educators who are responsible for supplying the service with qualified staff. The mandatory requirement of intellectual leadership is for professional schools to preserve and pass on existing knowledge, create new knowledge, and use both existing and new knowledge to define the objectives of the profession as best perceived. Periodically, the information thus generated are in conflict with the tradition and assumed norms in the profession because in most cases **change** is advocated, and sometimes the reform of the profession itself is theorised.

One possible explanation for the communication barrier is that the professionals are not eager to submit themselves and the service to the whims and caprices of intellectual prognosis and this reluctance often results in emotive debate and consequently inevitable rift between the two sides. For instance, Conant in pointing out the antipathy of service professions to change in the United States of America, observes that:

> Most service professions tend to develop static organisational forms and procedures that lend stability and continuity must from time to time give way to new discoveries and techniques that permit the profession to adapt to change. Librarianship benefits from stability and continuity in that the record of human knowledge requires procedures that guarantee against loss and destruction, but the adoption of new techniques of access are needed to balance the values of preservation and order.[45]

Implicit in the above quotation is the emphasis on the function of professional education to provide an intellectual disposition whereby new techniques of access may be explored, yet the tradition of practice could still be preserved within that new order. Swanson argues that intellectual access to information can be made possible through, for example, in-depth analysis of 'indexing, subject-analysis, reference, bibliography, classification and cataloguing.'[46] These are areas which deal with the conceptual realms of gaining intellectual access to information. Furthermore, one may argue that the intellectual aspects of the stated library tasks can be distinguished from the vocational aspects in terms of depth other than their mere application.

However, some practitioners are of the view that the activity as described above seems like forcing intellectualism into librarianship. The library schools, though, have a responsibility to prepare their students for change if libraries as learning institutions are not prepared to innovate their methods for information retrieval and dissemination to clientele. Lancaster[47] has uncompromisingly suggested disastrous consequences for libraries if they continue to resist change. Not that this is something new. In their concern to alert the librarian and information worker to the new technology, the doomsday merchants have predicted the demise of the library and information profession and the information media. It is arguable that whilst the librarian and information worker must recognise the technology and environment of the present decade (1980s) and not cling to the past two or three decades, change is not as rapid as some would have the profession to believe but the position of the library schools is quite understandable as they cannot afford to take chances else in future they will incur the wrath of this same profession for 'not being far-sighted' and lacking in 'intellectual leadership.'

Besides, there is evidence in literature[48,49] to show that libraries have rightly recognised the need to respond to new technology though they may not have been very united or systematic in the nature of their response.[50,51] For example, reference libraries and information units have embraced view data systems like Prestel, and systems which permit them to search both bibliographic and non-bibliographic computerised data bases. Therefore library schools cannot simply ignore these developments.

The library schools in providing professional education which is in consonance with current developments in the field need to take account of the several claims of writers on the future of libraries. Perhaps the point needs to be emphasised that the 'information science' element owes its present status and future possibilities almost entirely to computer and other ancillary electronic innovations. Licklider's concept of 'Symbiont'[52] visualised a little less than two decades ago, Landau's concept of the 'Library-in-a-desk,'[53] and Lancaster's 'paperless information systems,'[54] are all based on advanced computer technologies. According to Taylor, with further technological progress during the next couple of decades, a stage will be reached when the libraries of the traditional types will 'wither away, their historic duties done.'[55] The predictions of the 'prophets' on the future of library services seem possible enough, but perhaps Rowley's observation as quoted below sums up how the problem should presently be perceived:

> For most people, on most occasions when they might seek information or entertainment from text, accessibility of a computerised data base offers nothing to compete with a gentle stroll to the public library or neighbourhood bookshop or newsagent. Despite its limitations, the information available from these sources satisfies most users most of the time.[56]

It will be in the library schools' interest to preserve this balance in their programmes.

Control of Library Education

An important aspect of professional education in all disciplines is its form of control. The education system may be controlled either from within the professional schools or outside the institutions, say for example, through the general professional association working closely with the association of professional schools and educators, or a government or parastatal body set up to regulate the education system. However, with regards to librarianship, most institutions operate within the university system each of the institutions being independent and governed by different regulations. Another dimension is that whilst degrees in librarianship, as obtained for instance in the U.K., (Polytechnics now upgraded to universities), are subject to regulations of the academic board or the Council for National Academic Awards, the certification does not automatically guarantee that the graduate is professionally competent although sandwich courses incorporate practical elements. The accreditation remains the exclusive preserve of the profession, although nowadays the graduate librarian can seek employment without the necessity of being a 'chartered' or 'ordinary' member of the association. Even now the route towards chartered status has been narrowed through the Licentiate system. This form of control has various implications for professional development and the future of library education as a whole.

At present, the control of library education is diversified incorporating elements of pedagogics, manpower (in terms of demand and supply of librarians), and continuing education and training. However, in the literature of librarianship it is not exactly clear where the power base of control of the education system should be lodged. The library schools and educators, the general professional association, and perhaps the education authority, all stake their claims to control professional education.

Burell considers that:

> Professional education is, for the most part, firmly in the hands of the professional associations at the stages of teaching, examination, certification and accreditation. It is theirs since they created it at a time when the very few universities of any real note were institutions for the propagation of a social, rather than a working elite.[57]

Burell's view no doubt relates to the United Kingdom but surely in developing countries such as Nigeria such a statement will be viewed with skepticism, as the library schools in the country owe the library profession a 'political' rather than 'educational' debt. This factor *per se* throws the whole issue of control wide open in circumstances where the general professional association has demonstrated little or no effect on the professional education system. A few examples will suffice: the association (N.L.A) has no certification system of its own nor a curriculum for purposes of teaching and examination; it cannot accredit due to its lack of legal status.

The fact that the Zaria library school was planned and established in 1968 without due consultation with the profession greatly enhances the point made here. Rather, the Federal Government mandated the National Library of Nigeria to initiate a course in HND Library Studies.[58] The courses are designed to be taught and examined not by the profession but by the colleges of technology where such programmes are to be offered. Furthermore, non-viable statistics are presently available concerning the demand and supply of librarians in Nigeria — a factor which really ought to have been spearheaded by the profession.

Thus, it would seem that unless the library profession revitalises itself in this direction the control of library education will continue to slip away from them, thereby, affording the library schools a free hand in pursuing their own objectives. The millennium will be a crucial one for the survival of the profession in Nigeria if factors such as membership and education are taken into account:

However, another element of 'control' not examined in any detail here so far is the location of professional schools. There are divergent views on this issue i.e. as to whether professional schools should operate within the university system, or perhaps in colleges and polytechnics (under the control of local education authority), or whether professional education can be effectively handled by the profession itself (through external examining or internal validation in appointed institutions). Most of these routes, as stated here, are laudable and have proved practicable elsewhere. But perhaps the most enticing challenge is that of location at the universities – how does this affect recruitment into the profession? Would a university education produce 'elitist' tendency in the professional and how does this element affect his general practice, professional outlook, and job mobility?

While university education is a good thing for a professional, e.g. architect, librarian, accountant, or engineer, the fact remains that independent schools such as the Nigerian Law School and the independent library schools in Scandinavian countries are viable alternatives in support of the professional association's own education programmes. Nigeria shares the same higher education tradition with Britain as determined by history, thus the model of investigation here is based on the British traditional university.

The concept of the 'university' as a traditional centre of learning and teaching (a **stadium**), has been the focus of scholarly analysis in literature of every kind. Some considered writers seem to link past influence of early universities to current developments in university institutions. Professor Havard-Williams in his lecture (on the conferment of a doctoral degree *honoris causa* at Sung Kynn Kwan University, Korea, 27 September, 1982) relates how the evolution of the university in its formative period still influences university practice today, he argues:

> At Oxford (and at Paris) there were the three superior (and incidentally vocational) faculties of theology (the Queen of the Sciences), law and medicine, while arts was the junior faculty, where students first received their basic general education. The tradition of taking a BA before any other degree still exists at Oxford and Cambridge, though the degree is no longer a 'liberal arts' degree, but nearly always an honours degree in a specific subject (from Physiology to French, or German to Geology).[59]

The 'superior' nature of traditionally vocational faculties such as theology, law, and medicine is implicit in the above quotation but, on the other hand, the 'arts' came to dominate the organisation of the university as there were teachers of distinction particularly in philosophy and the arts at Oxford, and the graduates of the University had, according to Havard-Williams, *Ius ubique docendi i.e.* a right to teach everywhere in Western Europe. The emphasis was thus placed on teaching. But other than teaching, the 'liberal arts' curriculum in colleges had centred on providing the foundation for a general education depending on the level of the corresponding secondary or high school education. Certainly, many of the original library schools in the U.S.A. are attached to colleges where the American BA degree in Library Science are obtained.[60]

The university college system has wide implications, for example, the administration of university college create the positions of chancellors, vice-chancellors, deans, faculties, schools, matriculation, degrees of bachelor, master, and the ultimate academic accolade of doctor — all deriving from the concept of *studium generale*, or the *universitas magistrorum* (the corporation of masters). Many of the early graduates at the University College, Ibadan took influential positions in government while others took to teaching and rose to the rank of professors with time. The university has in this way often been perceived by the Nigerian observer as centres of learning *par excellence*. The certificates, diplomas, and degrees obtained from university institutions have therefore been recognised for employment and teaching, thereby conferring status not only on the individual but his profession as a whole. The university thus seems to have become an inevitable *tour de force* for acknowledging the status of a discipline.

Unlike 'management studies,' 'accountancy,' 'communications' (media) — all new comers to the traditional university education system — librarianship is fortunate to have been identified early in its formation with the traditional university. This is due largely to the energetic influence of the 'Founding Fathers' of librarianship in Nigeria such as the late Professor John Harris, F. A. Sharr, the late Harold Lancour and John Dean, all of whom contributed positively to provide a sound basis upon which the programmes of professional education are now based.

The decision to establish library schools as part of university education in Nigeria stems from the John Harris' school of thought who felt strongly with the Ibadan (1953) Seminar group that:

> ... library schools in Africa should require university graduation or its equivalent for admission to the programme of full-scale professional training at the leadership level.[61]

The author's argument follows the general belief in Africa that university education at graduate level seems to provide the most effective means and probably a most reliable measure for ensuring that persons aspiring to reach the highest levels of professional practice, such as in librarianship, shall be well educated individuals with formal schooling not less good than the best which the continent affords. In the light of this development, Sharr felt obliged to recommend in his 1963 Report to the Ministry of Information of the then Northern Nigeria, that a school of librarianship should be established at Ahmadu Bello University, Zaria to provide formal professional education which concentrates on undergraduate programmes leading to the award of a first degree or diploma.[62]

Thus it is possible to view the two concepts of 'profession' and 'university' as inter-related in terms of educational function. Control of professional education is therefore balanced as

(a) Independent control of content, teaching, and examining by the higher institutions offering librarianship programmes, and

(b) Professional control as exerted through recruitment of educational products, changes in the nature of practice and hence changes in career structure.

The empirical basis of the model which is presented here in (a) and (b) above have been relatively explored in an article by Adams.[63] who contends that in the case of the concept of a profession, social changes have made many of the old criteria on professionalism obsolete. According to Adams, three of these social changes include the following (as summarised by the present writer):

(i) Today, members of a profession instead of being solely employed to serve in the private sector have a great majority of their membership serving in public employment, central or local, for example, teaching, medical staff, and the more recently related professions in the social services which find their main activities in local or central government. Public employment therefore is absorbing an increasing proportion of 'surveyors and architects, of actuaries and statisticians, and of the legal and engineering' professions. Adams argues further that on the basis of this revolutionary changes, there must be some profound effects of the change upon all aspects of the professions — i.e. their recruitment, internal hierarchies, social status, discipline, and their relationships to clients. These effects are yet to be studied systematically.

(ii) The change in the institutional education structure, Adams observes that universal primary education was, in the last forty years, supplemented by compulsory secondary education, and a period in which tertiary education is becoming freely available to secondary school leavers — in universities, polytechnics, colleges of education, technical colleges, and the whole network of institutional training and education which is developing in the binary system. The age of entry to the professions has rapidly risen with some professions like the veterinary adopting a single portal entry, a university degree, thus entrusting their primary professional qualification to the universities. Against this new educational background, the professions are having to change their recruitment policies and the standard content of their qualifying demands and to adjust themselves to a different composition in terms of social classes and traditions.

(iii)   The explosion of organised knowledge, i.e. the advent of specialisation in the professions, some having been derived form historical accidents, such as the separation of barristers and lawyers, or the distinction between physicians and surgeons (and perhaps, one may add, between the librarian and information scientist). However, the kaleidoscopic changes in the past century lend weight to Adam's contention that specialisation has its origins mainly in 'the great explosion' of organised knowledge. Perhaps one could employ a less 'explosive' term and say simply that the situation as described portrays the 'historic advances of organised knowledge.'

It is this concern by profession with standards and with accredited knowledge that creates the mutual interest between the 'professions' and the 'universities.' White provides a neat summary of the distinct advantages of university education for professional librarians by stating that university sponsorship of the education of librarians has yielded two principal benefits. It has raised the level of scholarship, introduced research and research programs in a field where nothing of the sort had existed before. Second, it has broadened the education of the operating personnel, balancing instruction in the technology of the subject with supporting instruction in other fields. Libraries are concerned with the entire spectrum of knowledge; balanced instruction thus becomes of necessity an inter-departmental task. In this respect, educating librarians is something like educating writers. Each speciality, writing just as librarianship, presupposed a certain technical competence as well as a special language and some knowledge of a particular literature, all of which can be taught by a *single* department.[64]

Shera agrees that librarians require a well-rounded intellectual development. He considers that:

> ... the skill of the librarian will depend upon his ability to abstract a system from the intellectual, emotional, social, and physical world around him... the basis of the librarian's system is the communication of information, where information is to be understood as any graphic manifestation of intellectual activity.[65]

It would seem that in the context of libraries being related to the world of learning, a philosophy of library education evolves which specifies that the prime requisite of the well-qualified librarian is a university education. Assuming that this view is accepted, the function of a library school is therefore one of rounding off a general university education with that more specialised preparation, which is essential to intelligent practice of the library profession. University education in the professions affords facilities for promoting research and development. It may be true to assert that the resilience to change in library schools' programmes has been made possible through university affiliation which helps to establish in the public, the professional status of librarianship and its 'academic responsibility.' The strengthening of the curriculum and higher standards of teaching derive from contact with the rest of the academic community and accordingly with wider fields of knowledge. The dynamic occurrences in the past decade in relation to the growth of information technology is a case in point of the strengthening of the librarianship curriculum. The library schools could not have ignored this development in the field. Havard-Williams, in a forthcoming publication, describes the new challenge to librarianship as follows:

With the growing influence of automation and computerisation, the procedures in libraries have become much more complex in terms of house-keeping — acquisitions (in association with greatly increased computerisation introduced by the major periodical and book suppliers), cataloguing, classification and indexing generally, and circulation systems. More important for its long-term effect on libraries and information centres is the production of data-bases, the large number of which now equals the number of data banks. Data bases provide bibliographical details, and frequently abstracts of published materials in most of the subjects in which research is pursued, and open a new concept of information provision.

This supports the view that professional education when conducted in the university environment can beneficially develop both the academic and professional content of the curriculum for the advancement of library and information services. From the perspective of the old dichotomy of 'education' and 'training' it seems clear that professional education takes place in a university milieu, a locus whose residential fee is paid in the coin of theoretical emphasis. On the other hand, professional education has as its goal the pursuit of a vocation and this element can be clearly portrayed in independent educational circumstances.

The Knowledge-Base Theory and Librarianship

In the sociological literature, the core of the commonly accepted criteria on professionalism resides in the 'knowledge-base' theory. Usually, a profession is service-oriented, but the intellectual knowledge of its practitioners and the factors of skills which have been developed and theoretically derived, form the basis of practice in the profession. As competence in the skill must be demonstrated by passing a test in order that the practice of the profession be restricted, knowledge becomes 'internalised' in the course of professional development. It is this intellectual ingredient which defines the knowledge-base of the profession. By implication, the theory, laws, and principles of practice in a profession thus represent the knowledge-base of that profession.

Contributors to the analysis of the intellectual basis of the professions often use the term 'learned profession' to describe the knowledge-base criterion.

But as Flexner[67] and Sharr[68] have shown, the term 'learned profession' is tautologous since all professions must by the accepted criteria on professionalism be 'learned' if they are to measure up to required standard.[69, 70]

The skill upon which theory is usually derived should in turn require further enhancement through education and training. By tradition, the professional is expected to avail himself of every opportunity open to him by which he could update his knowledge, usually by participating in programmes of professional self-improvement such as short courses, residential tutorial/ seminar or workshop and continuing education in general. Summation of these activities by all professionals in a given field of activity usually form the broad knowledge-base.

Hughes observes that the knowledge-base of a profession is not always clear:

> The nature of the knowledge, substantive or theoretical, on which advice and action are based is not always clear; it is often a mixture of several kinds of practical and theoretical knowledge.[71]

However, as already analysed, there should be no ambiguity about the knowledge-base. The functioning of the profession and the inherent generation of information by professionals, through interchange of ideas, form the knowledge foundation within the profession. This generation and exchange of information through the 'invisible college' create a cyclical process whereby the functions and general practice of the profession are constantly under review.

Goode clarifies that 'doubts about a sufficient knowledge-base undermine occupational claims to professional status or reward.'[72] One may add that knowledge-base cannot be qualified as 'sufficient' or 'insufficient' as stated by Goode as this assessment is prone to be value-laden. Nevertheless, Goode's seven criteria for professional knowledge needs to be assessed:

(i) Ideally abstract skills with codified principles;

(ii) Knowledge applicable to concrete problems of living;

(iii) A public belief that the professional knowledge can deal with these;

(iv) The acceptance by the public that the profession should take charge of solving these problems;

(v) The profession itself should help to create, organise and transmit knowledge;

(vi) The profession has the final decision over the technical solution to the problems.

(vii) The knowledge and the skills are seen as a 'mystery' by the public.[73]

Most of the traits identified in Goode's criteria apply to all professions and can thus be validated. The firmer the theoretical framework of professional studies, the easier it will be to teach the subjects at the level of principles rather than through a detailed description of practice. For instance, the library school curriculum may be thought of, not only in terms of activity and experience but also in the context of knowledge to be acquired and facts to be stored. In the educational literature,[74, 75, 76] it has been suggested that life and its problems are not neatly divided into nicely-bounded subjects; they are multi-disciplinary and at times inter-disciplinary.

Similarly, in librarianship, the objectives of library education parallel closely those of other professional fields. A cursory look at library schools' brochures, prospectuses and other course material indicates that the library schools act as the vortex of the profession, by their description of programmes offered reflecting both broad and specific knowledge of librarianship, **and** as well presenting members of the teaching staff as authorised in various aspects of the discipline. As the knowledge accumulates, librarianship would according to Sharr, 'be the study of people on the one hand, and of ideas or knowledge on the other.'[77]

Stokes[78] points out (about British librarianship in the early sixties when the LA was still largely in control of professional examinations) that students have found it difficult to understand the complicated pattern of the government and administration of many existing types of libraries **without** some basic knowledge of the outlines of central and local government and yet this is a rare thing for a student to bring to his professional career. It has also been difficult for a student to understand the complexities of government publications even down to the purely professional problems of their cataloguing, unless the student knows something of the mechanism of government which produces these publications. Historical bibliography is another area found to be impossible for a student to study with any real sense of purpose when his knowledge of the history of Europe is to say the least, rudimentary.

The resultant effect of these deficiencies in students is for them to 'learn by rote' rather than by any real understanding of the bibliographical processes. This situation also pervades in the syllabus because a student could possibly sit for the paper on 'Bibliography of French Language and Literature' **without** producing evidence of any language of French.[79] In short, general education was lacking in the early sixties but this has more than been compensated for in the seventies as the content of the librarianship curriculum has increasingly reflected the subject expertise required of the librarian.[80]

According to Montgomery:

> If one considers librarianship on the basis of the strict sociological interpretation of professionalism then it does fall short, notably in the knowledge base and theoretical principles, and in the general role of the librarian and the specific duties or functions which he is competent and qualified to carry out.[81]

But the knowledge-base theory is synthetically rooted in the principles and practice of librarianship. Kaplan states that the Library symbolises:

... a means of education, an instrumentality by which special groups and classes in the society can take advantage of experiences not directly their own, and so improve their position in society.[82]

However, it is clear that an 'encyclopedic' knowledge is not required of the librarian in the fulfilment of his duties. There may have been a time in earlier generations of libraries when it could be expected that the librarian would know all there is to know, and the measure of his effectiveness in the discharge of his duties could have been provided to a significant extent by the measure of how completely he had mastered human knowledge and interest. Hughes concludes that, 'what kinds of general knowledge — human knowledge, scientific knowledge — and wisdom are essential for the profession I simply do not know.' But I would say that if library educators are not in a continual state of strain with their students over this point they are probably not doing their job very well. [83]

The suggestion that library educators should constantly explore the knowledge framework of librarianship with their students seems pertinent enough but how can this be best achieved? It is worth considering that knowledge is a universal attribute which applies to all strands of life; in the case of librarianship professional knowledge is based on humanistic perspectives of library practice such as 'library culture,' 'oral tradition and history', 'enhancement of individual values,' **and** on the generation of information, its use and dissemination. These factors are culture-specific and hence they must relate to the society.

As Phenix argues in his *Realms of Meaning*, society itself is fully aware of the inter-relationship between knowledge and information. He states:

... great advances have been made in the storage and retrieval of knowledge. Vast resources of information can be preserved on tapes, films, discs, and other devices, as well as in the more conventional forms of books and artifacts, and they may quickly and inexpensively be reproduced for wide distribution. Effective new methods of indexing, cataloguing, abstracting, and cross-referencing have also been developed, so that whatever is known will not be lost from sight and so that the relevance of any given item to many other items of knowledge may be kept in view.[84]

The task of the library educator is to plan and implement programmes of study which conform to the generation and processing of information in all formats suggested by Phenix. The library educator could choose from all forms of knowledge necessary to be learned in relation to the society in which the library school is located. Furthermore, it would be logical to assume that the student librarian living in a modern society is exposed to various manifestations of knowledge which are characterised by growth in inter-disciplinary studies and to an increasing need for awareness in understanding the process of knowledge transference as a whole. Hence the consequent harmonisation of knowledge elements [85] in the international approach to librarianship curriculum.

'Home' or 'Abroad'

The objective in this section is to provide additional background material that will enable greater appreciation of factors which determine the philosophy of education for librarianship. One such important factor is the location of the library schools which contribute to manpower development in the profession, especially form the viewpoint of Nigeria.

In Nigeria, as in many other 'developing' countries, the formal provision of library education is a recent phenomenon when compared with the advanced countries of Europe and North America. Many Nigerian librarians, prior to the first library school being established in 1960 gained their qualifications from overseas institutions, notably UK and North America. However, the creation of more library schools in the country has not stemmed the exodus of students (who still travel to European institutions in search of 'the golden fleece') as was first anticipated in the profession. Despite the efforts of pioneers in the field to ensure a truly indigenous system of education for library practitioners, facilities for 'home' study has proved comparatively inadequate, so many students still prefer to study 'abroad,' especially those whose specialisation are not catered for at home. This situation has varying implications for services and personnel, and the effects are yet to be quantitatively determined.

The education of library practitioners, if conducted abroad, is less likely to take account of the genesis of local problems and thus it has been argued by some that on return home the 'globally-qualified' librarian may turn out to be a misfit in challenging situations such as 'rural library service,' 'information work relating to Nigerian documentation,' and 'appreciation of users' needs' in general. The implications for service is therefore serious enough.

As libraries are set up, sooner or later an indigenous system of professional education has to be introduced to meet their staffing needs. In this respect, the practical needs of the library profession, as derived both locally and nationally, can be assessed and a curriculum designed for the educational preparation of the specialist staff required. The existing trend suggests a recent curriculum proposal for the training of specialist staff for Nigerian agricultural and rural development.[86] Despite this development, government provides their studies abroad in librarianship. Those who are unsuccessful to gain scholarship awards study abroad by benefiting through employer's sponsorship schemes. Few students still brave the daunting task of self-sponsorship and it is hardly surprising that they are overly critical of the government scholarship scheme and the apparent inability of the library profession to improve its educational provision.

Library schools in Nigeria offer programmes ranging from non-graduate diploma, first degree, master's degree and the doctorate. The bone of contention is the insensitivity of the governing institutions in making their admission policy for postgraduate studies rather inflexible for matured professionals who do not possess the minimum admission requirements for higher degrees. The universities, operating under the constraints of a developing economy, are reluctant to 'lower' their own standards considering the impact this would have on the quality of their certificates in the employment market. The Nigerian Library Association's overtures to the universities on this issues[87] have come to nothing since 1974. Many students who are ambitious of becoming full professionals therefore look for schools abroad where the regulations are in some instances flexible to enable the non-graduate diploma holders or the A.L.A./F.L.A. chartered librarian, and even those without any formal qualification but who are experienced to study for master's degree. Usually the F.L.A. holder can study for academic master's degree both in overseas and Nigerian library schools[88] but in this respect this is how far Nigerian universities have gone at present.

It would seem therefore, that students who cannot gain entry into Nigerian library schools would continue to explore the possibilities of furthering their education overseas regardless of factors of relevance to local practice and the inconveniences thus generated in terms of culture shock, separation from families, inadequate finance and the inevitable lack of appreciation of the host country's advanced library and information systems due to severe time restrictions in the duration of their stay.

Asheim, in commenting on the strict adherence of institutions to their regulations observes that, in the developing countries this attitude is inevitable in a society keen to preserve the special privilege which accrues to a class-conscious society where it is deemed that the educated possesses particular natural qualifications which are absent in others.[89] Such an education must, by the society's definition, be limited to the elect; to open it to others is virtually to destroy its basic tenets. Those who attain this educational lofty height in the society do not willingly relinquish it, and those who, in the present generation of rising expectations aspire to push up are much more motivated by the desire personally to enter this realm of privilege than to abolish it. This conflict of philosophies, i.e. the desire to indigenise **courses** preferably than its **education** system is one of the present unresolved crises facing many developing nations such as Nigeria.

The kind of education that any nation offers its nations tends to support its own beliefs and institutions, and formal education in Nigerian universities should no less be different. As evaluation studies in this present work reveal (Section 7.5), librarianship has fared well in terms of innovations to its curriculum in the university system. The course are structure at all levels to reflect social influences, ensure academic respectability, and relate to the overall objectives of the library profession.

A comprehensive article consisting of expert's views titled 'A Library Education Policy for the Developing Countries' was published in *UNESCO*

Bulletin for Libraries (1968).[90] In it salient points were made concerning the issue of 'training' students at home or overseas. In the summing up by Dean the comparative advantages and disadvantages of overseas training for library staff in the developing countries was discussed. Dean, assessed the credentials of all three contributors to the article — Salvan, Kirkegaard and Bousso — and reflected on their contribution, thus, the authors have wide experience of the problems of providing library education for the nationals of emergent territories. Paul Salvan and Preben Kirkegaard agree, with some reservations, that basic library education is best provided in the country of origin of the student, but that at a higher level, overseas training is to be preferred. Amadou Bousso would accept the first proposition, but he is clearly of the opinion that, while overseas training is in some circumstances valued for higher level staff, the prospects of providing library education at this level in the emergent counties should not be discounted.[91]

Both sides of the view on overseas 'training' as contained in Dean's summary are pertinent today. At present most students obtain their basic librarianship qualifications at diploma and degree levels in Nigerian library schools. Higher level programmes are also available for those who wish to further their education. However, despite these notable advances, technicians and specialists are still required to staff libraries in greater numbers than at present provided by the schools.

On the advantages of a **'metropolitan'** professional education (so defined because the library school is located in an 'advanced' environment in the host countries of e.g., U.K., Canada and the U.S.A.) Dean clarifies that the following factors are discernible:

(i)   The broadening experience of travel.

(ii)   The award of a qualification that is universally acceptable.

(iii)   A cadre of instructors with sufficient leisure to develop their specialities and undertake the research that is so important for the enrichment of teaching.

(iv)   Associations of lasting value with professionals of the sponsoring metropolitan country.

(v)   A diversity of libraries for field work and demonstration purposes; facilities which are all too often lacking in the emergent countries.

(vi)   An opportunity to become acquainted with those technologies closely associated with librarianship, such as printing, data processing, reprography, etc., in a highly developed form. [92]

More than a decade later, following Dean's enumeration of the above factors, all the points still bear considerable relevance especially for the postgraduate student. However, most students are inevitably too busy fulfilling the schedules of exacting coursework, projects, and examinations to even spare the time for assimilating the experience borne out from the stated advantages of their overseas stay.

As to the disadvantages of studying abroad mostly by students from developing countries, Dean observes that:

(i) Standards in the Library schools of metropolitan countries vary enormously and from time to time we find too great a flexibility in admission policy which is often a disservice to the student from overseas. (Elsewhere in the literature, Dean augments this view by clarifying that the student from the 'developing country is sometimes as a concession admitted to course for which he does not have the normally required admission qualifications, often with disastrous consequences during the course.*)

(ii) Although the world of librarianship may be one world, the emphasis placed upon various aspects of library education differs from place to place Library education in metropolitan countries often fails to place the emphasis specifically where it is required by the student from the developing countries.

(iii) Selection procedure for candidates in absentia, whether for fellowships or library school places, is often unsatisfactory. For example, fellowships are often awarded to library students form developing countries solely on the basis of academic ability and without adequate consideration of the candidate's motivation or sense of vocation.

(iv) Encouragement of overseas library training and the expense involved may well deprive the developing countries with an evolving library system of one basic essentials of such a system, i.e. a school of librarianship. It is the function of the school not only to teach and develop courses relevant to the needs of a region or country at all levels, but also to gather together a nucleus of specialists to undertake the various research projects which must be carried out if emergent countries are ever to provide library service of the highest order. Library schools must also take responsibility for adapting the body of library knowledge accumulated in the metropolitan countries for the benefit of the nation or region which they serve. A library school in a developing country, as in a developed country, also assists in giving leadership and unity to the profession. It is in fact a part of the standard library infrastructure and at a certain level in any country's development should be regarded as essential.[93]

Dwelling on the above thoughts, it is possible to deduce that there is distinct advantage to be gained from having **localised** professional education system which cuts across the broad spectrum of all professions, so that the system will produce the designed educational out-course, supported with professional test of competence as advocated by Morehead,[94] McGrath,[95] and Lee[96] in the appropriate field of activity. In the education of librarians, the localisation problem can be assiduously solved through integration of its factors in the undergraduate curriculum in particular since the duration of study can absorb such radical possibilities.

The undergraduate programmes that are offered abroad are naturally not geared to the local problems of library practice of the overseas student's country. In general, apart from this and other peripheral, important factors such as finance, competition for places with home applicants, and the residual problems of language and the capacity of the overseas student's ability to endure a rigorous academic tenure, library schools in places such as the U.K. are mostly reluctant to admit undergraduate candidates from overseas. Usually there is the problem, for 'metropolitan' library educators, of matching the student's home professional experience with the high standards inexorably set by the nature of the 'advanced' environment in which the library school operates.

Wise[98] observes that the problem of comprehending librarianship, set within an understanding of British tradition, poses psychological and other problems for the overseas student. However, Chan in a radical article,[99] has criticised library schools for 'teaching what is desirable rather than what is necessary.' He supports this claim by pointing out that for a newly qualified librarian in a developing country, 'the desirable is usually an impossible dream, while the reality is a nightmare for which he may be unprepared and largely untrained.' The author argues that:

> This is especially so if, as it is highly likely, he (the newly-qualified librarian) has been trained at a British, American, or Canadian library school. Few if any of their courses are likely to pay any attention to the special problems or needs of the developing countries, and there is no reason why they should. Consequently, the student may learn about O & M, MBO and PPBS, but he will not learn what to do when the library is infested with mice. He may learn about the different kinds of equipment which are available, but not which types are suitable for tropical conditions, not how to obtain them when every order must be approved by half a dozen different irrational bureaucrats ....[100]

Chan's argument seems obvious enough for reasons discussed in the early part of this work, but equally, there are variations between library schools which make some more suitable for others, but this is rarely a factor in the students choice of school. The cultural dominance, material comforts, technical sophistication, and bright prospect of obtaining a master's degree attract many students to British, American, or Canadian schools, whilst if the curriculum is taken into consideration, these schools tend to be unsuitable due to the academic emphasis in the content and the general sophistication of the library system. It may be argued, however, that the theory of librarianship is universal in nature but the point being emphasised here relates to the factor of relevance as the developing afford the empiricism which characterise library education in the 'metropolitan' schools.

Other reasons for selecting the level at which overseas students can, for example, study in Britain exist. These seem to be philosophical in outlook. According to Havard-Williams:

> ... we do not on the whole take undergraduates from overseas countries as the Department considers that they should primarily be trained in their own country.[101]

This view is supported, though in a wider context by New[102] in an article which examined environmental and other factors creating difficulties for the overseas student in his study abroad. The need was stressed for library education to be set up at local levels where the basic qualifications can best be taught. Elsewhere in the literature, New[103] amplifies the need for some form of library education in the student's own country. He is of the opinion that despite the advantages of study abroad, those who study and those who teach are painfully aware of the difficulties which it presents. These might be summarised as unsuitability of course content and the inevitable handicaps which an overseas student has to overcome. Both lead to a high risk of failure in a library school where there is a much greater number of overseas students than their proportion in any class would indicate. It is clear that a curriculum intended for, say, British or American students and therefore based on practice in those countries will pose extra problems to students from elsewhere in the world. Reference may be made, for instance, to the system of government, both national and local, or it may even be assumed that this is known. This, and many other examples (such as the educational pattern of the country) will be both irrelevant and confusing to the overseas student. Even where a topic is potentially relevant (e.g. computers in libraries), it may be so far outside the student's experience that it poses a study problem. For these reasons, the foreigner may have his choice of options within courses severely limited, for he will be well advised to leave alone topics which call for a national background which he does not have... topics of interest and importance (in the curriculum) to the student and his country may frequently be ignored. So one might find the student from the tropics required to have some knowledge of library heating, when his need is for information on air conditioning and storage of library materials in humid conditions.[104]

In the 'home' or 'abroad' situation the content of the curriculum of 'metropolitan' library schools is certainly a feature of concern as depicted in detail in the above quotation. Hardly can library schools in advanced countries be criticised for upholding their own priorities. It is therefore in the best interests of the profession to set up its own system of professional education to complement the services of professional schools. This is likely to considerably reduce the number of students leaving the country for their first qualification overseas.

Librarianship in modern Nigeria is no longer at the embryonic stage; most of the present pre-eminence was achieved in the past four decades. This is consistent with Asheim's criterion as stated in the mid-sixties: The essentials of good library education are seldom present where librarianship and publishing are still in their early stages.... There is much to be said for library education on the home ground rather than in another country, but not if it must be so far below standards as to offer no contribution to the profession of library service.'[105]

The library schools and professional education as a whole has contributed positively to the library profession in Nigeria by supplying it with the required manpower of the highest calibre; professional education has also contributed via the avenue of continuing education and training and through demonstrating intellectual leadership in the professional literature. But it is difficult to impose any form of control on students who wish to further their studies overseas.

Other professions in Nigeria such as the engineers and accountants have derived methods of associateship whereby any practitioner in the field including those who have been trained abroad, is required to register for practice on his return home through the institutions' own accreditation as soon as the profession secures the legal backing it is seeking from the government. However, whatever system is derived to encourage 'home' study for student librarians, it is clear that students will continue to travel abroad to further their education in library studies. This is especially so at the higher degree level where, as in other disciplines, specialisation has become global and the brighter students are inevitably attracted towards the foremost teachers and researchers wherever they may be — Africa, Asia, U.K. or U.S.A.

References

1. Shera, J. H., *The Foundation of Education for Librarianship*, New York: Wiley-Becker and Haynes, 1972: 202 - 203.

2. Maidment, W. R., *The Professions: Librarianship*, Newton Abbot/ London: David and Charles, 1975. (Especially chapters 1 and 2, pp. 9-41).

3. Broadfield, A., *A Philosophy of Librarianship*, Graton, 1946.

4. Butler, P., 'Librarianship as a Profession,' *Library Quarterly,* 21 (4). 195:235-247.

5. Emery, R., 'Philosophy, Purpose and Function in Librarianship,' *Library Association Record,* 73(7), 1971: 127-129.

6. Grimshaw, A., 'What is Librarianship?' *Library Review* 24 (7), 1974: 307-309.

7. Butler, P., *op. cit.* 246

8. Emery, R., *op. cit.:* 127

9-11. The transformation process of libraries from purely the traditional role is discussed in some detail in the following sources which are appropriately used in context in the chapter on professionalism.

   Benge, R. C., *Libraries and Cultural Change,* London: Clive Bingley, 1970.

   Becker, J., 'Libraries, Society, and Technological Change,' *Library Trends,* 27(3), 1978: 409-416.

   Bowden, R., *Public Libraries: Information Transmission and Social Responsibilities,* London: L. A., 1979. (mimeo).

12. Grimshaw, A., *op. cit.:* 307

13. Quoted in: Dean, J., 'Library Education and Curriculum Problems in the Developing Countries,' in: Parr, E. A. and E. J. Wainwright, eds., *Curriculum Design in Librarianship: An International Approach,* Perth: WAIT, 1974: 98-110.

14. Benge, R. C., *Cultural Crisis and Libraries in the Third World,* London: Clive Bingley, 1979: 210.

15. *Ibid.:* 2121

16. White, C. M., 'The Intertwined Destiny of Literate Society and Librarianship, in: White, C. M. ed., *Bases of Modern Librarianship,* Oxford: Pergamon

Press, 1964: 8-9.

17. Shera, J. H., *op. cit.:* 207

18. Line, M. B., 'Demystification in Librarianship and Information Science' in Barr, K and M. B. Line, eds., *Essays on Information and Libraries: A Festschrift for Donald Urquhart,* London: Clive Bingley, 1975: 105-116.

19. *Ibid.:* 107

20. Khan, R. R., 'From Library Economy to Information Science,' in: Agarwal, S. N. *et. al.,* eds. *Perspectives in Library and Information Science, Vol. 1 Viswanathan festschrift,* Lucknow (India): Print House, 1982: 57.

21. Butler, P., *op. cit:* 245.

22. Cubarain, O. S., 'Librarianship in the System of the Sciences,' *Libri,* 21(4), 1971: 336-349.

23. *Ibid.:* 343-344.

24. Aguolu, C. C., 'Librarianship in Francophone West Africa,' *International Library Review,* 14(2), 1982: 155.

25. Cory, R. M., 'The Undetermined Profession,' *American Library Association Bulletin,* 49(3), 1955: 110-118.

26. Gupta, R. K., 'The Long and Difficult Road Ahead for the Library Profession,' *Libri,* 19(1), 1969: 52-57.

27. Gwinup, T., 'The Failure of Librarians to Attain Profession: The Causes, the Consequences, and the Prospect,' *Wilson Library Bulletin,* 48 (6), 1974: 482-490.

28. Butler, P., *op. cit.:* 237.

29. Messenger, M: F., 'The Shortfall of Library Education,' in: *Proceedings, Papers and Summaries of Discussions at the National Conference, Scarborough, 1976,* London: L. A., 1976: 45-47.

30. Jeson, A. F., 'The Shortfall of Library Education,' *in: Proceedings, Papers and Summaries...* London: L. A., 1976: 41-44.

31. *Ibid.:* 41.

32. Dean, J., *Planning Library Education Programmes,* London: Andre Deutsch, 1972: 21.

33. *Ibid.*

34. Ifla, Standing Advisory Committee, Section of Library Schools, 'Standards for Library Schools,' 1976: xii. (mimeo).

35. *Ibid.:* xii

36. *United Nations Bibliographic Information System (UNBIS) Thesaurus, 1981,* New York: United nations, 1981: 109.

37. Churchwell, C. D., *The Shaping of American Library Education,* Chicago: A. L. A., 1975: 1.

38. McGlothlin, W. J., 'Insights from One Profession which may be Applied to Educating for Other Professions', in: Smith, G. K., ed., *Current Issues in Higher Education: Proceedings of the 16th Annual National Conference on Higher Education,* Washington, D. C.: Association for Higher Education, 1961: 120.

39. Evidence to this effect is provided in the work of: Mackenzie, W. J. M., 'The Ingredients of Professionalism,' *Universities Quarterly,* 20 (2), 1966: 147-208. (Part of the report of the Gulbenkian educational discussion on *Higher Education for the Professions.* 1965).

40. Blauch, L. E. ed., *Education for the Professions,* Washington: GPO, 1955: 9.

41. It is on record that the Department of Library Studies at Loughborough University favour this trend. *c.f.:* L. U. T., DLIS *Prospectus, 3rd ed.,* 1982: 1-2.

42. Havard-Williams, P., 'Professional Education: A Personal View,' *International Library Review,* 13(4), 1981: 351-356.

43. Conant, R. W., *The Conant Report: A Study of the Education of Libraries,* Massachusetts: MIT Press, 1980: 13.

44. Saunders, W. L., 'Professional Education: Some Challenges for the Next Decade," in: Barr, K. and M. Line, eds., *Essays on Information and Libraries...* London: Clive Bingley, 1975: 156.

45. Conant *op. cit.:* 17-18.

46. Swanson, D. R., 'Introduction,' in: Swanson, D. R. ed., *The Intellectual Foundations of Library Education,* Chicago: University of Chicago Press, 1965: 4.

47. Lancaster, F. W., 'Whither Libraries?' Or Wither Libraries, *College and Research Libraries,* 1978: 345-357.

48. Rowley, J., 'In Defence of the Book,' *Library Association Record,* 83(12), 1981: 576-577.

49. Horsnell, V., 'New Technology: A Personal View', *Library Association Record,* 82(8), 1980: 359

50. Gee, R., 'Database Versus Book: Creator and Recreator, No Sole Rights,' *Library Association Record,* 84(2), 1982: 55-56.

51. Rowley, J., 'Our Traditional Responsibility Remains But is Now Even Heavier,' *Library Association Record*, 84 (4), 1982: 143-144.

52. Licklider, O. C. R., *Libraries of the Future*, Cambridge, Mass.: MIT Press, 1965.

53. Landau, R. M., *Robot*, Kensington: Science Information Association, 1977.

54. Lancaster, F. W., *Toward Paperless Information Systems*, New York: Academic Press, 1978.

55. Taylor, R. S., 'Patterns Toward a User-centred Academic Library,' in; Josey, E. J., ed., *New Dimension for Academic Library Service*, Metuchen: The Scarecrow Press, 1975: 298-304.

56. Rowley, J., 'In Defence of the Book...' *op. cit.*: 576-577.

57. Burrell, T. W., 'Curriculum Development for Librarianship, ' (Ph.D thesis). University of Strathclyde, 1982: 70.

58. National Library of Nigeria, 'The Advisory Committee on Nigerian National Diploma in Library Studies,' *Report*. Lagos: NLN, 1979: 28.

59. Havard-Williams, P., 'The Tradition of British Higher Education.' Lecture on the conferment of an honorary degree at Sung Kynn Kwan University, Korea, 27 September, 1982: 3 (mimeo).

60. Reed, S. R., 'The Curriculum of Library Schools Today: A Historical Overview,' in: Goldhor, H. ed. *Education for Librarianship*, Urbana, Illinois: Graduate School of Library Science, 1971: 19-45.

61. Unseco, *Development of Public Libraries in Africa: The Ibadan Seminar*, Paris: UNESCO, 1954: 100-101.

62. Nigeria. Northern, 'Ministry of Information,' *The Library Needs of Northern Nigeria:* A report prepared under the special Commonwealth African Assistance Plan, by F. A. Sharr, Kaduna: Ministry of Information, 1963.

63. Adams, W., 'The Place of Professional Education in the Universities,' *Applied Social Studies*, 1(1), 1969: 3-11

64. White, C. M., 'The Intertwined Destiny of Literate Society and Librarianship...' *op. cit.*: 12.

65. Shera, J. H., 'The Foundation of Education for Librarianship' *op. cit.*: 197-198.

66. Havard-Williams, P., 'Library and Information Education in Britain,' Loughborough University of Technology, 1982: 1-2. (To be published in; Agarwal, *et. al.* eds. *Perspectives in Library and Information Science*, Vol. 2).

67. Flexner, A., 'Is Social Work a Profession?' *School and Society,* 1 (26), 1915:903.

68. Sharr, F. A., 'Presidential Address,' *Library Assistant,* 45 (6), 1952: 84.

69. Carr-Saunders; A. M. and P. A. Wilson, *The Professions,* London: O. U. P., 1933 (Reprinted by Cass, 1964.)

70. Millerson, G., *The Qualifying Associations: A Study in Professionalisation,* Lond: Routledge, 1964.

71. Hughes, E. C., 'The Professions,' *Daedalus* (N.Y.), 92 (4), 1963:655.

72. Goode, W.J., 'The Theoretical Limits of Professionalisation,' in: Etzioni, A., ed., *The Semiprofessions and their Organisation,* New York: Fress Press/Collier-Macmillan, 1969: 281.

73. *Ibid.*

74. Lawton, D., 'The Idea of an Integrated Curriculum,' University of London, *Institute of Education Bulletin,* 19, 1969: 5-11.

75. Pring, R. A., 'Curriculum Integration,' University of London, *Institutes of Education Bulletin,* 20, 1969: 4-8.

76. Musgrove, F., 'Power and the Integrated Curriculum,' *Journal of Curriculum Studies,* 5(1), 1973: 3-12.

77. Sharr, F. A., 'Presidential Address' ... *op. cit.* : 84.

78. Stokes, R., 'Education for Librarianship: Looking Ahead 3: Programme for Professionals," *Library Association Record,* 65 (8), 1963: 295-299.

79. *Ibid.:* 296

80. Lawal, O. O., 'Elements of Degree Courses in Librarianship and Information Science, LUT, 1979'. (M. A. thesis)

81. Montgomery, A. C., 'Professionalism in British Librarianship,' (FLA thesis). London: L. A., 1979: 264-265.

82. Kaplan, A., 'The Age of the Symbol: A Philosophy of Library Education,' *Library Quarterly,* 34(4), 1964: 297.

83. Hughes, E. C., 'Education for a Profession,' *Library Quarterly,* 31 (4), 1961:342.

84. Phenix, P. H., *Realms of Meaning,* New York: McGraw-Hill, 1964: 304.

85. c.f. Havard-Williams, P., 'Education for Library, Information, and Archive Studies' *IFLA Journal,* 2 (3), 1976: 137-145.

86. Aboyade, B. O., ed., 'Problems of Identifying Training Needs for Library and Information Services in a Predominantly Non-literate Society — With Particular Reference to Agricultural and Rural Development.' Paper presented at the FID/ET Technical Meeting, Ibadan, Nigeria 6-9 May, 1981. The Hague: FID, 1981. (Especially Professor Ogunsheye's paper, pp. 87-103).

87. Bankole, E. B., 'Report on Colloquium on Education and Training for Librarianship in Nigeria,' *Nigerian Libraries,* 9 (3), 1974: 169 - 171.

88. From an interview with a Nigerian library school Head who wishes to remain anonymous.

89. Asheim, L., *Librarianship in the Developing Countries,* Urbana: University of Illinois Press, 1966: 36.

90. Salvan, P. Kirkegaard, P., and Bousso, A., 'A Library Education Policy for the Developing Countries,' *UNESCO Bulletin for Libraries,* 22 (4), 1968: 173-188.

91. Dean, J., 'The Summing Up.' in: A Library Education Policy for the Developing Countries, *UNESCO Bulletin for Libraries,* 22 (4), 1968: 182.

92. *Ibid.:* 183.

93. *Ibid.:* 184

94. Morehead, J., *'Theory and Practice in Library Education,* Littleton, Colorado: Libraries Unlimited, 1980: 22-24.

95. McGrath, E. J., 'The Ideal Education for the Professional man,' in: Henry, N. B. ed., *Education for the Professions,* 61st Yearbook of the National Society for the study of Education, Part II. Chicago: University of Chicago Press, 1962: 290.

96. Lee, R. E., 'Theory and Practice in Training for the Law: Thinking like a Lawyer and Doing What He Does,' *University of Dayton Law Review,* 2, 1977: 3, 6.

97. Wise, M., 'Visitors to Britain,' *Library Review,* 28, 1979: 254-258.

98. Chan, G. K. L., 'Third World Libraries and Cultural Imperialism,' *Assistant Librarian,* 72 910, 1979: 134-140.

99. *Ibid.:* 138.

100. Havard-Williams, P., 'Postgraduate Work in Library and Information Studies at Loughborough University,' Loughborough: L. U. T., 1978/79: 4 (mimeo).

101. New, P. G., 'Education for Librarianship: Home or Abroad,' *Herald of Library Science,* 17 (2/3), 1978: 146-153.

102   New, P. G., *Education for Librarianship*, London: Clive Bingley, 1978.

103.   *Ibid.:* 11-12.

104.   Asheim, L., *Librarianship in the Developing Countries ... op. cit.:* 70-71.

7

The Future

In the preceding chapters a detailed survey of aspects of professional education for librarianship has been examined to show its evolution, structure, content and renewal capacities. The foundation for the study of library and information science is now firmly established globally. In comparative terms, it has been easier for the developed countries to assimilate current trend in communications technology as an important core of gaining professional competence for librarians.

Almost two decades after initiating this study, the element of information technology has surged in library schools' curriculum. This is a good thing if the monopoly of entry into the profession is to be maintained. Several librarians in Africa still graduate from schools without proficiency or competence in the use of computer for research and information sharing through network systems. For instance, important discoveries have been made in respect of patronage of African published journals in the universities (Alemna, A. A. *et at.*, 2000).[1]

Librarians and information scientists, who are professional partners, should explore ways and means of capitalising on the application of information technology in creating virtual libraries in the vast continent. An appraisal of prospects of digital libraries in Africa (Ojedokun, 2000)[2] is a compelling need for library educators in streamlining the nature of practice with modern education required in the preparation of librarians. It can no longer be doubted that the introduction of digital libraries in Africa has implications for improving educational standards, library and information services delivery and the creation of an informed society in an increasingly global world.

In retrospect, the slow development in first degrees in librarianship is definitely justified on the basis of the high level of role expectation of the professional librarian which should not be severely restricted to routine practice. The first professional qualification is now set at postgraduate level with a wider appreciation of change in the profession and development or enhancement of communication technological skills. A cogent and genuine fear would be the possible over-running of library personnel with technological staff who know next to nothing on the rudiments of librarianship. This situation poses a great challenge to library educators and curriculum planners.

Librarians should therefore engage in strategic plans within the framework of their institutions in order to ensure the sustainability of library services and assuring library staff of their relevance and strategic important information services to the social and academic community. A typical Master of Library Studies (M.L.S.) programme should have as its core the following elements:

(a)   Cataloguing, Classification and Indexing
(b)   Technologies for Information Management
(c)   Library Management
(d)   Advanced Bibliography and Physical Form of the Book
(5)   Automation Processes/Basic Computer Application in Libraries.

Ideally, the M.L.S. should be two full sessions in duration in order to ensure practical orientation of 'first entrants' into the profession. A situation whereby a fresh holder of M.I.L. or M.L.S. or M. Inf. Sc. perceives himself as an expert in librarianship above an information science 'guru' simply by being in the academic librarians' group is very misleading and impractical.

Another important element that should attract our attention resides in research in librarianship. For two decades now the research base in librarianship as practiced globally and in Africa has widened significantly. There are yardsticks for measuring this research growth. For instance more librarians are now academic in status and show keen interest in research for the purpose of widening the knowledge base of the profession through obtaining research grants at the universities, pursuing postgraduate research studies both at home and abroad with significant findings impacting on library development. The challenges of engaging in profitable research are enormous in terms of scarce funds, inadequate facilities and limited access to published and unpublished materials which could have provided the springboard for finding solutions to practical problems through indigenisation of the curriculum and work practices (Lawal, 1993).[3]

Library literature on Africa is increasing in quality and volumes. More scholars in library and information science are busy providing the necessary data for sharing experiences and ideas on national and international scales.[4] The doctoral programme in library schools need to be enhanced to provide the needed manpower for education and training and fostering international staff exchange in the African continent. The library profession in Africa would certainly gain a lot if there is fusion between the two bodies of library and information practitioners as now existing in the U.K. where it is most probable that the members of the Institute of Information Scientists would opt for merger with the Library Association, London.

References

1. Alemna, A. A., *et al.,* 'African Journals: An Evaluation of their use in African Universities,' *African Journal of Library, Archive & Inf. Science,* 10 (2)2000: 93-111.

2. Ojedokun, Ayoku. A., 'Prospects of Digital Libraries in Africa," *African Journal of Library, Archive & Inf. Science, 1*0(1) 2000: 12-21.

3. Lawal, O. O., 'Indigenisation of the Curriculum in Nigerian Library Schools: Survey of its Impact on Practitioners,' *African Journal of Library, Archive & Inf. Science,* 3(2) 1993: 141-150.

4. Amanqua, S. N., ed., *African University Libraries in the 21st Century,* Kumasi: SCAULWA/KNUST University Press, 2000:114p.

Index